# CHARGE!

# CHARGE!

## History's Greatest
## Military Speeches

*Edited by* Congressman Steve Israel

NAVAL INSTITUTE PRESS
*Annapolis, Maryland*

Naval Institute Press
291 Wood Road
Annapolis, MD 21402

Library of Congress Cataloging-in-Publication Data
Charge! : history's greatest military speeches / edited by Steve Israel.
    p. cm.
Includes bibliographical references and index.
ISBN 978-1-59114-399-4 (alk. paper)
1. Speeches, addresses, etc. 2. Military history. I. Israel, Steve.
    PN6122.C43 2007
    808.859'358--dc22

                                                                2007016457


Printed in the United States of America on acid-free paper

14 13 12 11 10 09 08 07    9 8 7 6 5 4 3 2

First printing

To Marlene, Carly, and Elana,
who have marched with me.

*The clearer vision which time and study bring
have shown that he used words almost as effectively as the sword,
and that throughout his career the address ably supported
the military maneuver.*

—IDA TARBELL, *Napoléon's Addresses*, 1897

# CONTENTS

## PART 2: LIBERTY OR DEATH

# PART 3: SAFE FOR DEMOCRACY

## PART 4: BEAR ANY BURDEN

## PART 5: 9/11 AND BEYOND

# ACKNOWLEDGMENTS

I am indebted to many people for their support and assistance with this project. First and foremost, my family. My wife, Judge Marlene Budd, and my daughters, Carly and Elana, have offered tolerance for yet another of my projects (in addition to serving in the U.S. Congress, working for my constituents, campaigning for reelection, writing constantly, and amassing a growing pile of "books to be read" in my study).

Brett Kunsch was an extraordinary research assistant. In addition to fact checking, writing, and editing, he made substantive creative contributions to the book that improved my early drafts.

Tom Cutler, of the Naval Institute Press, was a patient and dependable advocate of the project.

I also appreciate the military officials and historians who have guided my work. Congressman Ike Skelton (D-MO), the chairman of the House Armed Services Committee, fueled my interest in military history and encouraged me to pursue the issue of professional military education on the committee.

I am also fortunate to have a staff that is so deeply committed to my constituents that I was able to focus my personal time on *Charge!* without worrying about a diminution in the quality of service we provide. Jack Pratt is not only my chief of staff but also a friend. He reliably weathers my daily proclamations: "I have an idea for a project. . . ." And he leads a staff that patiently endures my many interests as well: Karen Agostisi, Alex Bacham, Swati Bindra, Nick Crocco, Lisa Deutsch, Silvana Diaz, Meghan Dubyak, Holli Dunayer, Beth Gabellini, Tracie Holmberg, Nicole Haber, Matt Jennings, Zach Kranitz, Caryn Lewi, Heather McHugh, Major Chris Meyers, Erin Murphy, Mike Ryan, Tricia Russell, Debra Solomon, Harris Wiener, and others who were kind enough to work for me before moving on to bigger and better things.

There are two other groups I must thank: the generations of men and women who have marched to protect us, and the people of New York's Second Congressional District. They have given me a seat in Congress and a seat on the House Armed Services Committee and therefore a front seat to history, which helps me contribute to shaping the future.

# INTRODUCTION

*The pen is mightier than the sword.*

EDWARD BULWER-LYTTON, 1839

O N A SULLEN DAY IN EARLY APRIL, the former commandant of
the U.S. Army War College led me up a gravel path to what he
called "sacred ground."

Low clouds hung over Gettysburg; a chilly wind swept across the battlefield, rustling the Wheatfield and the Peach Orchard and blowing against the
scarred rocks of Devil's Den. The battlefield was almost desolate; it would be
a few weeks and at least twenty degrees warmer before tourists swarmed the
famous landmarks, signed up for ghost tours, and lined up to buy coffee mugs
emblazoned with the images of famous generals.

All of that seemed distant as we climbed a lonely path. Finally, we arrived
at the wooded summit of a hill, and Maj. Gen. Robert Scales, USA (Ret.),
planted his feet near a tree stump. Not very far away, 142 years before, his
great-grandfather, Brig. Gen. Alfred Scales, stood with a Confederate bri-
gade. On the other side of the battlefield. On the other side of history.

"Welcome to Little Round Top," Robert Scales said, and then repeated,
"This is sacred ground."

Here on this hill, on July 2, 1863, Col. Joshua Chamberlain and his 20th
Maine were ordered to "hold this ground at all costs." The order was crucial,
complying with it almost impossible. If Chamberlain lost the hill, Robert E.
Lee's army could push across Union lines and threaten Washington, D.C.,
less than ninety miles away. Gettysburg would be lost, and perhaps even
the war. Yet, the 15th and 47th Alabama Infantry Regiments outnumbered
the 20th Maine and were positioned to attack them frontally and on their
left flank. After repelling several assaults, Chamberlain's men had nearly
exhausted their ammunition and seemed incapable of surviving another
attack. Chamberlain then decided to mount what many must have believed

would be a final, suicidal defense of the hill: a bayonet charge into apparently overwhelming firepower.

"Bayonet!" Chamberlain ordered, and he could hear the click of steel. Moments later, the 20th Maine rushed down the hill, executing a difficult maneuver that swept away the enemy, saved Little Round Top, and helped win Gettysburg for the Army of the Potomac.

Chamberlain on Little Round Top has become a hallowed moment in military history and the subject of passionate debate as well. Even today historians argue whether Chamberlain was really out of ammunition; whether he actually gave the order to advance or whether his men had an intuitive grasp of what had to be done, and when to do it; even whether the Confederates had commenced a retreat before or after the 20th Maine swept upon them.

The debate is academic. More important to me is this: How did that small band of brothers find the fortitude to charge against what they assumed to be superior force? What propelled them into the enemy, bayonets versus musketry?

What happened on Little Round Top has echoed throughout history: on other hills and on mountains, on beaches and deserts, in cities and plains. They are not simply stories; they demonstrate the importance of words in the story. History demonstrates—from the ancient spear to our new array of weapons, the Future Combat Systems—that weapons systems are lacking unless those who wield them know why they fight. Unless they fight with their hearts as well as their hands.

Words inspire, weapons implement.

Of course, words in battle have different purposes. They motivate populations against great odds . . . they explain why the fight and sacrifice are necessary . . . they give comfort and consolation . . . they help explain the unfathomable loss that occurs with war. They are sometimes written in safe places, far removed from the brutality of the battlefield—and many times simply blurted in the fog of battle. They become sharp and powerful weapons of victory, and sometimes they have blunted the fear of inevitable defeat. Queen Elizabeth I pledging to die with her soldiers as they faced the Spanish Armada . . . Patrick Henry choosing between liberty and death . . . Napoléon Bonaparte exhorting his troops as they traveled to Egypt . . . General Bernard Montgomery informing his men that they would not retreat from Egypt . . . Winston Churchill rallying his nation to "victory at all costs" . . . and Admiral David Farragut ordering his men: "Damn the torpedoes, full speed ahead."

As a Member of Congress, I spent four years on the House Armed Services Committee; I have witnessed the power of words. Almost every time I speak on the floor of the House, I am cognizant of the fact that I am standing in the same place where Franklin D. Roosevelt summoned America against tyranny and fascism in December 1941. Only days after 9/11, I was at Ground Zero with President George W. Bush when he stood atop a heap of rubble and said, "I can hear you. I can hear you. The rest of the world hears you. And the people who knocked these buildings down will hear all of us soon." I found that terse call to battle an inspirational (but soon to be squandered) moment. I have listened to the words of U.S. service members when I have visited them in Iraq and Kuwait, flown with them on C-130s and Blackhawk helicopters, and sat with them in military hospitals, at congressional committee hearings, and in my offices in Washington and Long Island. The memories of battle fresh in their minds, their words are the most powerful. Once, as I was struggling to decide my vote on whether the Geneva Convention should fully apply to so-called "enemy noncombatants," I sat privately with a U.S. Marine who had recently received the Bronze Star for his bravery in Fallujah. "How do you think I should vote?" I asked him. "Sir," he replied, "I want to fight for a country that has strong moral values." His words were more valuable to me than hours of long-winded, carefully scrubbed congressional briefings and PowerPoint maps.

Every day in Washington I reflect on the importance of words and deeds in meeting great challenges. Morton Kuntsler's *Hero of Little Round Top* dominates a wall facing my desk. It captures the moment when Chamberlain ordered his troops to fix bayonets and commence a charge against the odds. When visitors talk about the improbability of mastering the grave challenges we face—the war on terror, conquering our addiction to foreign oil, balancing our budgets, offering decent health care, and educating our children—I simply point to the painting. No words need to be spoken.

This book is not only history—it is about our future. I hope it will motivate and inspire its readers with the raw courage that moved people forward against critical challenges, toward new hope. On the battlefield. And off.

# PART I
# DISTANT ECHOES

*The Lord, your God He is the One Who goes with you.*

—MOSES IN DEUTERONOMY

# Moses

## INSTRUCTING HIS PEOPLE
## TO MARCH WITHOUT HIM,
## CIRCA 1260 BCE

*Be strong and resolute, be not in fear or in dread of them;*
*for the Lord your God Himself marches with you;*
*He will not fail you or forsake you.*

*Moses Smashing the Tables of the Law,* by Rembrandt (1601–1669).

ON THE PLAINS OF MOAB, east of the Jordan River, Moses confronted two immense tasks. First, he had to inspire his people to cross the Jordan and confront powerful militaries, fortified cities, and vast populations. Second, he had to announce that he would no longer lead them. "Today I am one hundred and twenty years old. I can no longer go or come, and the Lord said to me, 'You shall not cross this Jordan.'"

Moses achieves his objective by promising an even greater ally: God, Himself. Yet God's support of the Children of Israel does not come easily. It is not enough to simply rely on Him to carry them in battle; they must follow a strict moral and military code worthy of having God at their side. Moses thereby instills in his people a higher purpose; something worth fighting for.

Throughout history, military speeches have pushed men and women forward with the comforting promise that God marches with them. More important is the notion that they march for God. Here, excerpted from Deuteronomy, are portions of Moses's last words to the Children of Israel before they crossed the Jordan River for the Promised Land.

---

## DEVARIM—CHAPTER 10

1. Hear, O Israel: Today, you are crossing the Jordan to come in to possess nations greater and stronger than you, great cities, fortified up to the heavens.

2. A great and tall people, the children of the 'Anakim, whom you know and of whom you have heard said, "Who can stand against the children of 'Anak?"

3. You shall know this day, that it is the Lord your God Who passes over before you as a consuming fire He will destroy them, and He will subdue them before you; and you shall drive out them and destroy them quickly, as the Lord spoke to you.

4. Do not say to yourself, when the Lord, your God, has repelled them from before you, saying, "Because of my righteousness, the Lord has brought me to possess this land," and [that] because of the wickedness of these nations, the Lord drives them out from before you.

5. Not because of your righteousness or because of the honesty of your heart, do you come to possess their land, but because of the wickedness of these nations, the Lord your God drives them out from before you, and in order to establish the matter that the Lord swore to your forefathers, Abraham, Isaac, and Jacob. . . .

# DEVARIM—CHAPTER 20

1. When you go out to war against your enemies, and you see horse and chariot, a people more numerous than you, you shall not be afraid of them, for the Lord, your God is with you Who brought you up out of the land of Egypt.

2. And it will be, when you approach the battle, that the kohen shall come near, and speak to the people.

3. And he shall say to them, "Hear, O Israel, today you are approaching the battle against your enemies. Let your hearts not be faint; you shall not be afraid, and you shall not be alarmed, and you shall not be terrified because of them."

4. For the Lord, your God, is the One Who goes with you, to fight for you against your enemies, to save you.

5. And the officers shall speak to the people, saying, "What man is there who has built a new house and has not [yet] inaugurated it? Let him go and return to his house, lest he die in the war, and another man inaugurate it.

6. And what man is there who has planted a vineyard, and has not [yet] redeemed it? Let him go and return to his house, lest he die in the war, and another man redeem it.

7. And what man is there who has betrothed a woman and has not [yet] taken her? Let him go and return to his house, lest he die in the war, and another man take her."

8. And the officers shall continue to speak to the people and say, "What man is there who is fearful and fainthearted? Let him go and return to his house, that he should not cause the heart of his brothers to melt, as his heart."

9. And it shall be, that when the officials finish speaking to the people, they shall appoint officers of the legions at the edges of the people.

10. When you approach a city to wage war against it, you shall propose peace to it.

11. And it will be, if it responds to you with peace, and it opens up to you, then it will be, [that] all the people found therein shall become tributary to you, and they shall serve you.

12. But if it does not make peace with you, and it wages war against you, you shall besiege it,

13. and the Lord, your God, will deliver it into your hands, and you shall strike all its males with the edge of the sword.

14. However, the women, the children, and the livestock, and all that is in the city, all its spoils you shall take for yourself, and you shall eat the spoils of your enemies, which the Lord, your God, has given you.

15. Thus you shall do to all the cities that are very far from you, which are not of the cities of these nations.

16. However, of these peoples' cities, which the Lord, your God, gives you as an inheritance, you shall not allow any soul to live.

17. Rather, you shall utterly destroy them: The Hittites, and the Amorites, the Canaanites, and the Perizzites, the Hivvites, and the Jebusites, as the Lord, your God, has commanded you.

18. So that they should not teach you to act according to all their abominations that they have done for their gods, whereby you would sin against the Lord, your God.

19. When you besiege a city for many days to wage war against it to capture it, you shall not destroy its trees by wielding an ax against them, for you may eat from them, but you shall not cut them down. Is the tree of the field a man, to go into the siege before you?

20. However, a tree you know is not a food tree, you may destroy and cut down, and you shall build bulwarks against the city that makes war with you, until its submission.

# DEVARIM—CHAPTER 31

1. And Moses went, and he spoke the following words to all Israel.

2. He said to them, "Today I am one hundred and twenty years old. I can no longer go or come, and the Lord said to me, 'You shall not cross this Jordan.'

3. The Lord, your God He will cross before you; He will destroy these nations from before you so that you will possess them. Joshua he will cross before you, as the Lord has spoken.

4. And the Lord will do to them, as He did to the Amorite kings, Sihon and Og, and to their land, [all of] which He destroyed.

5. And [when] the Lord delivers them before you, you shall do to them according to all the commandment that I have commanded you.

6. Be strong and courageous! Neither fear, nor be dismayed of them, for the Lord, your God He is the One Who goes with you. He will neither fail you, nor forsake you."

7. And Moses called Joshua and said to him in the presence of all Israel, "Be strong and courageous! For you shall come with this people to the land which the Lord swore to their forefathers to give them. And you shall apportion it to them as an inheritance.

8. The Lord He is the One Who goes before you; He will be with you; He will neither fail you, nor forsake you. Do not fear, and do not be dismayed."

# Pericles

*We must resist our enemies in any and every way,
and try to leave to those who come after us
an Athens that is as great as ever.*

Marble bust of Pericles wearing Corinthian helmet, artist unknown.

THE MOST IMPORTANT DEBATES in which I participate as a Member of Congress focus on war and peace. Yet, those debates are not new to any deliberative institution. Indeed, they have raged for as long as war has been waged. And many have echoed Pericles' appeal for war against the Spartan Alliance.

Near the end of the fifth century BCE, the Athenian Empire and Spartan Alliance fought a war described by the historian Thucydides as "great and noteworthy above all the wars that had gone before." Late in the year 432 BCE, the Spartans offered Athens an ultimatum to avoid a clash: revoke a decree that excluded Megarian access to Athenian ports and markets; and grant autonomy for various Athenian allies.

The democratic Athenian assembly debated the proposal. Some believed that the Megarian decree was not worth a war. Others insisted that conceding on this issue would weaken Athens and invite war later. Finally, Pericles, described by Thucydides as "the leading man of his time among the Athenians and the more powerful both in action and in debate," rose to speak.

Pericles' arguments are important because they can be applied to contemporary debates over war and peace. He begins by directly rebuffing the argument that the Megarian Decree is not worth a war. He offers a detailed strategic and tactical assessment of military strengths and weaknesses. And he concludes with an emotional appeal to history and to the future: "When our fathers stood against the Persians they had no such resources as we have now; indeed, they abandoned even what they had, and then it was by wisdom rather than by good fortune, by daring rather than by material power, that they drove back the foreign invasion and made our city what it is today. We must live up to the standard they set: we must resist our enemies in any and every way, and try to leave to those who come after us an Athens that is as great as ever."

Pericles' oratory—in tone and tactic—is especially evident in the twentieth-century speeches of Winston Churchill.

---

ATHENIANS, my views are the same as ever: I am against making any concessions to the Peloponnesians, even though I am aware that the enthusiastic state of mind in which people are persuaded to enter upon a war is not retained when it comes to action, and that the people's minds are altered by the course of events. Nevertheless I see that on this occasion I must give you exactly the same advice as I have given in the past, and I call upon those of you who are persuaded by my words to give your full support to these resolutions which we are making all together, and to abide by them even if in some respect or other we find ourselves in difficulty; for, unless you do, you will be able to claim no credit for intelligence when things go well with us. There is often no more logic in the course of events than there is in the plans of men, and this is why we usually blame our luck when things happen in ways that we did not expect.

It was evident before that Sparta was plotting against us, and now it is even more evident. It is laid down in the treaty that differences between us should be settled by arbitration, and that, pending arbitration, each side should keep what it has. The Spartans have never once asked for arbitration, nor have they accepted our offers to submit to it. They prefer to settle their complaints by war rather than by peaceful negotiations, and now they come here not even making protests, but by trying to give us orders. They tell us to abandon the siege of Potidaea, to give Aegina her independence, and to revoke the Megarian Decree. And finally they come to us with a proclamation that we must give the Hellenes their freedom.

Let none of you think that we should be going to war for a trifle if we refuse the Megarian decree. It is a point they make much of, and say that war need not take place if we revoke this decree; but if we do go to war, let there be no kind of suspicion in your hearts that the war was over a small matter. For you this trifle is both the assurance and the proof of your determination. If you give in, you will immediately be confronted with some greater demand, since they will think that you only gave way on this point through fear. But if you take a firm stand you will make it clear to them that they have to treat you properly as equals. And now you must make up your minds what you are going to do—either to give way to them before being hurt by them, or, if we go to war—as I think we should do—to be determined that, whether the reason put forward is big or small, we are not in any case going to climb down nor hold our possessions under a constant threat of interference. When one's equals, before resorting to arbitration, make claims on their neighbors and put those claims in the form of commands, it would still be slavish to give in to them, however big or however small such claims may be.

Now, as to the war and to the resources available to each side, I should like you to listen to a detailed account and to realize that we are not the weaker party. The Peloponnesians cultivate their own land themselves; they have no financial resources either as individuals or as states; then they have no experience of fighting overseas, nor of any fighting that lasts a long time, since the wars they fight against each other are, because of their poverty, short affairs. Such people are incapable of often manning a fleet or often sending out any army, when that means absence from their own land, expense from their own funds, and, apart from this, when we have control of the sea. And wars are paid for by the possession of reserves rather than by a sudden increase in taxation. Those who farm their own land, moreover, are in warfare more anxious about their money than their lives; they have a shrewd idea that they themselves will come out safe and sound, but they are not at all sure that all their money will not have been spent before then, especially if, as is likely to happen, the war lasts longer than they expect. In a single battle the Peloponnesians and their allies could stand up to all the rest of Hellas, but they cannot fight a war against a power unlike themselves, so long as they have no central deliberative authority to produce quick decisive action, when they all have equal votes, though they all come from different nationalities and every one of these is mainly concerned with its own interests—the usual result of which is that nothing gets done at all, some being particularly anxious to avenge themselves on an enemy and others no less anxious to avoid coming to any harm themselves. Only after long intervals do they meet together at all, and then they devote only a fraction of their time to their general interests, spending most of it arranging their own separate affairs. It never occurs to any of them that the apathy of one will damage the interests of all. Instead each state thinks that the responsibility for its future belongs to someone else, and so, while everyone has the same idea privately, no one notices that from a general point of view things are going downhill.

But this is the main point: they will be handicapped by lack of money and delayed by the time they will have to take in procuring it. But in war opportunity waits for no man.

Then we have nothing to fear from their navy, nor need we be alarmed at the prospect of their building fortifications in Attica. So far as that goes, even in peace time it is not easy to build one city strong enough to be a check upon another, and this would be a much harder thing to accomplish in enemy territory and faced with our own fortifications, which are just as strong as anything that they could build. While if they merely establish some minor outpost, they could certainly do some harm to part of our land by raiding and by receiving deserters, but this could by no means prevent us from retaliating by the use of our sea-power and from sailing to their territory and building fortifications there. For we have acquired more experience of land fighting through our naval operations than they have of sea fighting through their operations on land. And as for seamanship, they will find that a difficult lesson to learn. You yourselves have been studying it ever since the end of the Persian wars, and have still not entirely mastered the subject. How, then, can it be supposed that they could ever make much progress? They are farmers, not sailors, and in addition to that they will never get a chance of practicing, because we shall be blockading them with strong naval forces. Against a weak blockading force they might be prepared to take a risk, bolstering up their ignorance by the thought of their numbers, but if they are faced with a large fleet they will not venture out, and so lack of practice will make them even less skillful than they were, and lack of skill will make them even less venturesome. Seamanship, just like anything else, is an art. It is not something that can be picked up and studied in one's spare time; indeed, it allows one no spare time for anything else.

Suppose they lay their hands on the money at Olympia or Delphi and try to attract the foreign sailors in our navy by offering higher rates of pay: that would be a serious thing if we were not still able to be a match for them by ourselves and with our resident aliens serving on board our ships. As it was, we can always match them in this way. Also—which is a very important point— we have among our own citizens more and better steersmen and sailors than all the rest of Hellas put together. Then, too, how many of our foreign sailors would, for the sake of a few days' extra pay, fight on the other side at the risk not only of being defeated but also of being outlawed from their own cities?

I have given, I think, a fair enough account of the position of the Peloponnesians. As for our own position, it has none of the weaknesses which I have noticed in theirs, and it also has a strength entirely of its own. If they invade our country by land, we will invade theirs by sea, and it will turn out that the destruction of a part of the Peloponnese will be worse for them than the destruction of the whole of Attica would be for us. For they can get no more land without fighting for it, while we have plenty of land both in the islands and on the continent.

Sea-power is of enormous importance. Look at it this way. Suppose we were an island, would we not be absolutely secure from attack? As it is we must try to think of ourselves as islanders; we must abandon our land and our houses, and safeguard the sea and the city. We must not, through anger at losing land and homes, join battle with the greatly superior forces of the Peloponnesians. If we won a victory, we should still have to fight them again in just the same numbers, and if we suffered a defeat, we should at the same time lose our allies, on whom our strength depends, since they will immediately revolt if we are left with insufficient troops to send against them. What we should lament is not the loss of houses or of land, but the loss of men's lives. Men come first; the rest is the fruit of their labor. And if I thought I could persuade you to do it, I would urge you to go out and lay waste your property with our own hands and show the Peloponnesians that it is not for the sake of this that you are likely to give in to them.

I could give you many other reasons why you should feel confident in ultimate victory, if only you will make up your minds not to add to the empire while the war is in progress, and not to go out of your way to involve yourselves in new perils. What I fear is not the enemy's strategy, but our own mistakes. However, I shall deal with this on another occasion when words and action will go together. For the present I recommend that we send back the Spartan ambassadors with the following answer: that we will give Megara access to our market and our ports, if at the same time Sparta exempts us and our allies from the operation of her orders for the expulsion of aliens (for in the treaty there is no clause forbidding either those orders of hers or our decree against Megara); that we will give their independence to our allies if they had it at the time that we made the treaty and when the Spartans also allow their own allies to be independent and have the kind of government each wants to have rather than the kind of government that suits Spartan interests. Let us say, too, that we are willing, according to the terms of the treaty, to submit to arbitration, that we shall not start the war, but that we shall resist those who do start it. This is the right reply to make and it is the reply that this city of ours ought to make. We must realize that this war is being forced upon us, and the more readily we accept the challenge the less eager to attack us our opponents will be. We must realize, too, that, both for cities and for individuals, it is from the greatest dangers that the greatest glory is to be won. When our fathers stood against the Persians they had no such resources as we have now; indeed, they abandoned even what they had, and then it was by wisdom rather than by good fortune, by daring rather than by material power, that they drove back the foreign invasion and made our city what it is today. We must live up to the standard they set: we must resist our enemies in any and every way, and try to leave to those who come after us an Athens that is as great as ever.

# Pericles

## AT THE FUNERAL OF FALLEN SOLDIERS, 431 BCE

*In the fighting, they thought it more honorable to stand their ground and suffer death than to give in and save their lives.*

Marble bust of Pericles, copy of Ktesilas.

**D**URING THE WARS in Afghanistan and Iraq, I was called upon to comfort families and to speak at military funerals and memorial services. Few questions are more profoundly difficult to answer than why a loved one has fallen in combat. Pericles' funeral oration during the first winter of the war between Sparta and Athens offers some answers.

Here, Pericles attempts to make sense of the great losses suffered by Athens while motivating his people to continue their sacrifices—even asking the sons and brothers of those who had fallen to take their place. Pericles appeals to patriotism and honor, promising eternal glory for all who join in battle. The speech's tone and structure are similar to Lincoln's Gettysburg Address. Over three thousand years separate both speeches, but they are poignantly connected in answering the profound question of "why we fight."

---

**I** SHALL BEGIN BY speaking about our ancestors, since it is only right and proper on such an occasion to pay them the honor of recalling what they did. In this land of ours there have always been the same people living from generation to generation up till now, and they, by their courage and their virtues, have handed it on to us, a free country. They certainly deserve our praise. Even more so do our fathers deserve it. For to the inheritance they had received they added all the empire we have now, and it was not without blood and toil that they handed it down to us of the present generation. And then we ourselves, assembled here today, who are mostly in the prime of life, have, in most directions, added to the power of our empire and have organized our State in such a way that it is perfectly well able to look after itself both in peace and in war.

I have no wish to make a long speech on subjects familiar to you all: so I shall say nothing about the warlike deeds by which we acquired our power or the battles in which we or our fathers gallantly resisted our enemies, Greek or foreign. What I want to do is, in the first place, to discuss the spirit in which we faced our trials and also our constitution and the way of life which has made us great. After that I shall speak in praise of the dead, believing that this kind of speech is not inappropriate to the present occasion, and that this whole assembly, of citizens and foreigners, may listen to it with advantage.

Let me say that our system of government does not copy the institutions of our neighbors. It is more the case of our being a model to others, than of our imitating anyone else. Our constitution is called a democracy because power is in the hands not of a minority but of the whole people. When it is a question of settling private disputes, everyone is equal before the law; when it is a question of putting one person before another in positions of public responsibility, what counts is not membership of a particular class, but the actual ability which the man possesses. No one, so long as he has it in him to be of service to the state, is kept in political obscurity because of poverty. And, just as our political life is free and open, so is our day-to-day life in our relations with each other. We do not get into a state with our next-door neighbor if he enjoys himself in his own way, nor do we give him the kind of black looks which, though they do no real harm, still do hurt people's feelings. We are free and tolerant in our private lives; but in public affairs we keep to the law. This is because it commands our deep respect.

We give our obedience to those whom we put in positions of authority, and we obey the laws themselves, especially those which are for the protection of the oppressed, and those unwritten laws which it is an acknowledged shame to break. . . .

And here is another point. When our work is over, we are in a position to enjoy all kinds of recreation for our spirits. There are various kinds of contests and sacrifices regularly throughout the year; in our own homes we find a beauty and a good taste which delights us every day and which drive away our cares. Then the greatness of our city brings it about that all the good things from all over the world flow in to us, so that to us it seems just as natural to enjoy foreign goods as our own local products.

Then there is a great difference between us and our opponents, in our attitude towards military security. Here are some examples: Our city is open to the world, and we have no periodical deportations in order to prevent people observing or finding out secrets which might be of military advantage to the enemy. This is because we rely, not on secret weapons, but on our own real courage and loyalty. There is a difference, too, in our educational systems. The Spartans, from their earliest boyhood, are submitted to the most laborious training in courage; we pass our lives without all these restrictions, and yet we are just as ready to face the same dangers as they are. Here is a proof of this: When the Spartans invade our land, they do not come by themselves, but bring all their allies with them; whereas we, when we launch an attack abroad, do the job by ourselves, and, though fighting on foreign soil, do not often fail to defeat opponents who are fighting for their own hearths and homes. As a matter of fact none of our enemies has ever yet been confronted with our total strength, because we have to divide our attention between our navy and the many missions on which our troops are sent on land. Yet if our enemies engage a detachment of our forces and defeat it, they give themselves credit for having thrown back our entire army; or, if they lose, they claim that they were beaten by us in full strength. There are certain advantages, I think, in our way of meeting danger voluntarily, with an easy mind, instead of with a laborious training, with natural rather than with state-induced courage. We do not have to spend our time practicing to meet sufferings which are still in the future; and when they are actually upon us we show ourselves just as brave as these others who are always in strict training. This is one point in which, I think, our city deserves to be admired. There are also others:

Our love of what is beautiful does not lead to extravagance; our love of the things of the mind does not make us soft. We regard wealth as something to be properly used, rather than as something to boast about. As for poverty, no one need be ashamed to admit it: the real shame is in not taking practical measures to escape from it. Here each individual is interested not only in his own affairs but in the affairs of the state as well: even those who are mostly occupied with their own business are extremely well-informed on general politics—this is a peculiarity of ours: we do not say that a man who takes no interest in politics is a man who minds his own business; we say that he has no business here at all. We Athenians, in our own persons, take our decisions on policy or submit them to proper discussions: for we do not think there is an incompatibility between words and deeds; the worst thing is to rush into action before the consequences have been properly debated. And this is another point where we differ from other people. We are capable at the same time of taking risks and of estimating them beforehand. Others are brave out of ignorance; and, when they stop to think, they begin to fear. But the man who can most truly be accounted brave is he who best knows the meaning of what is sweet in life and what is terrible, and then goes out undeterred to meet what is to come.

Again, in questions of general good feeling there is a great contrast between us and most other people. We make friends by doing good to others, not by receiving good from them. This makes our friendship all the more reliable, since we want to keep alive the gratitude of those who are in our debt by showing continued goodwill to them: whereas the feelings of one who owes us something lack the same enthusiasm, since he knows that, when he repays our kindness, it will be more like paying back a debt than giving something spontaneously. We are unique in this. When we do kindness to others, we do not do them out of any calculations of profit or loss: we do them without afterthought, relying on our free liberality. Taking everything together then, I declare that our city is an education to Greece, and I declare that in my opinion each single one of our citizens, in all the manifold aspects of life, is able to show himself the rightful lord and owner of his own person, and do this, moreover with exceptional grace and exceptional versatility. And to show that this is no empty boasting for the present occasion, but real tangible fact, you have only to consider the power which our city possesses and which has been won by those very qualities which I have mentioned. Athens, alone of the states we know, comes to her testing time in a greatness that surpasses what was imagined of her. In her case, and in her case alone, no invading enemy is ashamed at being defeated, and no subject can complain of being governed by people unfit for their responsibilities. Mighty indeed are the marks and monuments of our empire which we have left. Future ages will wonder at us, as the present age wonders at us now. We do not need the praises of a Homer, or of anyone else whose words may delight us for the moment, but the estimation of facts will fall short of what is really true. For our adventurous spirit has forced an entry into every sea and into every land: and everywhere we have left behind us everlasting memorials of good done to our friends or suffering inflicted on our enemies.

This, then, is the kind of city for which these men, who could not bear the thought of losing her, nobly fought and nobly died. It is only natural that every one of us who survive them should be willing to undergo hardships in her service. And it was for this reason that I have spoken at such length about our city, because I wanted to make it clear for us there is more at stake than there is for others who lack our advantages; also I wanted my words of praise for the dead to be set in the bright light of evidence. And now the most important of these words has been spoken. I have sung the praises of our city; but it was the courage and gallantry of these men, and people like them, which made her splendid. Nor would you find it true in the case of many of the Greeks, as it is true of them, that no words can do more than justice to their deeds.

To me it seems that the consummation which has overtaken these men shows us the meaning of manliness in its first revelation and in its final proof. Some of them, no doubt, had their faults; but what we ought to remember first is their gallant conduct against the enemy in defense of their native land. They have blotted out evil with good, and done more service to the commonwealth than they ever did harm in their private lives. No one of these men weakened because he wanted to go on enjoying his wealth: no one put off the awful day in the hope that he might live to escape his poverty and grow rich. More to be desired than such things, they chose to check the enemy's pride. This, to them, was a risk most glorious, and they accepted it, willing to strike down the enemy and relinquish everything else. As for success or failure, they left that in the doubtful hands of hope, and when the reality of battle was before their faces, they put their trust in their own selves. In the fighting, they thought it more honorable to stand their ground and suffer death than to give in and save their lives. So they fled from the reproaches of men, abiding with life and limb the brunt of battle; and, in a small moment of time, the climax of their lives, a culmination of glory, not of fear, were swept away from us.

So and such they were, these men—worthy of their city. We who remain behind may hope to be spared their fate, but must resolve to keep the same daring spirit against the foe. It is not simply a question of estimating the advantages in theory. I could tell you a long story (and you know it as well as I do) about what is to be gained by beating the enemy back. What I would prefer is that you should fix your eyes every day on the greatness of Athens as she really is, and should fall in love with her. When you realize her greatness, then reflect that what made her great was men with a spirit of adventure, men who knew their duty, men who were ashamed to fall below a certain standard. If they ever failed in an enterprise, they made up their minds that at any rate the city should not find their courage lacking to her, and they gave to her the best contribution that they could. They gave her their lives, to her and to all of us, and for their own selves they won praises that never grow old, the most splendid of sepulchers—not the sepulcher in which their bodies are laid, but where their glory remains eternal in men's minds, always there on the right occasion to stir others to speech or action. For famous men have the whole earth as their memorial: it is not only the inscription on their graves in their own country that mark them out; no, in foreign lands also, not in any visible form but in people's hearts, their memory abides and grows. It is for you to try to be like them. Make up your minds that happiness depends on being free, freedom depends on being courageous. Let there be no relaxation in face of the perils of the war. The people who have most excuse for despising death are not the wretched and unfortunate, who have no hope of doing well for themselves, but those who run the risk of a complete reversal in their lives, and who would feel the difference most intensely, if things went wrong for them. Any intelligent man would find a humiliation caused by his own slackness more painful to bear than death, when death comes to him unperceived, in battle, and in the confidence of this patriotism.

For these reasons I shall not commiserate with those parents of the dead, those who are present here. Instead I shall try to comfort them. They are well aware that they have grown up in a world where there are many changes and chances. But this is good fortune—for men to end their lives with honor, as these have done, and for you honorably to lament them: their life was set to a measure where death and happiness went hand in hand. I know that it is difficult to convince you of this. When you see other people happy you will often be reminded of what used to make you happy too. One does not feel sad at not having some good thing which is outside one's experience: real grief is felt at the loss of something which one is used to. All the same, those of you who are of the right age must bear up and take comfort in the thought of having more children. In your own homes these new children will prevent you from brooding over those who are no more, and they will be a help to the city, too, both in filling the empty places, and in assuring her security. For it is impossible for a man to put forward fair and honest views about our affairs if he has not, like everyone else, children whose lives may be at stake. As for those of you who are now too old to have children, I would ask you to count as gain the greater part of your life, in which you have been happy, and remember that what remains is not long, and let your hearts be lifted up at the thought of the fair fame of the dead. One's sense of honor is the only thing that does not grow old, and the last pleasure, when one is worn out with age, is not, as the poet said, making money, but having the respect of one's fellow man.

As for those of you who are sons or brothers of the dead, I can see a hard struggle in front of you. Everyone always speaks well of the dead, and, even if you rise to the greatest heights of heroism, it will be a hard thing for you to get the reputation of having come near, let alone equaled, their standard. When one is alive, one is always liable to the jealousy of one's competitors, but when one is out of the way, the honor one receives is sincere and unchallenged.

Perhaps I should say a word or two on the duties of women to those among you who are now widowed. I can say all I have to say in a short word of advice. Your great glory is not to be inferior to what God had made you, and the greatest glory of a woman is to be least talked about by men, whether they are praising you or criticizing you. I have now, as the law demanded, said what I had to say. For the time being our offerings to the dead have been made, and for the future their children will be supported at the public expense by the city, until they come of age. This is the crown and prize which she offers, both to the dead and to their children, for the ordeals which they have faced. Where the rewards of valor are the greatest, there you will find also the best and bravest spirit among the people. And now, when you have mourned for your dear ones, you must depart.

# Pericles

## LIFTING THE MORALE OF ATHENS, 430 BCE

*Not courage alone, therefore, but an actual sense of your superiority should animate you as you go forward against the enemy.*

Bust of Pericles, Roman copy of Greek work.

I N THE LATE SUMMER OF **430,** Pericles found himself in a maelstrom. The war with Sparta had turned unpopular, a plague had swept through Athens, and the Athenian assembly had defied its leader by voting to send diplomats to Sparta to negotiate an end to hostilities. At a critical time, it fell upon Pericles to lift the morale of an anxious population.

His technique was anything but defensive. He begins by noting: "You took my advice when you were still untouched by misfortune, and repented of your actions when things went badly with you; it is because your own resolution is weak that my policy appears to you to be mistaken." Then he returns to themes that inspired Athens at the start of war: their military superiority, their sea-power dominance, and their obligation to their fathers and to the future. He concludes by noting that conquest engenders two responses: a temporary hatred among those defeated and the permanent glory of the victory itself.

Pericles won the debate. Yet his political opposition continued to mount, and he was soon tried and convicted of embezzlement.

------◆◆◆------

I EXPECTED THIS OUTBREAK OF ANGER on your part against me, since I understand the reason for it; and I have called an assembly with this object in view, to remind you of your previous resolutions and to put forward my own case against you, if we find that there is anything unreasonable in your anger against me and in your giving way to your misfortunes. My own opinion is that when the whole state is on the right course it is a better thing for each separate individual than when private interests are satisfied but the state as a whole is going downhill. However well off a man may be in his private life, he will still be involved in the general ruin if his country is destroyed; whereas, so long as the state itself is secure, individuals have a much greater chance of recovering from their private misfortunes. Therefore, since a state can support individuals in their suffering, but no one person by himself can bear the load that rests upon the state, is it not right for us all to rally to her defense? Is it not wrong to act as you are doing now? For you have been so dismayed by disaster in your homes that you are losing your grip on the common safety; you are attacking me for having spoken in favor of war and yourselves for having voted for it.

So far as I am concerned, if you are angry with me you are angry with the one who has, I think, at least as much ability as anyone else to see what ought to be done and to explain what he sees, one who loves his city and one who is above being influenced by money. A man who has the knowledge but lacks the power clearly to express it is no better off than if he never had any ideas at all. A man who has both these qualities, but lacks patriotism, could scarcely speak for his own people as he should. And even if he is patriotic as well, but not able to resist a bribe, then this one fault will expose everything to the risk of being bought and sold. So that if at the time when you took my advice and went to war you considered that my record with regard to these qualities was even slightly better than that of others, then now surely it is quite unreasonable for me to be accused of having done wrong.

If one has a free choice and can live undisturbed, it is sheer folly to go to war. But suppose the choice was forced upon one—submission and immediate slavery or danger with the hope of survival: then I prefer the man who stands up to danger rather than the one who runs away from it. As for me, I am the same as I was, and do not alter; it is you who have changed. What has happened is this: you took my advice when you were still untouched by misfortune, and repented of your actions when things went badly for you; it is because your own resolution is weak that my policy appears to you to be mistaken. It is a policy which entails suffering, and each one of you already knows what this suffering is; but its ultimate benefits are still far away not yet clear for all to see. So, now that a great and sudden disaster has fallen on you, you have weakened in carrying out to the end the resolves which you made. When things happen suddenly, unexpectedly, and against all calculation, it takes the heart out of a man; and this certainly has happened to you, with the plague coming on top of everything else. Yet you must remember that you are citizens of a great city and that you were brought up in a way of life suited to her greatness; you must therefore be willing to face the greatest disasters and be determined never to sacrifice the glory that is yours. We all look with distaste on people who arrogantly pretend to a reputation to which they are not entitled; but equally to be condemned are those who, through lack of moral fiber, fail to live up to the reputation which is theirs already. Each of you, therefore, must try to stifle his own particular sorrow as he joins with the rest in working for the safety of us all.

And if you think that our war-time sufferings may grow greater and greater and still not bring us any nearer to victory, you ought to be satisfied with the arguments which I have often used on other occasions to show that there is no good reason for such fears. But there is this point also which I shall mention. In thinking of the greatness of your empire there is one advantage you have which, I think, you have never taken into consideration, nor have I mentioned it in my previous speeches. Indeed, since it sounds almost like boasting, I shall not be making use of this argument now if it were not for the act that I see that you are suffering from an unreasonable feeling of discouragement. Now, what you think is that your empire consists simply of your allies: but I have something else to tell you. The whole world before our eyes can be divided into two parts, the land and the sea, each of which is valuable and useful to man. Of the whole of one of these parts you are in control—not only of the area at present in your power, but elsewhere too, if you want to go further. With your navy as it is today there is no power on earth—not the King of Persia nor any people under the sun—which can stop you from sailing where you wish. This power of yours is something in an altogether different category from all the advantages of houses or of cultivated land. You may think that when you lose them you have suffered a great loss, but in fact you should not take things so hardly; you should weigh them in the balance with the real source of your power and see that, it comparison, they are no more to be valued than gardens and other elegances that go with wealth. Remember, too, that freedom, if we preserve our freedom by our own efforts, will easily restore us to our old position; but to submit to the will of others means to lose even what we still have. You must not fall below the standard of your fathers, who not only won an empire by their own toil and sweat, without receiving it from others, but went on to keep it safe so that they could hand it down to you. And, by the way, it is more of a disgrace to be robbed of what one has than to fail in some new undertaking. Not courage alone, therefore, but an actual sense of your superiority should animate you as you go forward against the enemy. Confidence, out of a mixture of ignorance and good luck, can be felt even by cowards; but this sense of superiority comes only to these who, like us, have real reasons for knowing they are better placed than their opponents. And when the chances on both sides are equal, it is intelligence that confirms courage—the intelligence that makes one able to look down on one's opponent, and which proceeds not by hoping for the best (a method only valuable in desperate situations), but by estimating what the facts are, and thus obtaining a clearer vision of what to expect.

Then it is right and proper for you to support the imperial dignity of Athens. This is something in which you all take pride, and you cannot continue to enjoy the privileges unless you also shoulder the burdens of empire. And do not imagine that what we are fighting for is simply the question of freedom or slavery: there is also involved the loss of our empire and the dangers arising from the hatred which we have incurred in administering it. Nor is it any longer possible for you to give up this empire, though there may be some people who in a mood of sudden panic and in a spirit of political apathy actually think that this would be a fine and noble thing to do. Your empire is now like a tyranny; it may have been wrong to take it; it is certainly dangerous to let it go. And the kind of people who talk of doing so and persuade others to adopt their point of view would very soon bring a state to ruin, and would still do so even if they lived by themselves in isolation. For those who are politically apathetic can only survive if they are supported by people who are capable of taking action. They are quite valueless in a city which controls an empire, though they would be safe slaves in a city that was controlled by others.

But you should not be led astray by such citizens as these; nor should you be angry with me, you who came to the same conclusion as I did about the necessity for making war. Certainly the enemy have invaded our country and done as one might have expected they would do, once you refused to give in to them; and then the plague, something which we did not expect, fell upon us. In fact out of everything else this has been the only case of something happening which we did not anticipate. And I know that is very largely because of this that I have become unpopular, quite unfairly, unless you are also going to put down to my credit every piece of unexpected good fortune that comes your way. But it is right to endure with resignation what the gods send, and to face one's enemies with courage. This was the old Athenian way: do not let any acts of yours prevent if from still being so. Remember, too, that the reason why Athens has the greatest name in all the world is because she has never given in to adversity, but has spent more life and labor in warfare than any other state, thus winning the greatest power that has ever existed in history, such a power that will be remembered forever by posterity, even if now (since all things are born to decay) there should come a time when we were forced to yield: yet still it will be remembered that of all the Hellenic powers we held the widest sway over the Hellenes, that we stood firm in the greatest wars against their combined forces and against individual states, that we lived in a city that had been perfectly equipped in every direction and which was the greatest in Hellas.

No doubt all of this will be disparaged by people who are politically apathetic; but those who, like us, prefer a life of action will try to imitate us, and, if they fail to secure what we have secured, they will envy us. All who have taken it upon themselves to rule over others have incurred hatred and unpopularity for a time; but if one has a great aim to pursue, this burden of envy must be accepted, and it is wise to accept it. Hatred does not last for long; but the brilliance of the present is the glory of the future stored up forever in the memory of man. It is for you to safeguard that future glory and to do nothing now that is dishonorable. Now, therefore, is the time to show your energy and to achieve both these objects. Do not send embassies to Sparta: do not give the impression that you are bowed down under your present sufferings! To face calamity with a mind as unclouded as may be, and quickly to react against it—that, in a city and in an individual, is real strength.

# Isocrates

## On Resisting Persia,
## 380 BCE

*And how great must we consider the fame,*
*and the memory, and the glory*
*which those will either have in their lives,*
*or leave behind them in their deaths,*
*who have been the bravest in such exploits?*

Engraving by an unknown artist (1778) from a marble bust at Rome.

A DISTANT ECHO OF THE REFRAIN "united we stand, divided we fall" is sounded in this speech by Isocrates, one of Athens' most famous orators. By 380 BCE, Greece had become unstable. Conflicts arose between city states, social tensions flared between rich and poor, and Athens' chief threat, Persia, stood ready to exploit these vulnerabilities.

Here, Isocrates, one of the most famous orators of Athens, attempts to garner support for a war against Persia. He reminds his listeners of the glory of Greece—its intellectual, political, cultural, and military achievements. He illustrates that Greece is one culture, one people. Isocrates calls for an end to internal divisions and a focus on Persia, a foe capable of conquering all of Greece. Unity of purpose, argues Isocrates, will allow Greece to defeat Persia, a triumph that will bring glory and concord to a nation troubled by internal weakness.

---

IT IS CONFESSED indeed that our state is the most ancient and the greatest, and the most celebrated among all men; and the foundation being thus glorious, on account of what follows these it is still more befitting that we should be honored. For we inhabit this city, not having expelled others, nor having found it deserted, nor collected promiscuously from many nations, but we are of such honorable and genuine birth that we continue for all time possessing this land from which we were born, being sprung from the soil, and being able to call our city by the same names as our nearest relations, for we alone of all the Greeks have a right to call the same—nurse and fatherland and mother. And yet it is right that those who with good reason entertain high thoughts, and who justly dispute the supremacy and who often make mention of their hereditary rights, should prove the origin of their race to be of this nature.

The advantages, then which we possessed from the beginning, and which were bestowed upon us by fortune, are so great in magnitude; but of how great advantages we have been the cause to the rest we should thus best investigate, if we should go through in detail the time from the commencement, and the exploits of the State in succession; for we shall find that she not only [delivered us] from the dangers in respect of war, but also is the cause of that established order besides in which we dwell and with which we live as free citizens, and by means of which we are able to live.

Of the wars, indeed, the Persian was the most famous; the old achievements, however, are not less strong proofs for those who dispute about hereditary institutions. For when Greece was still in a lowly condition, the Thracians indeed came to our land with Eumolpus the son of Poseidon, and Scythians with the Amazons the daughters of Mars, not at the same time, but at the time when each of them were rulers of Europe, hating, indeed, the whole race of the Greeks, but making charges against us separately, thinking that by this line of conduct they would incur danger against one state indeed, but would at the same time conquer all.

They did not, however, succeed, but having engaged with our ancestors separately, they were destroyed equally as if they had made war on all together. And the magnitude of the evils which befell them is manifest, for the speeches concerning them would never have lived on for so long a time had not also their achievements far excelled those of other men. It is recorded, then concerning the Amazons, that not one of those who came went back again, while those who were left at home were driven out of their government on account of their calamity here; and concerning the Thracians, [it is said] that although during the former times they dwelt beside us, on our borders, yet on account of that expedition they left so great an intervening space, that in the district between us, many nations and all kinds of races and great cities have been established.

Glorious indeed, then are these things, and befitting those who dispute for the supremacy, but akin to what has been said, and such as it is natural that those sprung from such men would perform, were the exploits of those who waged war against Darius and Xerxes.

Always indeed, then, both our ancestors and the Lacedæmonians acted in a spirit of rivalry to each other. Not but what in those times they contended for the most glorious objects, not thinking each other to be enemies, but rivals, not paying court to the foreigner with a view to the slavery of the Greeks, but being of one mind about the common safety, and engaging in a contest as to this, viz., which of the two shall be the authors of it. And they displayed their valor first, indeed, in the case of those sent by Darius. For when these had landed in Attica, the one did not wait for their allies, but making what was a common war a personal one, they went out to meet those who had treated contemptuously the whole of Hellas with their private force, a few against many myriads, as if about to brave the danger in the case of the lives of other, while the others no sooner heard of the war being in Attica than, neglecting everything else they came to assist us, making as great haste as if it was their own country which was being ravaged.

And after these things, when the subsequent expedition took place, which Xerxes led in person, after abandoning his palace and undertaking to become a general, and having collected all the men from Asia; and who, being anxious not to speak in extravagant terms, has spoken about him in language which fell short of the reality?—a man, who reached such a height of arrogance, that considering it to be a trifling achievement to subdue Greece, and wishing to leave behind such a monument as surpasses human nature, ceased not until he had devised and at the same time carried out by compulsion that which all talk of, so that with his armament he sailed through the mainland and marched over the sea, having bridged over the Hellespont and dug a canal through Athos. Against him, indeed, having such high thoughts, and having succeeded in accomplishing such great deeds and having become the lord of so many, they went forth, having divided amongst themselves the danger, the Lacedæmonians indeed to Thermopylae against the land force, having selected a thousand of themselves, and taking along with them a few of their allies with the intention of preventing them in the narrow pass from advancing farther, while our fathers went out to Artemisium, having manned sixty triremes to meet the whole naval force of the enemy. And they had the courage to do these things, not so much through contempt of the enemy as from a spirit of rivalry with each other, the Lacedæmonians indeed envying our state, for the battle at Marathon, and seeking to put themselves on an equality with us, and fearing lest our state should twice in succession become the author of deliverance to the Greeks, and our fathers wishing chiefly indeed to retain their present glory and to make it manifest to all that both in the former case it was through valor and not through fortune that they had conquered; in the next place also to induce the Greeks to maintain a sea-fight by showing to them that valor gets the better of numbers in naval dangers and enterprise equally as in those by land.

And to the king of Asia, indeed, nothing is more important than to consider by what means we shall never cease warring against one another, while we are so far from bringing any of his interest into collision or causing them to be distracted by factions, that we even endeavor to assist in putting an end to the troubles which have befallen him through fortune; since we also allow him to make use of one of the two armaments in Cyprus, and to blockade the other, though both of them belong to Hellas. For both those who have revolted are friendly disposed towards us and give themselves up to the Lacedæmonians, and the most useful part of those who are serving with Tiribazus and of the land army have been collected from these districts, and the greater part of the navy has sailed along with them from Ionia, who would much more gladly have ravaged Asia in concert than have fought against one another on account of trifles. Of these things we take no thought, but we are disputing about the islands of the Cyclades, and thus heedlessly have we surrendered to the foreign foe cities so many in number and so great in magnitude. Therefore, he is in possession of some, and is on the point of taking possessions of others, and is plotting against others, having despised all of us, and with good reason. For he has effected what no one of his ancestors ever did; for it has been agreed on, both by us and by the Lacedæmonians, that Asia belongs to the king, and he has taken possession of the Grecian cities with such authority as to raze some of them to the ground, and in others to fortify citadels. And all these things have happened through our folly and not on account of his power.

Our citizens are at this time reconciled with all the others with whom they have been at war, and forget the hostility which has arisen, but to the inhabitants of the continent they do not feel grateful, even when they receive benefits [from them], so undying is the anger they feel toward them. And our fathers condemned many to death for favoring the Medes; and even at the present day, in their public assemblies, they make imprecations, before they transact any other business, on whomsoever of the citizens makes proposals for peace to the Persians. And the Eumolpidæ and the Heralds, in the celebration of the mysteries, on account of their hatred for them, proclaim publicly also to all other foreigners, as they do to homicides, that they are excluded from the sacred rites. And such hostile feelings do we entertain by nature toward them, that even in our legends, we occupy ourselves with most pleasure with those relating to the Trojan and Persian wars, by which it is possible to hear of the calamities. And one might find hymns composed in consequence of the war against the foreigners, but dirges produced for us in consequence of that against the Greeks, and might find the former sung at the festivals, while we call to mind the latter in our calamities. And I think that even the poetry of Homer received greater honors, because he nobly extolled those who made war against the foreign foe; and that for this reason our ancestors wished to make his art honored, both in the contest in poetry and in the education of the younger generation, in order that, hearing frequently his poems, we may learn by heart the enmity which existed toward them, and, emulating the deeds of valor of those who made war upon them, may set our hearts upon the same exploits as they achieved.

Wherefore there appear to me to be very many things which encourage us to make war against them, and especially the present favorable opportunity, than which nothing is more clear. And we must not let it slip. For, in fact, it is disgraceful not to use it when present, but to remember it when it is past. For what additional advantage could we even wish to have, if intending to go to war with the king, beyond what we already possess? Has not Egypt revolted from him, as well as Cyprus; and have not Phœnicia and Syria been devastate owing to the war; and has not Tyre, on account of which he was greatly elated, been seized by his enemies? And the majority of the cities in Cilicia those on our side possess, and the rest it is not difficult to acquire. But Lycia no one of the Persians ever conquered. And Hecatomnos, the overseer of Caria, in reality indeed has revolted for a long time already, and will confess it whenever we may wish. And from Cnidus to Sinope the Greeks inhabit the coasts of Asia, who it is not necessary to persuade to go to war but [only] not to prevent them.

And yet, as we already possess so many bases of operation, and as so great a war encircles Asia, what need is there to accurately scrutinize what are likely to be the results? For where they are inferior to small portions, it is not uncertain how they would be disposed, if they should be compelled to war with all of us. Now the case stands thus. If, indeed, the king occupy in greater force the cities on the sea-coast, establishing in them greater garrisons than at present, perhaps also those of the islands which are near the mainland, as Rhodes and Samos and Chios, might lean to his fortunes; but if we be the first to seize them, it is probable that those inhabiting Lydia and Phrygia, and the rest of the country which lies above them would be in the power of those who make these their base of operations. Wherefore it is necessary to hasten and to make no loss of time, that we may not suffer what our fathers did.

And it is fitting to make the expedition in the present age, in order that those who participate in the calamities may also have the enjoyment of the advantages, and may not continue to live unfortunate during all their lifetime. For the time past is sufficient—in which what horror is there which has not happened?—for though there are many evils already existing in the nature of man, we ourselves have invented in addition more than the necessary evils, having created wars and factions among ourselves, so that some are perishing lawlessly in their own cities, and some are wandering in a foreign land with their children and wives, and many being compelled, through want of the daily necessaries of life, to serve as mercenaries, are dying fighting against their friends on behalf of their enemies. And at this not one has ever been indignant, but they think it becoming to shed tears at the calamites composed by poets, but, though gazing upon many dreadful genuine sufferings happening on account of the war, they are so far from pitying them, that they even take more pleasure in the misfortunes of one another than in their own personal advantages. And perhaps, also, many might laugh at my simplicity, if I were to lament the misfortunes of individuals at such critical times, in which Italy has been devastated, and Sicily reduced to slavery, and so many cities have been surrendered to the foreigners, and the remaining portions of the Greeks are in the greatest dangers.

Now it is necessary to put out of the way these plottings, and to attempt those deeds from which we shall both inhabit our cities in greater security, and be more faithfully disposed to one another, and what is to be said about these matters is simple and easy. For it is neither possible to enjoy a secure peace, unless we make war in concert against the foreign enemy, nor for the Greeks to be of one mind until we consider both our advantages to come from one another, and our dangers to be against the same people.

But when these things have been done, and the embarrassment with regard to our means of living has been taken away, which both dissolves friendships and perverts relationships into enmity, and involves all men in wars and factions, it is not possible that we shall not be of one mind, and entertain toward one another genuine feelings of good will. For which reasons we must esteem it of the greatest importance how we shall, as soon as possible, banish the war from hence to the continent, as this is the only advantage we should reap from the dangers in fighting against one another, namely, if it should seem good to us to employ against the foreign foe the experience which we have derived from them.

And truly we shall not even annoy the cities by enrolling soldiers from them, a thing which is not most troublesome to them in the war against one another; for I think that those who will wish to stay at home will be much fewer in number than those who will desire to follow with us. For who, whether young or old, is so indifferent that he will not wish to have a share in this expedition, commanded indeed by the Athenians and Lac, but collected in defense of the liberty of the allies, and sent out by the whole of Hellas, and marching to take vengeance upon the foreign foe? And how great must we consider the fame, and the memory, and the glory which those will either have in their lives, or leave behind them in their deaths, who have been the bravest in such exploits? For where those who made war against Alexander, and captured one city, were deemed worthy of such praises, what panegyrics must we expect that they will obtain who have conquered the whole of Asia? For who, either of those able to write poetry, or of those who understand how to speak, will not labor and study, wishing to leave behind him a memorial for all ages, at the same time of his own intellect and of their valor?

# Hannibal

## To His Soldiers, 218 BCE

*Here, soldiers, where you have first met the enemy,
you must conquer or die.*

Portrait bust of Hannibal.

Hannibal's march across the Alps during the Second Punic War (218–201 BCE) is considered one of the boldest and most difficult military exploits in history. Just as inspiring as the march itself is how Hannibal prepared his troops for battle when they descended into Italy.

After Rome declared war on Carthage, Hannibal left Spain on a five-month, forty-thousand-man march to Italy. After a fifteen-day crossing of the Alps—in severe weather and against hostile populations—they arrived in Italy's northern hills, decimated and weary. Hannibal was required to motivate them for a difficult battle. He begins by acknowledging their ominous position—surrounded by water and mountains, with no escape route. Hannibal strengthens their confidence by comparing them with their foes; and personalizes his argument by contrasting his skills as a general to those of his opponents': "Shall I compare myself—almost born, and certainly bred, in the tent of my father, that most illustrious commander, myself the subjugator of Spain and Gaul, the conqueror too not only of the Alpine nations, but, what is much more, of the Alps themselves—with this six-months' general, the deserter of his army?" Then he reminds them that they are fighting not for material reward alone, but for their destiny. Finally, he tells them that if they are willing to conquer or to die in battle, they have already triumphed: "no stronger incentive to victory has been given to man by the immortal gods."

Some two thousand years later, Napoléon Bonaparte would follow Hannibal across the Alps and echo many of his words.

———◆———

If, soldiers, you shall by and by, in judging of your own fortune, preserve the same feelings which you experienced a little before in the example of the fate of others, we have already conquered; for neither was that merely a spectacle, but, as it were, a certain representation of your consideration. And I know not whether fortune has not thrown around you still stronger chains and necessities than around your captives. On the right and left two seas enclose you, without your possessing even a single ship for escape. The river Po around you, the Po larger and more impetuous than the Rhone; the Alps behind, scarcely passed by you when fresh and vigorous, hem you in.

Here soldiers, where you have first met the enemy, you must conquer or die; and the same fortune which has imposed the necessity of fighting holds out to you, if victorious, rewards than which men are not wont to desire greater, even from the immortal gods. If we were only about to recover by our valor Sicily and Sardinia, wrested from our fathers, the recompense would be sufficiently ample; but whatever, acquired and amassed by so many triumphs, the Romans possess, all, with its masters themselves, will become yours. To gain this rich reward, hasten, then, and seize your arms, with the favor of the gods.

Long enough, in pursuing cattle among the desert mountains of Lusitania and Celtiberia, you have seen no emolument from so many toils and dangers; it is time to make rich and comfortable campaigns, and to gain the great reward of your labors, after having accomplished such a length of journey over so many mountains and rivers, and so many nations in arms. Here fortune has granted you the termination of your labors; here she will bestow a reward worthy of the service you have undergone. Nor, in proportion as the war is great in name, ought you to consider that the victory will be difficult. A despised enemy has often maintained a sanguinary contest, and renowned States and kings have been conquered by a very slight effort.

For, setting aside only the splendor of the Roman name, what remains with which they can be compared to you? To pass over in silence your service for twenty years, distinguished by such valor and success, you have made your way to this place from the pillars of Hercules, from the ocean and the remotest limits of the world, advancing victorious through so many of the fiercest nations of Gaul and Spain; you will fight with a raw army, which this very summer was beaten, conquered, and surrounded by the Gauls, as yet unknown to its general, and ignorant of him. Shall I compare myself—almost born, and certainly bred, in the tent of my father, that most illustrious commander, myself the subjugator of Spain and Gaul, the conqueror too not only of the Alpine nations, but, what is much more, of the Alps themselves—with this six-months' general, the deserter of his army?—to whom, if anyone, having taken away their standards, should today show the Carthaganians and Romans, I am sure that he would not know of which army he was consul.

I do not regard it, soldiers, as of small account, that there is not a man among you before whose eyes I have not often achieved some military exploit; and to whom, in like manner, I, the spectator and witness of his valor, could not recount his own gallant deeds, particularized by time and place. With soldiers who have a thousand times received my praises and gifts, I, who was the pupil of you all before I became your commander, will march out in battle-array against those who are unknown to and ignorant of each other.

On whatever side I turn my eyes I see nothing but what is full courage and energy: a veteran infantry; cavalry, both those with and those without the bridle; composed of the most gallant nations—you our most faithful and valiant allies, you Carthaginians, who are about to fight as well for the sake of your country as from the justest resentment. We are the assailants in the war, and descend into Italy with hostile standards, about to engage so much more boldly and bravely than the foe, as the confidence and courage of the assailants are greater than those of him who is defensive. Besides, suffering, injury, and indignity inflame and excite our minds: they first demanded me, your leader, for punishment, and then all of you who had laid siege to Saguntum; and had we been given up they would have visited us with the severest tortures.

That most cruel and haughty nation considers everything its own, and at its own disposal; it thinks it right that it should regulate with whom we are to have war, with whom peace; it circumscribes and shuts us up by the boundaries of mountains and rivers which we must not pass, then does not adhere to those boundaries which it appointed. Pass not the Iberius; have nothing to do with the Saguntines. Saguntum is on the Iberius: you must not move a step in any direction. Is it a small thing that you take away my most ancient provinces—Sicily and Sardinia? Will you take Spain also? And should I withdraw thence, will you cross over into Africa?

Will cross, did I say? They have sent the two consuls of this year, one to Africa, the other to Spain; there is nothing left to us in any quarter except what we can assert ourselves by arms. Those may be the cowards and dastards who have something to look back upon; whom, flying through safe and unmolested roads, their own lands and their own country will receive: there is a necessity for you to be brave, and, since all between victory and death is broken off from you by inevitable despair, either to conquer, or if fortune should waver, to meet death rather in battle than in flight. If this be well fixed and determined in the minds of you all, I will repeat, you have already conquered; no stronger incentive to victory has been given to man by the immortal gods.

# Catiline

## To His Troops,
## 62 BCE

*But, if Fortune be unjust to your valor,*
*take care not to lose your lives unavenged;*
*take care not to be taken and butchered like cattle,*
*rather than, fighting like men, to leave to your enemies*
*a bloody and mournful victory.*

*Cicero Denounces Catiline*, by Cesare Maccari (1840–1919).

CAN WORDS INSPIRE men to commit unnatural acts of bravery? Catiline casts doubt on this as he begins his final address to his soldiers before battle. Yet, by the time he concludes, he instills them with the confidence necessary to advance against overwhelming power.

Accused of conspiring against Rome, Catiline has fled the city to organize an army against it. After maneuvering between Rome and Gaul, he finds himself surrounded, and his only hope is an advance against the army of Antonius. Catiline's speech inspires his troops to surge forward . . . and into defeat. However, Catiline died true to his words: his body was found on the battlefield, far in front of his own lines.

For a more contemporary—in every sense of the word—version of Catiline's speech, see Gen. George Patton's address to the Third Army.

---

I AM WELL AWARE, soldiers, that words cannot inspire courage, and that a spiritless army cannot be rendered active, or a timid army valiant, by the speech of its commander. Whatever courage is in the heart of a man, whether from nature or from habit, so much will be shown by him in the field; and on him whom neither glory nor danger can move, exhortation is bestowed in vain; for the terror in his breast stops his ears.

I have called you together, however, to give you a few instructions, and to explain to you, at the same time, my reasons for the course which I have adopted. You all know, soldiers, how severe a penalty the inactivity and cowardice of Lentulus has brought upon himself and us; and how, while waiting for reinforcements from the city, I was unable to march into Gaul. In what situation our affairs now are, you all understand as well as myself. Two armies of the enemy, one on the side of Rome and the other on that of Gaul, oppose our progress; while the want of corn and of other necessaries prevents us from remaining, however strongly we may desire to remain, in our present position. Whithersoever we would go, we must open a passage with our swords. I conjure you, therefore, to maintain a brave and resolute spirit; and to remember, when you advance to battle that on your own right hands depend riches, honor, and glory, with the enjoyment of liberty and of your country. If we conquer, all will be safe; we shall have provisions in abundance; and the colonies and corporate towns will open their gates to us. But if we lose the victory through want of courage, those same places will turn against us; for neither place nor friend will protect him whom his arms have not protected. Besides, soldiers, the same exigency does not press upon our adversaries as presses upon us; we fight for our country, for our liberty, for our life; they contend for what little concerns them, the power of a small party. Attack them, therefore, with so much the greater confidence, and call to mind your achievements of old.

We might, with the utmost ignominy, have passed the rest of our days in exile. Some of you, after losing your property, might have waited at Rome for assistance from others. But because such a life, to men of spirit, was disgusting and unendurable, you resolved upon your present course. If you wish to quit it, you must exert all your resolution, for none but conquerors have exchanged war for peace. To hope for safety in flight when you have turned away from the enemy the arms by which the body is defended is indeed madness. In battle those who are most afraid are always in most danger; but courage is equivalent to a rampart.

When I contemplate you, soldiers, and when I consider your past exploits, a strong hope of victory animates me. Your spirit, your age, your valor, give me confidence; to say nothing of necessity, which makes even cowards brave. To prevent the numbers of the enemy from surrounding us, our confined situation is sufficient. But should Fortune be unjust to your valor, take care not to lose your lives unavenged; take care not to be taken and butchered like cattle, rather than, fighting like men, to leave to your enemies a bloody and mournful victory.

# Eleazar ben Yair

## DEATH, NOT SLAVERY,
## MAY 73

*Let us die unenslaved by our enemies,*
*and leave this world as free men*
*in company with our wives and children.*

Aerial view of the ruins of the Masada in the Judean Desert, Israel.

**W**ORDS HAVE BEEN USED to motivate people to overcome their fears, risk their lives, and charge headlong into seemingly unbeatable foes. On the mountaintop fortress Masada, Eleazar ben Yair exhorted 960 followers—the last remnant of the Jewish revolt against Rome—to defeat their enemy not by attacking, but by taking their own lives. Jerusalem had been devastated, the Second Temple destroyed, and now, the Tenth Legion was preparing its final assault of Masada after a three-year siege. Knowing that the Romans would breach the summit within a day, Ben Yair asked his people to demonstrate the ultimate act of defiance: burn their fortress to the ground, commit mass suicide, but leave their food supplies intact. "It will bear witness . . . to the fact that we perished not through want, but because, as we resolved at the beginning, we chose death rather than slavery."

Ben Yair employs a variety of rhetorical devices to persuade his followers. First he must convince them that they have no chance of defeating the enemy: "God Himself, without a doubt, has taken away all hope of survival." The choice for them is stark: suicide or surrender. He then uses graphic imagery to describe both. Death is portrayed as divine, when the soul is liberated from the body. In contrast, the plight of those who submitted to Roman conquest is grotesquely described: "Some of them have been broken on the rack or tortured to death at the stake or by the lash; some have been half-eaten by savage beasts and then kept alive to be their food a second time, after providing amusement and sport for their enemies. Of them all we have most cause to pity those who are still alive; for they pray and pray for the death that never comes." If the examples of others are not sufficiently persuasive, ben Yair projects what his followers will experience if they are alive when the Romans reach the fortress: "A man will see his wife violently carried off; he will hear the voice of his child crying, 'Father!' when his own hands are fettered. Come! While our hands are free and can hold a sword, let them do a noble service!"

When the Romans finally breached the summit, the only thing left for them to despoil was the food.

---

**M**Y LOYAL FOLLOWERS, long ago we resolved to serve neither the Romans nor anyone else but only God, who alone is the true and righteous Lord of men: now the time has come that bids us prove our determination by our deeds. At such a time we must not disgrace ourselves; hitherto we have never submitted to slavery, even when it brought danger with it: we must not choose slavery now, and with it penalties that will mean the end of everything if we fall alive into the hands of the Romans. For we were the first of all to revolt, and shall be the last to break off the struggle. And I think it is God who has given us this privilege, that we can die nobly and as free men, unlike others who were unexpectedly defeated. In our case it is evident that daybreak will end our resistance, but we are free to choose an honorable death with our loved ones. This our enemies cannot prevent, however earnestly they may pray to take us alive; nor can we defeat them in battle.

From the very first, when we were bent on claiming our freedom but suffered such constant misery at each other's hands and worse at the enemy's, we ought perhaps to have read the mind of God and realized that His once beloved Jewish race had been sentenced to extinction. For if He had remained gracious or only slightly indignant with us, He would not have shut His eyes to the destruction of so many thousands or allowed His most holy City to be burnt to the ground by our enemies. We hoped, or so it would seem, that of all of the Jewish race we alone would come through safely still in possession of our freedom, as if we had committed no sin against God and taken part in no crime—we who had taught the others! Now see how He shows the folly of our hopes, plunging us into miseries more terrible than any we had dreamt of. Not even the impregnability of our fortress has sufficed to save us, but though we have food in abundance, ample supplies of arms, and more than enough of every other requisite, God Himself without a doubt has taken away all hope of survival. The fire that was being carried into the enemy lines did not turn back of its own accord towards the wall we had built: these things are God's vengeance for the many wrongs that in our madness we dared to do to our own countrymen.

For those wrongs let us pay the penalty not to our bitterest enemies, the Romans, but to God—by our own hands. It will be easier to bear. Let our wives die unabused, our children without knowledge of slavery: after that, let us do each other an ungrudging kindness, preserving our freedom as a glorious winding-sheet. But first let our possessions and the whole fortress go up in flames: it will be a bitter blow to the Romans, that I know, to find our persons beyond their reach and nothing left for them to loot. One thing only let us spare—our store of food it will bear witness when we are dead to the fact that we perished, not through want but because, as we resolved at the beginning, we chose death rather than slavery.

I made a sad mistake in thinking I had the support of loyal followers in the struggle for freedom, men resolved to live honorably or die. You are not a bit different from the common herd in courage and boldness, you who fear death even when it means the end of utter misery, although you ought not to hesitate or wait for someone to urge you on. Ever since primitive man began to think, the words of our ancestors and of the gods, supported by the actions and spirit of our forefathers, have constantly impressed on us that life is the calamity for man, not death. Death gives freedom to our souls and lets them depart to their own pure home where they will know nothing of any calamity; but while they are confined within a mortal body and share its miseries, in strict truth they are dead. For association of the divine with the mortal is most improper. Certainly the soul can do a great deal even when imprisoned in the body: it makes the body its own organ of sense, moving it invisibly and impelling it in its actions further than mortal nature can reach. But when, freed from the weight that drags it down to earth and is hung about it, the soul returns to its own place, then in truth it partakes of a blessed power and an utterly unfettered strength, remaining as invisible to human eyes as God Himself. Not even while it is in the body can it be viewed; it enters undetected and departs unseen, having itself one imperishable nature, but causing a change in the body; for whatever the soul touches lives and blossoms, whatever it deserts withers and dies; such a superabundance it has of immortality.

Sleep will provide you with the clearest proof of what I say. In sleep souls left to themselves and free from bodily distractions enjoy the most blissful repose, and consorting with God whose kin they are, they go wherever they will and foretell many of the things to come. Why, pray, should we fear death if we love to repose in sleep? And isn't it absurd to run after the freedom of this life and grudge ourselves the freedom of eternity?

It might be expected that we, so carefully taught at home, would be an example to others of readiness to die. But if we do need the testimony of foreigners, let us look to those Indians who profess to practice philosophy. They are men of true courage, who, regarding this life as a kind of service that we must render to nature, undergo it with reluctance and hasten to release their souls from their bodies; and though no misfortune presses or drives them away, desire for immortal life impels them to inform their friends that they are going to depart. No one tries to stop them, but everyone congratulates them and gives them messages for his dear ones: so confidently and so truly do they believe that the souls share a common life. Then after receiving these commissions they consign their bodies to the flames, that the soul may be as pure as possible when it is separated from the body, and hymns are sung to them as they die. In fact they are sent off more happily by their dearest ones to death than other men are sent by their fellow-citizens on a long journey: the bereaved may weep for themselves, but the departed they deem happy, ranked now among the immortals. Well then! Are we not ashamed to show a poorer spirit than the Indians, and by our want of courage to bring the Law of our fathers, the envy of all the world, into utter contempt?

Even if from the very first we had been taught the contrary belief, that life is indeed the greatest good of mankind and death a disaster, the situation is such that we should still be called upon to bear it with a stout heart, for God's will and sheer necessity doom us to death. Long ago, it seems, God issued this warning to the whole Jewish race together, that life would be taken from us if we misused it. Do not fasten the blame on yourselves or give the Romans the credit for the fact that we are all ruined by the war against them: it is not through their power that these things have happened—a mightier hand has intervened to give them the outward shape of victory. What Roman weapons slew the Jews who lived in Caesarea? Why, they had no thought of rebelling against Rome, but were in the middle of their seventh-day ceremonies when the Caesarean mob rushed at them, and though they offered no resistance, butchered them with their wives and children, paying no heed to the Romans who were treating none as enemies except ourselves, who had in fact rebelled. No doubt I shall be told that the Caesareans had a permanent quarrel with the Jews in their midst and simply seized their chance to vent their old hatred. Then what are we to say of the Jews in Scythopolis? They had the effrontery to make war on us to please the Greeks, and would not join with us, their own kith and kin, to drive out the Romans. Much good they got from their faithful support of the Greeks! They were brutally massacred by them, they and their entire households—such was the reward their alliance brought them! What they saved the Greeks from suffering at our hands they themselves endured as if it was they who had wished to inflict it! It would take too long to speak now about every individual case: you know that of all the towns in Syria there isn't one that hasn't exterminated its Jewish inhabitants, though they were more hostile to us than the Romans. As a single instance, the Damascenes, though they couldn't even fake a plausible excuse, made their own city reek with the most loathsome slaughter, butchering eighteen thousand Jews and their wives and families as well. As for those tortured to death in Egypt, it was stated that the number was something over sixty thousand.

They, perhaps, died in this way because in a foreign land they could find no answer to their enemies; but all those who took up arms against Rome in their own had everything, hadn't they, that could give them hope of certain victory? Weapon, walls, impregnable fortresses, and a spirit that in the cause of liberty no danger could shake, encouraged all to rebel. But these things were effective for a very short time: they raised our hopes only to prove the beginning of worse misfortunes. All were captured; all came into the enemy's hands as if provided specially to make their victory more splendid, not to save the lives of those who fashioned them! Those who died in battle we may well congratulate: they died defending their freedom, not betraying it. But the masses who are now under the thumb of Rome who would not pity? Who would not hasten to die rather than share their fate? Some of them have been broken on the rack or tortured to death at the stake or by the lash; some have been half-eaten by savage beasts and then kept alive to be their food a second time, after providing amusement and sport for their enemies. Of them all we have most cause to pity those who are still alive; for they pray and pray for the death that never comes.

Where is the mighty city, the mother-city of the whole Jewish race, secure within so many encircling walls, sheltering behind so many forts and lofty towers, chock-full of equipment for war and defended by the thousands and thousands of determined men? Where now is the city that was believed to have God for her Founder? She has been torn up by the roots, and the only memorial of her that is left is the camp of her destroyers that still occupies her ruins! Old men with streaming eyes sit by the ashes of the Shrine, with a few women kept by the enemy as victims of their lust.

Which of us, realizing these facts, could bear to see the light of day, even if he could live free from danger? Who is such an enemy to his country, who so unmanly and so wedded to live as not to be sorry that he is alive today? If only we had all died before seeing the Sacred City utterly destroyed by enemy hands, the Holy Sanctuary so impiously uprooted! But since an honorable ambition deluded us into thinking that perhaps we should succeed in avenging her of her enemies, and now all hope has fled, abandoning us to our fate, let us at once choose death with honor and do the kindest thing we can for ourselves, our wives and children, while it is still possible to show ourselves any kindness. After all, we were born to die, we and those we brought into the world: this even the luckiest must face. But our children—these are not evils to which man is subject by the laws of nature: men undergo them through their own cowardice, if they have a chance to forestall them by death and will not take it. We were very proud of our courage, so we revolted from Rome: now in the final stages they have offered to spare our lives and we have turned the offer down. Is anyone too blind to see how furious they will be if they take us alive? Pity the young whose bodies are strong enough to survive prolonged torture; pity the not-so-young whose old frames would break under such ill-usage. A man will see his wife violently carried off; he will hear the voice of his child crying "Father!" when his own hands are fettered. Come! While our hands are free and can hold a sword, let them do a noble service! Let us die unenslaved by our enemies, and leave this world as free men in company with our wives and children. That is what the Law ordains, that is what our wives and children demand of us, the necessity of God has laid on us, the opposite of what the Romans wish—they are anxious that none of us should die before the town is captured. So let us deny the enemy their hoped-for pleasure at our expense, and without more ado leave them to be dumbfounded by our death and awed by our courage.

# Empress Theodora

## FIGHT, NOT FLIGHT,
## JANUARY 18, 532

*It is impossible for a person, having been born into this world, not to die;*
*but for one who has reigned it is intolerable to be a fugitive.*

Byzantine mosaic depicting Empress Theodora
flanked by a chaplain and court lady.

IN 532 A REBELLION under Hypatius threatened to overthrow and kill the Byzantine emperor, Justinian. Certain the rebels would succeed, Justinian's advisers urged him to flee to safety with his wife, Theodora. As Justinian anxiously prepared his departure, the empress rose from her throne, acknowledged the rarity that a woman would "speak in a man's council," and exhorted a different course of action: death with honor. Although her words were succinct, they altered history. Justinian remained, defeated the rebels, and preserved the Byzantine Empire.

———•◦•———

MY LORDS, THE PRESENT OCCASION is too serious to allow me to follow the convention that a woman should not speak in a man's council. Those whose interests are threatened by extreme danger should think only of the wisest course of action, not of conventions.

In my opinion, flight is not the right course, even if it should bring us to safety. It is impossible for a person, having been born into this world, not to die; but for one who has reigned it is intolerable to be a fugitive. May I never be deprived of this purple robe, and may I never see the day when those who meet me do not call me empress.

If you wish to save yourself, my lord, there is no difficulty. We are rich; over there is the sea, and yonder are the ships. Yet reflect for a moment whether, when you have once escaped to a place of security, you would not gladly exchange such safety for death. As for me, I agree with the adage that the royal purple is the noblest shroud.

# St. Bernard

## ON THE SECOND CRUSADE,
## 1146

*Christian warriors, He who gave His life for you,*
*today demands yours in return. These are combats worthy of you,*
*combats in which it is glorious to conquer and advantageous to die.*

From *A Short History of Monks and Monasteries*,
by Alfred Wesley Wishart (1865–1933).

W HEN THE CRUSADER STATE EDESSA FELL, Pope Eugenius turned to one of Christendom's foremost leaders to preach in favor of a Second Crusade. Bernard of Clairvaux rallied men to march to Jerusalem, warning soldiers that they could not be redeemed by dressing themselves "in sackcloth" but only with "the din of arms, the dangers, the labors, the fatigues of war" and declares that victory will expiate their sins. Bernard's powerful voice was critical in mobilizing an army for a battle that lacked the popular support of the First Crusade. The Second Crusade proved a failure. The armies of Louis VII of France and Conrad III of Germany were defeated, Jerusalem ultimately fell, and a Third Crusade was later launched.

---

YOU CANNOT BUT KNOW that we live in a period of chastisement and ruin; the enemy of mankind has caused the breath of corruption to fly over all regions; we behold nothing but unpunished wickedness. The laws of men or the laws of religion have no longer sufficient power to check depravity of manners and the triumph of the wicked. The demon of heresy has taken possession of the chair of truth, and God has sent forth his malediction upon his sanctuary.

Oh, ye who listen to me, hasten then to appease the anger of Heaven, but no longer implore His goodness by vain complaints; clothe not yourselves in sackcloth, but cover yourselves with your impenetrable bucklers; the din of arms, the dangers, the labors, the fatigues of war are the penances that God now imposes upon you. Hasten then to expiate your sins by victories over the infidels, and let the deliverance of holy places be the reward of your repentance.

If it were announced to you that the enemy had invaded your cities, your castles, your lands; had ravished your wives and your daughters, and profaned your temples—which among you would not fly to arms? Well, then, all these calamities, and calamities still greater, have fallen upon your brethren, upon the family of Jesus Christ, which is yours. Why do you hesitate to repair so many evils—to revenge so many outrages? Will you allow the infidels to contemplate in peace the ravages they have committed on Christian people? Remembering that their triumph will be a subject for grief of all ages and an eternal opprobrium upon the generation that has endured it. Yes, the living God has charged me to announce to you that He will punish them who shall not have defended Him against His enemies.

Fly then to arms; let a holy rage animate you in the fight, and let the Christian world resound with these words of the prophet: "Cursed be he who does not stain his sword with blood!" If the Lord calls you to the defense of His heritage think not that His hand has lost its power. Could He not send twelve legions of angels or breathe one word and all His enemies would crumble away into dust? But God has considered the sons of men, to open for them the road to His mercy. His goodness has caused to dawn for you a day of safety by calling on you to avenge His glory and His name.

Christian warriors, He who gave His life for you, today demands yours in return. These are combats worthy of you, combats in which it is glorious to conquer and advantageous to die. Illustrious knights, generous defenders of the Cross, remember the examples of your fathers who conquered Jerusalem, and whose names are inscribed in Heaven; abandon then the things that perish, to gather unfading palms, and conquer a Kingdom which has no end.

# William Shakespeare

## BATTLE OF AGINCOURT, 1599

*We few, we happy few, we band of brothers;*
*For he today that sheds his blood with me*
*Shall be my brother.*

Portrait of William Shakespeare, 1623.

WILLIAM SHAKESPEARE, in his play *Henry V,* imagines the king of England on the muddy plains of Agincourt on October 25, 1415, outnumbered by French opposition, yet still prepared for battle. Shakespeare's admiration for the bond between warriors is vividly displayed in this excerpt from his play. Shakespeare's words may have been unspoken in actual battle, but they ring in the ears of those who have . . . and those who will. They are an immortal tribute to those who sought victory against all odds.

If we are marked to die, we are enow
To do our country loss; and if to live,
The fewer men, the greater share of honour.
God's will! I pray thee, wish not one man more.
By Jove, I am not covetous for gold,
Nor care I who doth feed upon my cost;
It yearns me not if men my garments wear;
Such outward things dwell not in my desires.
But if it be a sin to covet honour,
I am the most offending soul alive.
No, faith, my coz, wish not a man from England:
God's peace! I would not lose so great an honour
As one man more methinks, would share from me
For the best hope I have. O, do not wish one more!
Rather proclaim it, Westmoreland, through my host,
That he which hath no stomach to this fight,
Let him depart; his passport shall be made,
And crowns for convoy put into his purse:
We would not die in that man's company
That fears his fellowship to die with us.
This day is called the feast of Crispian:
He that outlives this day, and comes safe home,
Will stand a tiptoe when this day is named,
And rouse him at the name of Crispian.
He that shall live this day, and see old age,
Will yearly on the vigil feast his neighbours,
And say "To-morrow is Saint Crispian:
Then will he strip his sleeve and show his scars,
And say "These wounds I had on Crispian's day."
Old men forget; yet all shall be forgot,
But he'll remember, with advantages,

What feats he did that day: Then shall our names,
Familiar in his mouth as household words
Harry the King, Bedford and Exeter,
Warwick and Talbot, Salisbury and Gloucester—
Be in their flowing cups freshly remember'd.
This story shall the good man teach his son;
And Crispin Crispian shall ne'er go by,
From this day to the ending of the world,
But we in it shall be remembered;
We few, we happy few, we band of brothers;
For he to-day that sheds his blood with me
Shall be my brother; be he ne'er so vile,
This day shall gentle his condition;
And gentlemen in England now-a-bed
Shall think themselves accursed they were not here,
And hold their manhood's cheap whiles any speaks
That fought with us upon Saint Crispin's day.

# Queen Elizabeth I

## Supporting Her Troops against the Spanish Armada, July 1588

*I am come amongst you at this time,*
*not as for my recreation or sport,*
*but being resolved,*
*in the midst and heat of the battle,*
*to live or die amongst you all;*
*to lay down, for my God,*
*and for my kingdom, and for my people,*
*my honor and my blood, even the dust.*

Coronation portrait of Elizabeth I, ca. 1558, artist unknown.

A CALL FOR SACRIFICE is diluted when it travels across vast distances from safe places. Words cannot mobilize courage unless they are accompanied by deed. Not unlike that of Empress Theodora over a thousand years earlier, Queen Elizabeth I's exhortation demonstrates her willingness to endure the very sacrifice she seeks of her forces and helps turn the tide of history.

In the sixteenth century, Protestant England and Catholic Spain battled over control of the seas and trade in the New World. In July 1588, King Philip II sent his Spanish Armada—130 ships and 30,000 men—to invade England, end the rivalry, and stop England's attacks on Spanish ships. Expecting the invasion, Queen Elizabeth visited troops positioned against the Spanish Armada at Tilbury in Essex.

Imagine what they saw that day. Their beloved queen arrives from her throne, acknowledges that her body is feeble that that she is prepared "to live and die amongst you all."

Elizabeth's stunning presence on the battlefield instilled her troops with the confidence—and loyalty—to fight with honor and strength against seemingly overpowering force. After nine days of battle, England would prove victorious.

---

MY LOVING PEOPLE, we have been persuaded by some, that are careful of our safety, to take heed how we commit ourselves to armed multitudes, for fear of treachery; but I assure you, I do not desire to live to distrust my faithful and loving people. Let tyrants fear; I have always so behaved myself that, under God, I have placed my chiefest strength and safeguard in the loyal hearts and good will of my subjects. And therefore I am come amongst you at this time, not as for my recreation or sport, but being resolved, in the midst and heat of the battle, to live or die amongst you all; to lay down, for my God, and for my kingdom, and for my people, my honor and my blood, even the dust. I know I have but the body of a weak and feeble woman; but I have the heart of a king, and of a king of England, too; and think foul scorn that Parma or Spain, or any prince of Europe, should dare to invade the borders of my realms: to which, rather than any dishonor should grow by me, I myself will take up arms; I myself will be your general, judge, and rewarder of every one of your virtues in the field. I know already, by your forwardness, that you have deserved rewards and crowns; and we do assure you, on the word of a prince, they shall be duly paid you. In the mean my lieutenant general shall be in my stead, than whom never prince commanded a more noble and worthy subject;

not doubting by your obedience to my general, by your concord in the camp, and by your valor in the field, we shall shortly have a famous victory over the enemies of my God, of my kingdom, and of my people.

# Frederick the Great

## BEFORE INVADING SILESIA, DECEMBER 11, 1740

*Go forth. I will follow you straightway
to the rendezvous of glory which awaits you.*

Frederick the Great of Prussia.

Some MILITARY SPEECHES inspire soldiers by soaring to great heights; others go to great lengths. Frederick the Great, king of Prussia, motivated his generals to invade Silesia through the power of simple clarity. This basic appeal helped the Prussian army's swift defeat of Silesia—the first step in Frederick's ambitious plan to turn the unassuming Prussia into a formidable European power.

---

GENTLEMAN, I am undertaking a war in which I have no allies but your valor and your good will. My cause is just; my resources are what we ourselves can do; and the issue lies in fortune. Remember continually the glory which your ancestors acquired in the plain of Warsaw, at Fehrbellin and in the expedition to Preussen. Your lot is in your own hands; distinctions and rewards await upon your fine actions which shall merit them.

But what need have I to excite you to glory? It is the one thing you keep before your eyes; the sole object worthy of your labor. We are going to front troops, who, under Prince Eugene, had the highest reputation. Though Prince Eugene is gone, we shall have to measure our strength against brave soldiers; the greater will be the honor if we can conquer. Adieu. Go forth. I will follow you straightway to the rendezvous of glory which awaits you.

# Frederick the Great

*The cavalry regiment that does not on this instant, on orders given, dash full plunge into the enemy, I will, directly after the battle, unhorse and make it a garrison regiment. The infantry battalion which, meet with what it may, shows the least sign of hesitancy, loses its colors, and sabers; and I cut the trimmings from its uniform!*

Frederick the Great.

FREDERICK THE GREAT achieved one of his greatest victories by expelling the Austrian army from Silesia at the Battle of Leuthen. The battle was a tactical triumph involving a highly disciplined, close-order infantry march and artful screening by the cavalry. Frederick's army marched toward the center of a five-mile Austrian front at the town of Leuthen; feigned an attack on its right flank; and attacked on the left, using a series of precision movements. Executing this complicated attack—which Frederick himself acknowledged was contrary to "the rules of art"—required troops instilled with a sense of discipline, honor, and above all, unity of purpose and movement. Before the battle, Frederick plainly tells his troops they are about to attack a stronger army. His address then emphasizes the concepts of honor and dishonor. Offering that the fearful may leave the battle without retribution, he quickly proclaims: "Hah! I knew it; none of you would desert me. I depend on your help, then, and on victory as sure." In this way, Frederick imbues his troops with the unit cohesion that will be critical to execute a tactical masterpiece against numerically superior opponents.

---

IT IS NOT UNKNOWN TO YOU, gentleman, what disasters have befallen here while we were busy with the French and Reichs army. Schweidnitz is gone; Duke of Bavern beaten; Breslau gone, and all our war stories there; a good part of Silesia is gone; and in fact my embarrassment would be at the impossible pitch, had not I boundless trust in you and your qualities which have been so often manifested as soldiers and sons of your country. Hardly one among you but has distinguished himself by some nobly memorable action: all these services to the State and to me I know well and will never forget.

I flatter myself, therefore, that, in this case, too, nothing will be wanting which the State has a right to expect of your valor. The hour is at hand. I should think I had done nothing if I left the Austrians in possession of Silesia. Let me apprise you, then: I intend, in spite of the rules of art, to attack Prince Karl's army, which is nearly twice our strength, wherever I find it. The question is not of his numbers or the strength of his position; all this by courage, by the skill of our methods, we will try to make good. This step I must risk, or everything is lost. We must beat the enemy, or perish all of us before his batteries. So I read the case; so I will act in it.

Make this, my determination, known to all officers of the army; prepare the men for what work is now to ensure and say that I hold myself entitled to demand exact fulfillment of orders. For you, when I reflect that you are Prussians, can I think that you will act unworthily? But if there should be one or another who dreads to share all dangers with me, he can have his discharge this evening, and shall not suffer the least reproach from me! Hah! I knew it; none of you would desert me. I depend on your help, then, and on victory as sure.

The cavalry regiment that does not on this instant, on orders given, dash full plunge into the enemy, I will, directly after the battle, unhorse and make it a garrison regiment. The infantry battalion which, meet with what it may, shows the least sign of hesitancy, loses its colors, and sabers; and I cut the trimmings from its uniform! Now, good night gentleman: shortly we will have either beaten the enemy, or we never see one another again.

# PART 2
# LIBERTY OR DEATH

*I know not what course others may take;*
*but as for me, give me liberty, or give me death!*

—Patrick Henry, 1775

# John Hancock

## On the Boston Massacre, March 5, 1774

*I conjure you, by all that is dear, by all that is honorable,*
*by all that is sacred, not only that ye pray,*
*but that ye act; that, if necessary,*
*ye fight, and even die, for the prosperity of our Jerusalem.*
*Break in sunder, with noble disdain, the bonds*
*with which the Philistines have bound you.*

*Jean Hancock, President au Congres des XIII*
*Provinces Unies d'Amerique, né à Boston*, copy of an English print by C. Corbutt.

HE BOSTON MASSACRE of March 5, 1770, inflamed American passion against British tyranny. On the fourth anniversary of the massacre, John Hancock delivered an oration intended to stoke those flames. Hancock begins by invoking the memory of those who died. To sharpen his point, he graphically describes the injuries rendered to Christopher Monk: "Observe his tottering knees, which scarce sustain his wasted body; look on his haggard eyes; mark well the death-like palences on his fallen cheek, and tell me, does not the sight plant daggers in your souls? Unhappy Monk! cut off, in the gay morn of manhood, from all the joys which sweeten life, doomed to drag on a pitiful existence, without even a hope to taste the pleasures of returning health!"

Hancock then transforms his scathing indictment into a religious fervor. Like Moses, he promises his followers that God will protect them against a powerful enemy: "Let us humbly commit our righteous cause to the great Lord of the universe, who loveth righteousness and hateth iniquity."

One year later, on April 19, 1775, seventy Massachusetts militiamen stood against a British advanced guard on Lexington Green. The shots that day echoed the thunder of John Hancock's speech—and changed the world.

———◆———

LET NOT THE HISTORY of the illustrious House of Brunswick inform posterity that a king, descended from that glorious monarch, George II, once sent his British subjects to conquer and enslave his subjects in America. But be perpetual infamy entailed upon that villain who dared to advise his master to such execrable measures; for it was easy to foresee the consequences which so naturally followed upon sending troops into America, to enforce obedience to acts of the British Parliament, which neither God nor man ever empowered them to make. It was reasonable to expect that troops, who knew the errand they were sent upon, would treat the people whom they were to subjugate, with a cruelty and haughtiness which too often buried the honorable character of a soldier in the disgraceful name of an unfeeling ruffian. The troops, upon their first arrival, took possession of our senate house, and pointed their cannon against the judgment hall, and even continued them there whilst the supreme court of judicature for this province was actually sitting to decide upon the lives and fortunes of the king's subjects. Our streets nightly resounded with the noise of riot and debauchery; our peaceful citizens were hourly exposed to shameful insults, and often felt the effects of their violence and outrage. But this was not all: as though they thought it not enough to violate our civil rights, they endeavored to deprive us of the enjoyment of our religious privileges, to vitiate our morals, and thereby render us deserving of destruction. Did not a reverence for religion sensibly decay? Did not our infants almost learn to lisp out curses before they knew their horrid import? Did not our youth forget they were Americans, and regardless of the admonitions of the wise and aged, servilely copy from their tyrants those vices which finally must overthrow the empire of Great Britain? And must I be compelled to acknowledge that even the noblest, fairest part of all the lower creation did not entirely escape the cursed snare? When virtue has once erected her throne within the female breast, it is upon so solid a basis that nothing is able to expel the heavenly inhabitant. But have there not been some, few, indeed, I hope, whose youth and inexperience have rendered them a prey to wretches, whom, upon the least reflection, they would have despised and hated as foes to God and their country? I fear there have been some such unhappy instances, or why have I seen an honest father clothed with shame? Or why a virtuous mother drowned in tears?

But I forbear, and come reluctantly to the transactions of that dismal night, when in such quick succession we felt the extremes of grief, astonishment, and rage; when Heaven in anger, for a dreadful moment, suffered hell to take the reins; when Satan with his chosen band opened the sluices of New England's blood, and sacrilegiously polluted our land with the dead bodies of her guiltless sons! Let this sad tale of death never be told without a tear; let not the heaving bosom cease to burn with a manly indignation at the barbarous story through the long tracts of future time; let every parent tell the shameful story to his listening children until tears of pity glisten in their eyes, and boiling passions shake their tender frames; and whilst the anniversary of that ill-fated night is kept a jubilee in the grim court of pandemonium, let all America join in one common prayer to Heaven, that the inhuman, unprovoked murders of the fifth of March, 1770, planned by Hillsborough, and a knot of treacherous knaves in Boston, and executed by the cruel hand of Preston and his sanguinary coadjutors, may ever stand in history without a parallel. But what, my countrymen, withheld the ready arm of vengeance from executing instant justice on the vile assassins? Perhaps you feared promiscuous carnage might ensure, and that the innocent might share the fate of those who had performed the infernal deed. But were not all guilty? Were you not too tender of the lives of those who came to fix a yoke on your necks? But I must not too severely blame a fault, which great souls only can commit. May that magnificence of spirit which scorns the low pursuits of malice, may that generous compassion which often preserves from ruin, even a guilty villain, forever actuate the noble bosoms of Americans! But let not the miscreant host vainly imagine that we feared their arms. No, them we despised; we dread nothing but slavery. Death is the creature of a poltroon's brains; 'tis immortality to sacrifice ourselves for the salvation of our country. We fear not death. That gloomy night, the pale-faced moon, and the affrighted stars that hurried through the sky, can witness that we fear not death. Our hearts which, at the recollection, glow with rage that four revolving years have scarcely taught us to restrain, can witness that we fear not death; and happy it is for those who dared to insult us, that their naked bones are not now piled up an everlasting monument of Massachusetts' bravery. But they retired, they fled, and in that flight they found their only safety. We then expected that the hand of public justice would soon inflict that punishment upon the murderers which, by the laws of God and man, they had incurred. But let the unbiased pen of a Robertson, or perhaps of some equally famed American, conduct this trial before the great tribunal of succeeding generations. And though the murderers may escape the just resentment of an enraged people, though drowsy justice, intoxicated by the poisonous draught prepared for her cup, still nods upon her rotten seat, yet be assured, such complicated crimes will meet their due reward. Tell me, ye bloody butchers! Ye villains high and low! Ye wretches who contrived, as well as you who executed the inhuman deed! Do you not feel the goads and stings of conscious guilt pierce through your savage bosoms? Though some of you may think yourselves exalted to a height that bids defiance to human justice; and others shroud yourselves beneath the mask of hypocrisy, and build your hopes of safety on the low arts of cunning, chicanery, and falsehood; yet do you not sometimes feel the gnawings of that worm which never dies? Do not the injured shades of Maverick, Gray, Caldwell, Attucks, and Carr, attend you in your solitary walks; arrest you even in the midst of your debaucheries, and fill even your dreams with terror? But if the unappeased manes of the dead should not disturb their murderers, yet surely even your obdurate hearts must shrink, and your guilty blood must chill within your rigid veins, when you behold the miserable Monk, the wretched victim of your savage cruelty. Observe his tottering knees, which scarce sustain his wasted body; look on his haggard eyes; mark well the death-like palences on his fallen cheek, and tell me, does not the sight plant daggers in your souls? Unhappy Monk! cut off, in the gay morn of manhood, from all the joys which sweeten life, doomed to drag on a pitiful existence, without even a hope to taste the pleasures of returning health! Yet, Monk, thou livest not in vain; thou livest a warning to thy country, which sympathizes with thee in thy sufferings; thou livest an affecting, an alarming instance of the unbounded violence which lust of power, assisted by a standing army, can lead a traitor to commit.

Ye dark designing knaves, ye murderers, parricides! How dare you tread upon the earth, which has drunk in the blood of slaughtered innocents, shed by your wicked hands? How dare you breathe that air which wafted to the ear of Heaven the groans of those who fell a sacrifice to your accursed ambition? But if the laboring earth doth not expand her jaws; if the air you breathe is not commissioned to be the minister of death; yet, hear it and tremble! The eye of Heaven penetrates the darkest chambers of the soul, traces the leading clue through all the labyrinths which your industrious folly has devised; and you, however you may have screened yourselves from human eyes, must be arraigned, must lift your hands, red with the blood of those whose death you have procured, at the tremendous bar of God!

Surely you never will tamely suffer this country to be a den of thieves. Remember, my friends, from whom you sprang. Let not a meanness of spirit, unknown to those whom you boast of as your fathers, excite a thought to the dishonor of your mothers. I conjure you, by all that is dear, by all that is honorable, by all that is sacred, not only that ye pray, but that ye act; that, if necessary, ye fight, and even die, for the prosperity of our Jerusalem. Break in sunder, with noble disdain, the bonds with which the Philistines have bound you.

I have the most animating confidence that the present noble struggle for liberty will terminate gloriously for America. And let us play the man for our God, and for the cities of our God; while we are using the means in our power, let us humbly commit our righteous cause to the great Lord of the universe, who loveth righteousness and hateth iniquity.

# Patrick Henry

## LIBERTY OR DEATH,
## MARCH 23, 1775

*I know not what course others may take;*
*but as for me, give me liberty, or give me death.*

Painting by George Bagby Matthews (1857–1943).

O N MARCH 23, 1775—less than a month before the Battles of Lexington and Concord—thirty-nine-year-old Patrick Henry rose to address the Virginia House of Burgesses in St. John's Church in Richmond. Before the house was a resolution authorizing defensive preparations for war with Britain—and its fate was uncertain. Britain's military presence was growing in the colonies, yet many delegates remained opposed to war. One of the colony's most effective orators, Henry systematically rebuffs the arguments that war could be avoided: "Our petitions have been slighted; our remonstrance's have produced additional violence and insult; our supplications have been disregarded; and we have been spurned, with contempt, from the foot of the throne. In vain, after these things, may we indulge the fond hope of peace and reconciliation. There is no longer any room for hope." He directly challenges the notion that the colonies are unprepared for battle: "They tell us, sir, that we are weak; unable to cope with so formidable an adversary. But when shall we be stronger? Will it be the next week, or the next year? Will it be when we are totally disarmed, and when a British guard shall be stationed in every house? Shall we gather strength by irresolution and inaction? Shall we acquire the means of effectual resistance, by lying supinely on our backs, and hugging the delusive phantom of hope, until our enemies shall have bound us hand and foot?"

Henry reportedly spoke without notes, his voice growing stronger until climaxing with his famous pronouncement about liberty or death. The resolution passed, albeit narrowly, setting the course for Virginia's entry into the American Revolution.

Henry weaves his speech with concepts introduced by Pericles ("We must realize that this war is being forced upon us, and the more readily we accept the challenge the less eager to attack us our opponents will be"), Eleazar ben Yair at Masada ("Let us die unenslaved by our enemies"), and Frederick the Great at Leuthen ("Shortly we will have either beaten the enemy, or we never see one another again.")

⁂

MR. PRESIDENT: No man thinks more highly than I do of the patriotism as well as abilities, of the very worthy gentlemen who have just addressed the House. But different men often see the same subject in different lights; and, therefore, I hope that it will not be thought disrespectful to those gentlemen, if, entertaining as I do, opinions of a character very opposite to theirs, I shall speak forth my sentiments freely and without reserve. This is no time for ceremony. The question before the House is one of awful moment to this country. For my own part I consider it as nothing less than a question of freedom or slavery; and in proportion to the magnitude of the subject ought to be the freedom of the debate. It is only in this way that we can hope to arrive at truth, and fulfill the great responsibility which we hold to God and our country. Should I keep back my opinions at such a time, through fear of giving offense, I should consider myself as guilty of treason towards my country and of an act of disloyalty towards the majesty of heaven, which I revere above all earthly kings.

Mr. President, it is natural to man to indulge in the illusions of hope. We are apt to shut our eyes against a painful truth, and listen to the song of that siren, till she transforms us into beasts. Is this the part of wise men, engaged in a great and arduous struggle for liberty? Are we disposed to be of the number of those who, having eyes, see not, and having ears, hear not, the things which so nearly concern their temporal salvation? For my part, whatever anguish of spirit it may cost, I am willing to know the whole truth; to know the worst and to provide for it.

I have but one lamp by which my feet are guided; and that is the lamp of experience. I know of no way of judging of the future but by the past. And judging by the past, I wish to know what there has been in the conduct of the British ministry for the last ten years, to justify those hopes with which gentlemen have been pleased to solace themselves and the House? Is it that insidious smile with which our petition has been lately received? Trust it not, sir; it will prove a snare to your feet. Suffer not yourselves to be betrayed with a kiss. Ask yourselves how this gracious reception of our petition comports with these war-like preparations which cover our waters and darken our land. Are fleets and armies necessary to a work of love and reconciliation? Have we shown ourselves so unwilling to be reconciled, that force must be called in to win back our love? Let us not deceive ourselves, sir. These are the implements of war and subjugation; the last arguments to which kings resort. I ask gentlemen, sir, what means this martial array, if its purpose be not to force us to submission? Can gentlemen assign any other possible motives for it? Has Great Britain any enemy, in this quarter of the world, to call for all this accumulation of navies and armies? No sir, she has none. They are meant for us; they can be meant for no other. They are sent over to bind and rivet upon us those chains which the British ministry have been so long forging. And what have we to oppose them? Shall we try argument? Sir, we have been trying that for the last ten years. Have we anything new to offer on the subject? Nothing. We have held the subject up in every light of which it is capable; but it has been all in vain. Shall we resort to entreaty and humble supplication? What terms shall we find which have not been already exhausted? Let us not, I beseech you, sir, deceive ourselves longer. Sir, we have done everything that could be done, to avert the storm which is now coming on. We have petitioned; we have remonstrated; we have supplicated; we have prostrated ourselves before the throne, and have implored its interposition to arrest the tyrannical hands of the ministry and Parliament. Our petitions have been slighted; our remonstrances have produced additional violence and insult; our supplications have been disregarded; and we have been spurned, with contempt, from the foot of the throne. In vain, after these things, may we indulge the fond hope of peace and reconciliation. There is no longer any room for hope. If we wish to be free—if we mean to preserve inviolate those inestimable privileges for which we have been so long contending—if we mean not basely to abandon the noble struggle in which we have been so long engaged, and which we have pledged ourselves never to abandon until the glorious object of our contest shall be obtained, we must fight! I repeat it, sir, we must fight! An appeal to arms and to the God of Hosts is all that is left us!

They tell us, sir, that we are weak; unable to cope with so formidable an adversary. But when shall we be stronger? Will it be the next week, or the next year? Will it be when we are totally disarmed, and when a British guard shall be stationed in every house. Shall we gather strength by irresolution and inaction? Shall we acquire the means of effectual resistance, by lying supinely on our backs, and hugging the delusive phantom of hope, until our enemies shall have bound us hand and foot? Sir, we are not weak, if we make a proper use of the means which the God of nature hath placed in our power. Three millions of people, armed in the holy cause of liberty, and in such a country as that which we possess, are invincible by any force which our enemy can send against us. Besides, sir, we shall not fight our battles alone. There is a just God who presides over the destinies of nations; and who will raise up friends to fight our battles for us. The battle, sir, is not to the strong alone it is to the vigilant, the active, the brave. Besides, sir, we have no election. If we were base enough to desire it, it is now too late to retire from the contest. There is no retreat, but in submission and slavery! Our chains are forged! Their clanking may be heard on the plains of Boston! The war is inevitable—and let it come! I repeat it, sir, let it come!

It is in vain, sir, to extenuate the matter. Gentlemen may cry peace, peace—but there is no peace. The war is actually begun! The next gale that sweeps from the north will bring to our ears the clash of resounding arms! Our brethren are already in the field! Why stand we here idle? What is it the gentlemen wish? What would they have? Is life so dear, or peace so sweet, as to be purchased at the price of chains and slavery? Forbid it, Almighty God! I know not what course others may take; but as for me, give me liberty, or give me death!

# George Washington

## CALMING HIS REBELLIOUS TROOPS,
## MARCH 15, 1783

*You will, by the dignity of your conduct, afford occasion for posterity to say,
when speaking of the glorious example you have exhibited to mankind,
"Had this day been wanting, the world had never seen the last stage
of perfection to which human nature is capable of attaining.*

The Lansdowne Portrait.

NEARLY A YEAR AND A HALF after the British surrender to Washington, the Continental Army had significant grievances, aimed not at Great Britain but at their own nascent republic. The Continental Congress had promised financial rewards for enlistment but now dragged its feet in keeping its commitments. The Army's discontent gave rise to talk of insurrection, a true danger to the fragile new nation. George Washington confronted his officers at a church in Newburgh, New York, in a crucial attempt to calm a rebellion against the very government they fought to create.

Here, Washington balances his disapproval of their aims with empathy for their distress. He appeals to the overwhelming pride they have in their newfound reputation, arguing that their efforts will "cast a shade over that glory which has been so justly acquired; and tarnish the reputation of an army which is celebrated through all Europe." He urges patience with Congress and warns that those who pursue an insurrection will "overturn the liberties of our country, and . . . open the floodgates of civil discord and deluge our rising empire in blood."

In *Lend Me Your Ears*, former presidential speechwriter William Safire points to a single, spontaneous moment that may have turned animosity into affection. As he ended his speech, Washington reached for a letter from a Member of Congress supporting his appeal. He squinted at the writing, fumbled for his spectacles, and said, "Gentlemen, you will permit me to put on my spectacles, for I have not only grown gray but almost blind in the service of my country." This sign of humility and sacrifice softened the hostility in the room and strengthened the bond between the warriors and their general.

The officers agreed to Washington's appeal, demonstrating yet another example of their continued sacrifice for liberty.

---

GENTLEMEN: By an anonymous summons, an attempt has been made to convene you together; how inconsistent with the rules of propriety, how unmilitary, and how subversive of all order and discipline, let the good sense of the army decide. . . .

If my conduct heretofore has not evinced to you that I have been a faithful friend to the army, my declaration of it at this time would be equally unavailing and improper. But as I was among the first who embarked in the cause of our common country. As I have never left your side one moment, but when called from you on public duty. As I have been the constant companion and witness of your distresses, and not among the last to feel and acknowledge your merits. As I have ever considered my own military reputation as inseparably connected with that of the army. As my heart has ever expanded with joy, when I have heard its praises, and my indignation has arisen, when the mouth of detraction has been opened against it, it can scarcely be supposed, at this late stage of the war, that I am indifferent to its interests.

But how are they to be promoted? The way is plain, says the anonymous addresser. If war continues, remove into the unsettled country, there establish yourselves, and leave an ungrateful country to defend itself. But who are they to defend? Our wives, our children, our farms, and other property which we leave behind us. Or, in this state of hostile separation, are we to take the two first (the latter cannot be removed) to perish in a wilderness, with hunger, cold, and nakedness? If peace takes place, never sheathe your swords, says he, until you have obtained full and ample justice; this dreadful alternative, of either deserting our country in the extremest hour of her distress or turning our arms against it (which is the apparent object, unless Congress can be compelled into instant compliance), has something so shocking in it that humanity revolts at the idea. My God! What can this writer have in view, by recommending such measures? Can he be a friend to the army? Can he be a friend to this country? Rather, is he not an insidious foe? Some emissary, perhaps, from New York, plotting the ruin of both, by sowing the seeds of discord and separation between the civil and military powers of the continent? . . .

I cannot, in justice to my own belief, and what I have great reason to conceive is the intention of Congress, conclude this address, without giving it as my decided opinion, that that honorable body entertain exalted sentiments of the services of the army; and, from a full conviction of its merits and sufferings, will do it complete justice. That their endeavors to discover and establish funds for this purpose have been unwearied, and will not cease till they have succeeded, I have not a doubt. But, like all other large bodies, where there is a variety of different interests to reconcile, their deliberations are slow. Why, then, should we distrust them? And, in consequence of that distrust, adopt measures which may cast a shade over that glory which has been so justly acquired; and tarnish the reputation of an army which is celebrated through all Europe, for its fortitude and patriotism? And for what is this done? To bring the object we seek nearer? No! most certainly, in my opinion, it will cast it at a greater distance.

For myself—and I take no merit in giving the assurance, being induced to it from principles of gratitude, veracity, and justice—a grateful sense of the confidence you have ever placed in me, a recollection of the cheerful assistance and prompt obedience I have experienced from you, under every vicissitude of fortune, and the sincere affection I feel for an army I have so long had the honor to command will oblige me to declare, in this public and solemn manner, that, in the attainment of complete justice for all your toils and dangers, and in the gratification of every wish, so far as may be done consistently with the great duty I owe my country and those powers we are bound to respect, you may freely command my services to the utmost of my abilities.

While I give you these assurances, and pledge myself in the most unequivocal manner to exert whatever ability I am possessed of in your favor, let me entreat you, gentlemen, on your part, not to take any measures which, viewed in the calm light of reason, will lessen the dignity and sully the glory you have hitherto maintained; let me request you to rely on the plighted faith of your country, and place a full confidence in the purity of the intentions of Congress; that, previous to your dissolution as an army, they will cause all your accounts to be fairly liquidated, as directed in their resolutions, which were published to you two days ago, and that they will adopt the most effectual measures in their power to render ample justice to you, for your faithful and meritorious services. And let me conjure you, in the name of our common country, as you value your own sacred honor, as you respect the rights of humanity, and as you regard the military and national character of America, to express your utmost horror and detestation of the man who wishes, under any specious pretenses, to overturn the liberties of our country, and who wickedly attempts to open the floodgates of civil discord and deluge our rising empire in blood.

By thus determining and thus acting, you will pursue the plain and direct road to the attainment of your wishes. You will defeat the insidious designs of our enemies, who are compelled to resort from open force to secret artifice. You will give one more distinguished proof of unexampled patriotism and patient virtue, rising superior to the pressure of the most complicated sufferings. And you will, by the dignity of your conduct, afford occasion for posterity to say, when speaking of the glorious example you have exhibited to mankind, "Had this day been wanting, the world had never seen the last stage of perfection to which human nature is capable of attaining."

# Napoléon Bonaparte

## SPEECHES OF 1796–1815

*The flash of Napoléon Bonaparte's sword so blinded men
in his lifetime, and indeed, long after, that they were unable to
distinguish a second weapon in his hand. The clearer vision
which time and study bring have shown that he used words
almost as effectively as the sword, and that throughout
his career the address ably supported the military maneuver.*

— IDA TARBELL

*Napoléon in His Study,* by Jacques-Louis David (1748–1825).

IN THE MID-NINETEENTH CENTURY, a commission was appointed to collect and publish the entirety of Napoléon Bonaparte's writings and speeches. The resulting *Correspondence de Napoléon* yielded thirty-two volumes, including forty thousand documents from the archives of Paris alone.

Forty years later, Ida Tarbell published *Napoléon's Addresses* and described the earlier work this way: "Across the pages of the great tomes file the mighty procession of soldiers and generals, priests and cardinals, kings and peoples who, in the twenty years in which Napoléon was the preeminent figure of Europe, fell captive to his charms or his power. Here are the words by which he fired starving armies to battle, bullied obstinate powers to follow his plans, put hope into despot-ridden people, told kings their duties."

Indeed, more than any other figure in history, Napoléon grasped the power of words as an indispensable instrument of military success. And he used words just as he used weapons: tactically and selectively, choosing the right caliber depending on his target.

For example, Napoléon used clear and accessible detail to brief his troops on the outcome of many battles. These reports did not simply recite fact, but also recognized each soldier's contribution to victory. Nor did they merely declare victory; they used that victory to motivate each soldier to aspire to even greater victory in the next battle. Consider what Napoléon's battle-weary army heard at the conclusion of the First Italian Campaign in 1797: "You have been victorious in fourteen pitched battles and seventy actions. You have taken more than a hundred thousand prisoners, five hundred field pieces, two thousand heavy guns, and four pontoon trains. You have maintained the army during the whole campaign. In addition to this, you have sent six millions of dollars to the public treasury, and have enriched the National Museum with three hundred masterpieces of the arts of ancient and modern Italy, which it has required thirty centuries to produce. You have conquered the finest countries in Europe. The French flag waves for the first time upon the Adriatic opposite to Macedon, the native country of Alexander. Still higher destinies await you. I know you will not prove unworthy of them."

Napoléon's addresses emphasize the supreme pride associated with the French army. Serving is not a sacrifice; it is as privilege, and an immortal privilege at that. On entering Milan, Napoléon promises his army that after battle, "You will then return to your homes and your country. Men will say, as they point you out, 'He belonged to the army of Italy.'" Conversely, expressing his dissatisfaction with his soldiers during the Siege of Mantua, Napoléon declares: "Quarter-master general, let it be inscribed on their colors, 'They no longer form part of the Army of Italy!'"

Tarbell wrote: "The flash of Napoléon Bonaparte's sword so blinded men in his lifetime, and indeed, long after, that they were unable to distinguish a second weapon in his hand. The clearer vision which time and study bring have shown that he used words almost as effectively as the sword, and that throughout his career the address ably supported the military maneuver."

True, but commentary falls short of the sheer power of Napoléon's own words. He speaks for himself.

---

# THE FIRST COALITION

IN 1792 AUSTRIA AND PRUSSIA organized a coalition of European nations to overthrow the revolutionary government of France. Four years later, Napoléon Bonaparte found himself in command of an underequipped, highly demoralized army in northern Italy. His proclamations—acknowledging hardship and promising renown—helped motivate his men to form a cohesive and determined fighting force that ultimately defeated their enemies and secured vast territorial gains for Paris.

## BEFORE THE ITALIAN CAMPAIGN, MARCH 1796

SOLDIERS: You are naked and ill-fed! Government owes you much and can give you nothing. The patience and courage you have shown in the midst of these rocks are admirable; but they gain you no renown; no glory results to you from your endurance. It is my design to lead you into the most fertile plains of the world. Rich provinces and great cities will be in your power; there you will find honor, glory, and wealth. Soldiers of Italy! will you be wanting in courage or perseverance?

## Proclamation to the Army, May 1796

*You have gained battles without cannon, passed rivers without bridges, performed forced marches without shoes, and bivouacked without strong liquors, and often without bread.*

SOLDIERS:  You have in fifteen days won six victories, taken twenty-one stand of colors, fifty-five pieces of cannon, and several fortresses, and overrun the richest part of Piedmont; you have made fifteen thousand prisoners, and killed or wounded upwards of ten thousand men. Hitherto you have been fighting for barren rocks, made memorable by your valor, though useless to your country, but your exploits now equal those of the armies of Holland and the Rhine. You were utterly destitute, and you have supplied all your wants. You have gained battles without cannon, passed rivers without bridges, performed forced marches without shoes, and bivouacked without strong liquors, and often without bread. None but Republican phalanxes, the soldiers of liberty, could have endured what you have done; thanks to you, soldiers, for your perseverance! Your grateful country owes its safety to you; and if the taking of Toulon was an earnest of the immortal campaign of 1794, your present victories foretell one more glorious. The two armies which lately attacked you in full confidence, now fly before you in consternation; the perverse men who laughed at your distress, and inwardly rejoiced at the triumph of your enemies, are now confounded and trembling. But, soldiers, you have yet done nothing, for there still remains much to do. Neither Turin nor Milan are yours; the ashes of the conquerors of Tarquin are still trodden underfoot by the assassins of Basseville. It is said that there are some among you whose courage is shaken, and who would prefer returning to the summits of the Alps and Apennines. No, I cannot believe it. The victors of Montenotte, Millesimo, Dego, and Mondovi are eager to extend the glory of the French name!

## On Entering Milan, May 1796

*Men will say, as they point you out, "He belonged to the army of Italy."*

SOLDIERS:  You have rushed like a torrent from the top of the Apennines; you have overthrown and scattered all that opposed your march. Piedmont, delivered from Austrian tyranny, indulges her natural sentiments of peace and friendship toward France. Milan is yours, and the Republican flag waves throughout Lombardy. The Dukes of Parma and Modena owe their political existence to your generosity alone. The army which so proudly threatened you can find no barrier to protect it against your courage; neither the Po, the Ticino, nor the Adda could stop you for a single day. These vaunted bulwarks of Italy opposed you in vain; you passed them as rapidly as the Apennines. These great successes have filled the heart of your country with joy. Your representatives have ordered a festival to commemorate your victories, which has been held in every district of the Republic. There your fathers, your wives, sisters, and mistresses rejoiced in your good fortune and proudly boasted of belonging to you. Yes, soldiers, you have done much—but remains there nothing more to do? Shall it be said of us that we know how to conquer, but not how to make use of victory? Shall posterity reproach us with having found Capau in Lombardy? But I see you already hasten to arms. An effeminate response is tedious to you; the days which are lost to glory are lost to your happiness. Well, then, let us set forth! We have still forced marches to make, enemies to subdue, laurels to gather, injuries to revenge. Let those who have sharpened the daggers of civil war in France, who have basely murdered our ministers, and burnt our ships at Toulon, tremble! The hour of vengeance has struck; but let the people of all countries be free from apprehension; we are the friends of the people everywhere, and those great men whom we have taken for our models. To restore the capitol, to replace the statues of the heroes who rendered it illustrious, to rouse the Roman people, stupefied by several ages of slavery—such will be the fruit of our victories; they will form an era for posterity, you will have the immortal glory of changing the face of the finest part of Europe. The French people, free and respected by the whole world, will give to Europe a glorious peace, which will indemnify them for the sacrifices of every kind which for last six years they have been making. You will then return to your homes and your country. Men will say, as they point you out, "He belonged to the army of Italy."

## At the Conclusion of the First Italian Campaign, March 1797

*Still higher destinies await you.*
*I know that you will not prove unworthy of them.*

**Soldiers:** The campaign just ended has given you imperishable renown. You have been victorious in fourteen pitched battles and seventy actions.

You have taken more than a hundred thousand prisoners, five hundred fieldpieces, two thousand heavy guns, and four pontoon trains. You have maintained the army during the whole campaign. In addition to this, you have sent six millions of dollars to the public treasury, and have enriched the National Museum with three hundred masterpieces of the arts of ancient and modern Italy, which it has required thirty centuries to produce. You have conquered the finest countries in Europe. The French flag waves for the first time upon the Adriatic opposite to Macedon, the native country of Alexander. Still higher destinies await you. I know that you will not prove unworthy of them. Of all the foes that conspired to stifle the Republic in its birth, The Austrian Emperor alone remains before you. To obtain peace we must seek it in the heart of his hereditary State. You will there find a brave people, whose religion and customs you will respect, and whose prosperity you will hold sacred. Remember that it is liberty you carry to the brave Hungarian nation.

## On the Signing of the Treaty of Campo Formio, October 17, 1797

*When you talk of the Princes you have conquered,*
*of the nations you have set free, and the battles you have fought*
*in two campaigns say: In the next two we shall do still more!*

SOLDIERS: I set out tomorrow for Germany. Separated from the army, I shall sigh for the moment of my rejoining it, and brave fresh dangers. Whatever post Government may assign to the soldiers of the Army of Italy, they will always be the worthy supporters of liberty and of the glory of the French name. Soldiers, when you talk of the Princes you have conquered, of the nations you have set free, and the battles you have fought in two campaigns say: In the next two we shall do still more!

# THE EGYPTIAN EXPEDITION

ALMOST IMMEDIATELY after the First Coalition War, Bonaparte advocated an assault on Egypt to undermine British interests in the region. He led a massive expeditionary force in May 1798, and within three months occupied Malta, landed at Egypt, assaulted Alexandria, fought the Battle of the Pyramids and the Battle of the Nile, and occupied Cairo. Seeking to extend his influence, Napoléon began a march on Syria, spending the first months of 1799 fighting in El Arish, Jaffa, Acre, and Mount Tabor. In May Napoléon began a retreat from Syria. He eventually returned to Paris and became first consul of France in December 1799.

## On Embarking for Egypt, June 1798

SOLDIERS, you are about to undertake a conquest the effects of which, on civilization and commerce, are incalculable. The blow you are about to give to England will be the best aimed, the most sensibly felt, she can receive until the time arrives when you can give her death-blow.

We must make some fatiguing marches; we must fight several battles; we shall succeed in all we undertake. The destinies are with us. The Mameluke beys, who favor exclusively English commerce, whose extortions oppress our merchants, and who tyrannize over the unfortunate inhabitants of the Nile, a few days after our arrival will no longer exist.

The people amongst whom we are going to live are Mahometans. The first article of their faith is this: "There is but one God and Mahomet is His prophet." Do not contradict them. Behave to them as you behaved to the Jews—to the Italians. Pay respect to their muftis and their imams, as you did to the rabbis and the bishops. Extend to the ceremonies prescribed by the Koran and the mosques the same toleration which you showed to the synagogues, to the religion of Moses and of Jesus Christ.

The Roman legions protect all religions. You will here find customs different from those of Europe. You must accommodate yourselves to them. The people amongst whom we are about to mix differ from us in the treatment of women; but in all countries he who violates is a monster. Pillage only enriches a small number of men; it dishonors us; it destroys our resources; it converts into enemies the people whom it is our interest to have for friends.

The first town we shall come to was built by Alexander. At every step we shall meet with grand recollections, worthy of exciting the emulation of Frenchmen.

## THE SECOND COALITION

WITH BONAPARTE on the Egyptian campaign, various European powers mobilized a Second Coalition to defeat France. By the time Napoléon returned to Paris, in October 1799, many of the territories he gained in Italy three years before had been lost. As first consul, he determined to reverse those losses with a daring march across the Alps in May 1800.

## BEFORE THE BATTLE OF MARENGO, JUNE 14, 1800

*Will you permit the army to escape which
has carried terror into your families?
You will not. March, then, to meet him.*

WHEN WE BEGAN OUR MARCH, one department of France was in the hands of the enemy. Consternation pervaded the south of the Republic. You advanced. Joy and hope in our country have succeeded to consternation and fear. The enemy, terror-struck, seeks only to regain his frontiers. You have taken his hospitals, his magazines, his reserve parks. The first act of the campaign is finished. Millions of men address you in strains of praise. But shall we allow our audacious enemies to violate with impunity the territory of the Republic? Will you permit the army to escape which has carried terror into your families? You will not. March, then, to meet him. Tear from his brows the laurels he has won. Teach the world that a malediction attends those that violate the territory of the Great People. The result of our efforts will be unclouded glory, and a durable peace.

## ON PRESENTING THE COLORS, DECEMBER 3, 1804

SOLDIERS: Behold your colors! These eagles will always be your rallying point! They will always be where your Emperor may think them necessary for the defense of his throne and of his people. Swear to sacrifice your lives to defend them, and by your courage to keep them constantly in the path of victory. Swear!

## THE THIRD COALITION

THE 1805 ATTEMPT by European powers to defeat France would be as spectacularly unsuccessful as the first two. In November, Bonaparte entered Vienna; a month later he defeated the Austrians at the decisive Battle of Austerlitz.

## Before the Battle of Austerlitz, December 1, 1805

*But should victory appear for a moment uncertain,*
*you will see your Emperor expose himself to the first strokes.*

THE RUSSIAN ARMY has presented itself before you to revenge the disasters of the Austrians at Ulm. They are the same men that you conquered at Hollabrunn, and on those flying trails you have followed. The positions which they occupy are formidable. While they are marching to turn my right, they must present their flank to your blows.

I will myself direct all your battalions. I will keep myself at a distance from the fire, if, with your accustomed valor, you carry disorder and confusion into the enemies' ranks. But should victory appear for a moment uncertain, you will see your Emperor expose himself to the first strokes. Victory must not be doubtful on this occasion.

## After the Battle of Austerlitz, December 3, 1805

*It will be enough for one of you to say, "I was at the battle of Austerlitz";*
*for all your fellow citizens to exclaim, "There is a brave man."*

I AM SATISFIED with you. In the Battle of Austerlitz you have justified all that I expected from your intrepidity. You have decorated your eagles with immortal glory. An army of one hundred thousand men, commanded by the Emperors of Russia and Austria, has been, in less than four hours, either cut in pieces or dispersed. Thus in two months the third coalition has been vanquished and dissolved. Peace can not now be far distant. But I will make only such a peace as gives us guarantee for the future, and secures rewards to our allies. When everything necessary to secure the happiness and prosperity of our country is obtained, I will lead you back to France. My people will behold you again with joy. It will be enough for one of you to say, "I was at the battle of Austerlitz;" for all your fellow citizens to exclaim, "There is a brave man."

# THE RUSSIAN CAMPAIGN

Napoléon's designs on Russia were crushed in 1812. For most of the spring, his army pushed Russian forces toward Moscow. In September the Russians finally turned and fought at Borodino. Although Napoléon won the battle and soon occupied Moscow, victory would be short lived. In October his army commenced a retreat, devastated by early snows and Russian attacks. The surviving remnant of Napoléon's army finally left Russian territory in December.

## Before the Battle of Borodino, September 7, 1812

*Let them say of you, "He was at the battle under the walls of Moscow."*

This is the battle you have so much desired. The victory depends upon you! It is now necessary to us. It will give us abundance of good winter quarters, and a prompt return to our country. Behave as at Austerlitz, at Friedland, at Witepsk, at Smolensk, and let the latest posterity recount with pride your conduct on this day; let them say of you, "He was at the battle under the walls of Moscow."

# THE INVASION OF FRANCE AND THE END OF AN ERA

Eighteen years after forming their first coalition against France, an alliance of Europeans finally defeated Napoléon. In 1814 the Sixth Coalition (Great Britain, Russia, Prussia, Sweden, Austria, and German states) invaded France, occupying Paris in March. Napoléon abdicated his throne and began an exile in Elba in May. In February 1815, Napoléon escaped Elba and landed at Cannes with six hundred guardsmen. His march toward Paris attracted thousands of veterans wishing to be reunited with the leader who had attained improbable victories in the past. Napoléon retook Paris in March and built an army of nearly three hundred thousand to launch a preemptive strike on the Sixth Coalition. On June 18, 1815, he battled the Duke of Wellington at the legendary Battle of Waterloo. The defeat marked the final chapter in Napoléon's brilliant military career. He abdicated the throne in June and soon sailed for St. Helena. He would die within six years.

## Address to the Guard, April 2, 1814

*Let us swear to conquer or die.*

**SOLDIERS:** The enemy has stolen three marches on us, and has made himself master of Paris. We must drive him thence. Frenchmen, unworthy of the name, emigrants whom we have pardoned, have mounted the white cockade and joined the enemy. The wretches shall receive the reward due to this new crime. Let us swear to conquer or die, and to enforce respect to the tri-colored cockade, which has for twenty years accompanied us on the path of glory and honor.

## Farewell Address to the Old Guard, April 20, 1814

*Do not regret my fate;*
*if I have consented to survive,*
*it is to serve your glory.*

**SOLDIERS OF MY OLD GUARD:** I bid you farewell. For twenty years I have constantly accompanied you on the road to honor and glory. In these latter times, as in the days of our prosperity, you have invariably been models of courage and fidelity. With men such as you our cause could not be lost; but the war would have been interminable; it would have been civil war, and that would have entailed deeper misfortunes on France. I have sacrificed all of my interests to those of the country. I go, but you, my friends, will continue to serve France. Her happiness was my only thought. It will still be the object of my wishes. Do not regret my fate; if I have consented to survive, it is to serve your glory. I intend to write the history of the great achievements we have performed together. Adieu, my friends. Would I could press you all to my heart. . . . I embrace you all in the person of your general. Adieu, soldiers! Be always gallant and good.

# On Returning from Exile, March 5, 1815

*Victory shall march at a charging step;*
*the eagle, with the national colors, shall fly from steeple to steeple,*
*till it reaches the towers of Notre Dame.*
*Then you will be able to show your scars with honor;*
*then you will be able to boast of what you have done;*
*you will be the liberators of your country!*

WE HAVE NOT BEEN CONQUERED; two men, sprung from our ranks, have betrayed our laurels, their country, their benefactor, and their prince. Those whom we have beheld for twenty-five years traversing all Europe to raise up enemies against us, who have spent their lives in fighting against us in the ranks of foreign armies, and in cursing our beautiful France, shall they pretend to command or enchain our eagles?—they, who have never been able to look them in the face. Shall we suffer them to inherit the fruit of our glorious toils, to take possession of our honors, of our fortunes; to calumniate and revile our glory? If their reign were to continue all would be lost, even the recollection of those memorable days. With what fury they misrepresent them! They seek to tarnish what the world admires; and if there still remain defenders of our glory, they are to be found among those very enemies whom we have confronted in the field of battle.

Soldiers: in my exile I have heard your voice; I have come back in spite of all obstacles, and all dangers. Your general, called to the throne by the choice of the people, and raised on your shields, is restored to you; come and join him. Mount the tri-colored cockade; you wore it in the days of our greatness. We must never forget that we have been the masters of nations; but we must not suffer any to intermeddle with our affairs. Who would pretend to be master over us? Who would have the power? Resume those eagles which you had at Ulm, at Austerlitz, at Jena, at Eylau, at Wagram, at Friedland, at Tudela, at Eckmuhl, at Essling, at Smolensk, at the Moskowa, at Lutzen, at Wurtchen, at Montmirail. The veterans of the armies of the Sambre and Meuse, of the Rhine, of Italy, of Egypt, of the West, of the Grand Army, are illuminated; their honorable scars are stained; their successes would be crimes; the brave would be rebels, if, as the enemies of the people pretend, the legitimate sovereigns were in the midst of foreign armies. Honors, recompenses, favors, are reserved for those who have served against the country and against us.

Soldiers: Come and range yourselves under the banners of your chief; his existence is only made up of yours; his interest, his honor, his glory, are no other than your interest, your honor, and your glory. Victory shall march at a charging step; the eagle, with the national colors, shall fly from steeple to steeple, till it reaches the towers of Notre Dame. Then you will be able to show your scars with honor; then you will be able to boast of what you have done; you will be the liberators of your country! In your old age, surrounded and looked up to by your fellow citizens, they will listen to you with respect as you recount your high deeds; you will each of you be able to say with pride, "And I also made part of that grand army which entered twice within the walls of Vienna, within those of Rome, of Berlin, of Madrid, of Moscow, and which delivered Paris from the stain which treason and the presence of the enemy had imprinted upon it." Honor to those brave soldiers, the glory of their country!

## Anniversary Proclamation on the Battles of Marengo and Friedland, June 14, 1815

**Soldiers:** This day is the anniversary of Marengo and Friedland, which twice decided the destiny of Europe. Then, as after the battles of Austerlitz and Wagram, we were too generous. We believed in the protestations and oaths of princes to whom we left their thrones. Now, however, leagued together, they strike at the independence and sacred rights of France. They have committed unjust aggressions. Let us march forward and meet them; are we not still the same men?

At Jena, these Prussians, now so arrogant, were three to one; at Montmirail six to one. Let those who have been captive to the English describe the nature of their prison ships, and the sufferings they endured. The Saxons, the Belgians, the Hanoverians, the soldiers of the Confederation of the Rhine, lament that they are obliged to use their arms in the cause of princes who are the enemies of justice, and the destroyers of the rights of nations. They well know the coalition to be insatiable. After having swallowed up twelve millions of Poles, twelve millions of Italians, one million Saxons, and six millions of Belgians, they now wish to devour the States of the second order among the Germans. Madmen! one moment of prosperity has bewildered them. To oppress and humble the people of France is out of their power; once entering our territory, there they will find their doom.

Soldiers: We have forced marches before us, battles to fight, and dangers to encounter; but firm in resolution, victory must be ours. The honor and happiness of our country are at stake! And, in short, Frenchmen, the moment is arrived when we must conquer or die!

# Giuseppe Garibaldi

## FAREWELL ADDRESS: FIGHT ON!
## SEPTEMBER 1860

*To arms, then, all of you! All of you!*
*And the oppressors and the mighty shall disappear like dust.*
*You, too, women, cast away all the cowards from your embraces;*
*they will give you only cowards for children,*
*and you who are the daughters of the land of beauty*
*must bear children who are noble and brave.*

From *Portrait Gallery of Eminent Men and Women in Europe and America*,
by Evert A. Duyckinick.

O N THE BANKS OF THE JORDAN RIVER, Moses inspired his followers to continue their battles even in his absence. The same task fell
to Giuseppe Garibaldi in 1860.

No one fought harder for the unification and liberation of Italy than
Giuseppe Garibaldi did. A patriot and warrior, Garibaldi inspired his troops
with the powerful lessons of example. At twenty-six, he joined the revolutionary movement to free Italy from Austrian rule. He was condemned to death
in 1834, escaped to South America, lived in the United States, and returned
to Italy in 1854 to resume his fight.

Garibaldi's "red shirts" conquered Sicily in the summer of 1860, crossed
to the Italian mainland, and defeated Naples in October of that year. There,
joyous crowds celebrated his conquest by singing the national anthem, now
known as "Garibaldi's Hymn." A year later, he gave control of Naples to Victor Emanuel and prepared to return home.

In this farewell speech, Garibaldi inspires his forces to continue their march
for Italian liberation without him. He celebrates victories already achieved,
but warns that if one million soldiers are not gathered by March 1861, hope
for total reunification will be lost. He then promises to rejoin them in battle:
"Today I am obliged to retire, but for a few days only. The hour of battle will
find me with you again, by the side of the champions of Italian liberty."

---

WE MUST NOW CONSIDER the period which is just drawing to a close as
almost the last stage of our national resurrection, and prepare ourselves to
finish worthily the marvelous design of the elect of twenty generations, the
completion of which Providence has reserved for this fortunate age.

Yes, young men, Italy owes to you an undertaking which has merited
the applause of the universe. You have conquered and you will conquer still,
because you are prepared for the tactics that decide the fate of battles. You are
not unworthy of the men who entered the ranks of a Macedonian phalanx,
and who contended not in vain with the proud conquerors of Asia. To this
wonderful page in our country's history another more glorious still will be
added, and the slave shall show at last to his free brothers a sharpened sword
forged from the links of his fetters.

To arms, then, all of you! All of you! And the oppressors and the mighty
shall disappear like dust. You, too, women, cast away all the cowards from your
embraces; they will give you only cowards for children, and you who are the
daughters of the land of beauty must bear children who are noble and brave.
Let timid doctrinaires depart from among us to carry their servility and their

miserable fears elsewhere. This people is its own master. It wishes to be the brother of other peoples, but to look on the insolent with a proud glance, not to grovel before them imploring its own freedom. It will no longer follow in the trail of men whose hearts are foul. No! No! No!

Providence has presented Italy with Victor Emmanuel. Every Italian should rally round him. By the side of Victor Emmanuel every quarrel should be forgotten, all rancor depart. Once more I repeat my battle cry: "To arms, all—all of you!" If March, 1861, does not find one million of Italians in arms, then alas for liberty, alas for the life of Italy. Ah, no, far be from me a thought which I loathe like poison. March of 1861, or if need be February, will find us all at our post-Italians of Calatafimi, Palermo, Ancona, the Volturno, Castelfidardo, and Isernia, and with us every man of this land who is not a coward or a slave. Let all of us rally round the glorious hero of Palestro and give the last blow to the crumbling edifice of tyranny. Receive, then, my gallant young volunteers, at the honored conclusion of ten battles, one word of farewell from me.

I utter this word with deepest affection and from the very bottom of my heart. Today I am obliged to retire, but for a few days only. The hour of battle will find me with you again, by the side of the champions of Italian liberty. Let those only return to their homes who are called by the imperative duties which they owe to their families, and those who by their glorious wounds have deserved the credit of their country. These, indeed, will serve Italy in their homes by their counsel, by the very aspect of the scars which adorn their youthful brows. Apart from these, let all others remain to guard our glorious banners. We shall meet again before long to march together to the redemption of our brothers who are still slaves of the stranger. We shall meet again before long to march to new triumphs.

# Frederick Douglass

## MEN OF COLOR, TO ARMS!
## MARCH 21, 1863

*I urge you to fly to arms, and smite with death
the power that would bury the government
and your liberty in the same hopeless grave.*

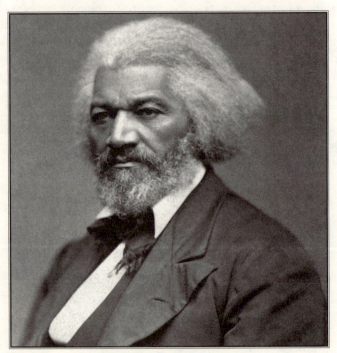

Photograph taken ca. 1879.

I N JULY 1862, Congress passed measures allowing the enlistment of African Americans in the Union Army and Navy. It wouldn't be until January 1, 1863—when the Emancipation Proclamation became effective—that official enlistment began. And it would be even longer before African American troops received equal pay and benefits with their counterparts.

Even still, some 200,000 African Americans joined the fight. When the abolitionist governor of Massachusetts, John A. Andrew, wanted to recruit then-called "Colored Troops" to the newly formed 54th Massachusetts Infantry Regiment, he turned to fellow abolitionist Frederick Douglass for assistance.

Douglass—an escaped slave and prominent orator and writer—crafted a rousing editorial that was reprinted in newspapers and posters throughout the North. Evocative of Eleazar ben Yair at Masada, and Patrick Henry's "Liberty or Death" speech, Douglass declares, "Better even die free, than to live slaves." He also addresses, in plain terms, a specific concern of potential soldiers: "I am authorized to assure you that you will receive the same wages, the same rations, and the same equipments, the same protection, the same treatment, and the same bounty, secured to the white soldiers." Finally, like so many others seeking to motivate and mobilize, he suggests God as an ally: "Remember that in a contest with oppression, the Almighty has no attribute which can take sides with oppressors."

Douglass inspired many, including his two sons, to enlist in the 54th Massachusetts. On July 18, 1863, the regiment led an assault on Fort Wagner, near Charleston, South Carolina. Nearly half the regiment was killed, captured, or wounded in an inspiring battle. The 1989 film *Glory* popularized their heroic deeds.

---

WHEN FIRST THE REBEL CANNON shattered the walls of Sumter and drove away its starving garrison, I predicted that the war then and there inaugurated would not be fought out entirely by white men. Every month's experience during these dreary years has confirmed that opinion. A war undertaken and brazenly carried on for the perpetual enslavement of colored men, calls logically and loudly for colored men to help suppress it. Only a moderate share of sagacity was needed to see that the arm of the slave was the best defense against the arm of the slaveholder. Hence with every reverse to the national arms, with every exulting shout of victory raised by the slaveholding rebels, I have implored the imperiled nation to unchain against her foes, her powerful black hand. Slowly and reluctantly that appeal is beginning to be heeded. Stop not now to complain that it was not heeded sooner. It may or it may not have been best that it should not. This is not the time to discuss that question. Leave it to the future. When the war is over, the country is saved, peace is established, and the black man's rights are secured, as they will be, history with an impartial hand will dispose of that and sundry other questions. Action! Action! not criticism, is the plain duty of this hour. Words are now useful only as they stimulate to blows. The office of speech now is only to point out when, where, and how to strike to the best advantage. There is no time to delay. The tide is at its flood that leads on to fortune. From East to West, from North to South, the sky is written all over, "Now or never." Liberty won by white men would lose half its luster. "Who would be free themselves must strike the blow." "Better even die free, than to live slaves." This is the sentiment of every brave colored man amongst us. There are weak and cowardly men in all nations. We have them amongst us. They tell you this is the white man's war; and you will be "no better off after than before the war;" that the getting of you into the army is to "sacrifice you on the first opportunity." Believe them not; cowards themselves, they do not wish to have their cowardice shamed by your brave example. Leave them to their timidity, or to whatever motive may hold them back. I have not thought lightly of the words I am now addressing you. The counsel I give comes of close observation of the great struggle now in progress, and of the deep conviction that this is your hour and mine. In good earnest then, and after the best deliberation, I now for the first time during this war feel at liberty to call and counsel you to arms. By every consideration which binds you to your enslaved fellow—countrymen, and the peace and welfare of your country; by every aspiration which you cherish for the freedom and equality of yourselves and your children; by all the ties of blood and identity which make us one with the brave black men now fighting our battles in Louisiana and in South Caroline, I urge you to fly to arms, and smite with death the power that would bury the government and your liberty in the same hopeless grave. I wish I could tell you that the State of New York calls you to this high honor. For the moment her constituted authorities are silent on the subject. They will speak by and by, and doubtless on the right side; but we are not compelled to wait for her. We can get at the throat of treason and slavery through the State of Massachusetts. She was the first in the War of Independence; first to break the chains of her slaves; first to make the black man equal before the law; first to admit colored children to her common schools, and she was first to answer with her blood the alarm cry of the nation, when its capital was menaced by rebels. You know her patriotic governor, and you know Charles Sumner. I need not add more.

Massachusetts now welcomes you to arms as soldiers. She has but a small colored population from which to recruit. She has full leave of the general government to send one regiment to the war, and she has undertaken to do it. Go quickly and help fill up the first colored regiment from the North. I am authorized to assure you that you will receive the same wages, the same rations, and the same equipments, the same protection, the same treatment, and the same bounty, secured to the white soldiers. You will be led by able and skillful officers, men who will take especial pride in your efficiency and success. They will be quick to accord to you all the honor you shall merit by your valor, and see that your rights and feelings are respected by other soldiers. I have assured myself on these points, and can speak with authority. More than twenty years of unswerving devotion to our common cause may give me some humble claim to be trusted at this momentous crisis. I will not argue. To do so implies hesitation and doubt, and you do not hesitate. You do not doubt. The day dawns; the morning star is bright upon the horizon! The iron gate of our prison stands half open. One gallant rush from the North will fling it wide open, while four millions of our brothers and sisters shall march out into liberty. The chance is now given you to end in a day the bondage of centuries, and to rise in one bound from social degradation to the place of common equality with all other varieties of men. Remember Denmark Vesey of Charleston; remember Nathaniel Turner of Southampton; remember Shields Green and Copeland, who followed noble John Brown, and fell as glorious martyrs for the cause of the slave. Remember that in a contest with oppression, the Almighty has no attribute which can take sides with oppressors. The case is before you. This is our golden opportunity. Let us accept it, and forever wipe out the dark reproaches unsparingly hurled against us by our enemies. Let us win for ourselves the gratitude of our country, and the best blessings of our posterity through all time. The nucleus of this first regiment is now in camp at Readville, a short distance from Boston. I will undertake to forward to Boston all persons adjudged fit to be mustered into the regiment, who shall apply to me at any time within the next two weeks.

# Abraham Lincoln

## GETTYSBURG ADDRESS,
## NOVEMBER 19, 1863

*From these honored dead we take increased devotion*
*to that cause for which they gave the last full measure of devotion.*

Photograph taken November 8, 1863.

**W**HY DO WE FIGHT? The question has lingered over battlefields ancient and new. It has galvanized and divided populations throughout history. Leaders have struggled to answer the question—in the scorching heat of battle and the hot television lights of Washington; at boisterous rallies and the still reverence of military funerals. Whenever "Taps" is sounded, the question arises.

Only a few leaders in history—Pericles, Napoléon Bonaparte, Winston Churchill, and Franklin D. Roosevelt among them—have given true voice to the question. Only one—Abraham Lincoln—has done so within three minutes and 272 words.

Between July 1 and July 3, 1863, over fifty thousand people were killed, wounded, or captured at Gettysburg, Pennsylvania. Four months later a cemetery was dedicated at a program headlined by Pastor Edward Everett of Massachusetts and offering secondary "remarks" by the president of the United States. After Everett's three-hour address, Lincoln stood. His speech echoes with the classic oratory of Pericles' "Oration At the Funeral of Fallen Soldiers." Its ancient rhythms remind us of the timelessness of war, the eternal search for peace.

That day Lincoln did not simply dedicate a cemetery. He rededicated America to the pursuit of noble goals even in the shadow of great and grave sacrifice. He achieved his goal by invoking our history, our purpose, and our future.

Lincoln's Gettysburg Address is a powerful tonic to today's television-clicker culture, where life and death decisions are reduced to spin and sound bite.

---

**F**OUR SCORE AND SEVEN YEARS AGO our fathers brought forth on this continent a new nation, conceived in Liberty, and dedicated to the proposition that all men are created equal.

Now we are engaged in a great civil war, testing whether that nation, or any nation so conceived and so dedicated, can long endure. We are met on a great battlefield of that war. We have come to dedicate a portion of that field as a final resting place for those who here gave their lives that that nation might live. It is altogether fitting and proper that we should do this.

But, in a larger sense, we cannot dedicate . . . we cannot consecrate . . . we cannot hallow . . . this ground. The brave men, living and dead, who struggled here, have consecrated it far above our poor power to add or detract. The world will little note nor long remember what we say here, but it can never forget what they did here. It is for us the living, rather, to be dedicated here to the unfinished work which they who fought here have thus far so nobly advanced. It is rather for us to be here dedicated to the great task remaining before us . . . that from these honored dead we take increased devotion to that cause for which they gave the last full measure of devotion; that we here highly resolve that these dead shall not have died in vain; that this nation, under God, shall have a new birth of freedom; and that government of the people, by the people, for the people, shall not perish from the earth.

# Abraham Lincoln

## To the 166th Ohio Regiment, August 22, 1864

*It is for this the struggle should be maintained,
that we may not lose our birthright.*

Photograph taken February 9, 1864.

IN THE BLISTERING AUGUST SUN, on the lawn of the White House, a fatigued Abraham Lincoln addressed a group of men serving a short term of service to ease troop shortages: the 166th Ohio Regiment. Hat in hand, Lincoln succinctly spoke of the importance of maintaining America's freedom not only for their generation, but for the future. Even shorter than his Gettysburg Address nine months earlier, Lincoln proved once again that it is not the length but the content of a speech that truly matters.

———◦•◦•◦———

I SUPPOSE YOU ARE GOING HOME to see your families and friends. For the service you have done in this great struggle in which we are engaged I present you sincere thanks for myself and the country. I almost always feel inclined, when I happen to say anything to soldiers, to impress upon them in a few brief remarks the importance of success in this contest. It is not merely for today, but for all time to come that we should perpetuate for our children's children this great and free government, which we have enjoyed all our lives. I beg you to remember this, not merely for my sake, but for yours. I happen temporarily to occupy this big White House. I am a living witness that any one of your children may look to come here as my father's child has. It is in order that each of you may have through this free government which we have enjoyed, an open field and a fair chance for your industry, enterprise and intelligence; that you may all have equal privileges in the race of life, with all its desirable human aspirations. It is for this the struggle should be maintained, that we may not lose our birthright—not only for one, but for two or three years. The nation is worth fighting for, to secure such an inestimable jewel.

# Abraham Lincoln

## SECOND INAUGURAL ADDRESS,
## MARCH 4, 1865

*Fondly do we hope, fervently do we pray, that this mighty scourge of war
may speedily pass away. Yet, if God wills that it continue, until all the wealth
piled by the bond-man's two hundred and fifty years of unrequited toil shall be
sunk, and until every drop of blood drawn with the lash, shall be paid by another
drawn with the sword, as was said three thousand years ago, so still it must be said
"the judgments of the Lord, are true and righteous altogether."*

Herline & Hensel lithograph, ca. 1860–70.

IN WAR, THERE ARE THREE CENTERS OF GRAVITY: the population for which the war is fought; the population in which the war is fought; and the population that actually does the fighting. In an extended conflict, an even greater force—the inexorable passage of time—pulls at those three centers of gravity.

The bravado that heralds conflict is worn down by the grinding inevitabilities of battle, and the call to go to war is often easier than the call to remain there. President Abraham Lincoln realized this when he took the oath of office for his second term. Here, he departs from the usual techniques to sustain support for war. Rather than offering false optimism, Lincoln establishes credibility by acknowledging the unexpected pain and duration of the war. Rather than reducing and vilifying the enemy, he humanizes them. He demonstrates his unequivocal belief in the struggle, promising to continue it "until every drop of blood drawn with the lash, shall be paid by another drawn with the sword"; but then exudes the values of compassion and righteousness that make the struggle worth supporting: "With malice toward none; with charity for all; with firmness in the right, as God gives us to see the right, let us strive on to finish the work we are in; to bind up the nation's wounds; to care for him who shall have borne the battle, and for his widow, and his orphan—to do all which may achieve and cherish a just and a lasting peace, among ourselves, and with all nations."

A month later—nearly four years after the war began—that peace was achieved, the Union was preserved, and Lincoln was assassinated.

———— ·•· ————

**FELLOW COUNTRYMEN:**

At this second appearing to take the oath of the presidential office, there is less occasion for an extended address than there was at the first. Then a statement, somewhat in detail, of a course to be pursued, seemed fitting and proper. Now, at the expiration of four years, during which public declarations have been constantly called forth on every point and phase of the great contest which still absorbs the attention, and engrosses the energies of the nation, little that is new could be presented. The progress of our arms, upon which all else chiefly depends, is as well known to the public as to myself; and it is, I trust, reasonably satisfactory and encouraging to all. With high hope for the future, no prediction in regard to it is ventured.

On the occasion corresponding to this four years ago, all thoughts were anxiously directed to an impending civil war. All dreaded it—all sought to avert it. While the inaugural address was being delivered from this place, devoted altogether to saving the Union without war, insurgent agents were in the city seeking to destroy it without war—seeking to dissolve the Union, and divide effects, by negotiation. Both parties deprecated war; but one of them would make war rather than let the nation survive; and the other would accept war rather than let it perish. And the war came.

One eighth of the whole population were colored slaves, not distributed generally over the Union, but localized in the Southern part of it. These slaves constituted a peculiar and powerful interest. All knew that this interest was, somehow, the cause of the war. To strengthen, perpetuate, and extend this interest was the object for which the insurgents would rend the Union, even by war; while the government claimed no right to do more than to restrict the territorial enlargement of it. Neither party expected for the war, the magnitude, or the duration, which it has already attained. Neither anticipated that the cause of the conflict might cease with, or even before, the conflict itself should cease. Each looked for an easier triumph, and a result less fundamental and astounding. Both read the same Bible, and pray to the same God; and each invokes His aid against the other. It may seem strange that any men should dare to ask a just God's assistance in wringing their bread from the sweat of other men's faces; but let us judge not that we be not judged. The prayers of both could not be answered; that of neither has been answered fully. The Almighty has His own purposes. "Woe unto the world because of offences; for it must needs be that offences come; but woe to that man by whom the offence cometh!" If we shall suppose that American Slavery is one of those offences which, in the providence of God, must needs come, but which, having continued through His appointed time, He now wills to remove, and that He gives to both North and South, this terrible war, as the woe due to those by whom the offence came, shall we discern therein any departure from those divine attributes which the believers in a Living God always ascribe to Him? Fondly do we hope—fervently do we pray—that this mighty scourge of war may speedily pass away. Yet, if God wills that it continue, until all the wealth piled by the bond-man's two hundred and fifty years of unrequited toil shall be sunk, and until every drop of blood drawn with the lash, shall be paid by another drawn with the sword, as was said three thousand years ago, so still it must be said "the judgments of the Lord, are true and righteous altogether."

With malice toward none; with charity for all; with firmness in the right, as God gives us to see the right, let us strive on to finish the work we are in; to bind up the nation's wounds; to care for him who shall have borne the battle, and for his widow, and his orphan—to do all which may achieve and cherish a just and a lasting peace, among ourselves, and with all nations.

# PART 3
# SAFE FOR DEMOCRACY

*The world must be made safe for democracy.*
*Its peace must be planted upon the tested foundations of political liberty.*

— WOODROW WILSON, 1917

# Woodrow Wilson

## TO THE U.S. NAVAL ACADEMY, JUNE 5, 1914

*It ought to be one of your thoughts all the time
that you are sample Americans—not merely sample Navy men,
not merely sample soldiers, but sample Americans—
and that you have the point of view of America
with regard to her Navy and her Army; that she is using them
as the instruments of civilization, not as the instruments of aggression.*

Photograph taken 1919.

ONE OF THE CRITICAL "LESSONS LEARNED" from the war in Iraq was the difficulty of asking a military trained as warriors to become nation builders. Soldiers found themselves playing the role of diplomats, economic development experts, educators, political scientists, and cultural anthropologists. As one commander told me during a Blackhawk helicopter ride over Balad, "I wasn't trained to do the things I have to do."

In 1914 President Woodrow Wilson foretold the broad demands that would be placed on our military. His commencement address to the Naval Academy urged the graduates not to narrow their professional military scope. He asked them not simply to fight, but to "come back and tell us … where you can, where you see men suffering; tell us where you think advice will lift them up; tell us where you think that the counsel of statesmen may better the fortunes of unfortunate men."

Wilson then uses the presence of the U.S. military in Vera Cruz, Mexico, as an example: "The lasting impression that those boys are going to leave is this, that they exercise self-control; that they are ready and diligent to make the place where they went fitter to live in than they found it."

His words were as relevant in Iraq today as they were in Vera Cruz in 1914.

---

**MR. SUPERINTENDENT, YOUNG GENTLEMEN, LADIES AND GENTLEMEN:**

During the greater part of my life I have been associated with young men, and on occasions it seems to me without number have faced bodies of youngsters going out to take part in the activities of the world, but I have a consciousness of a different significance in this occasion from that which I have felt on other similar occasions. When I have faced the graduating classes at universities I have felt that I was facing a great conjecture. They were going out into all sorts of pursuits and with every degree of preparation for the particular thing they were expecting to do; some without any preparation at all, for they did not know what they expected to do. But in facing you I am facing men who are trained for a special thing. You know what you are going to do, and you are under the eye of the whole Nation in doing it. For you, gentlemen, are to be part of the power of the Government of the United States. There is a very deep and solemn significance in that fact, and I am sure that every one of you feels it. The moral is perfectly obvious. Be ready and fit for anything that you have to do. And keep ready and fit. Do not grow slack. Do not suppose that your education is over because you have received your diplomas from the academy. Your education has just begun. Moreover, you are to have a very peculiar privilege which not many of your predecessors have had. You are yourselves going to become teachers. You are going to teach those 50,000 fellow-countrymen of yours who are the enlisted men of the Navy. You are going to make them fitter to obey your orders and to serve the country. You are going to make them fitter to see what the orders mean in their outlook upon life and upon the service; and that is a great privilege, for out of you is going the energy and intelligence which are going to quicken the whole body of the United States Navy.

I congratulate you upon that prospect, but I want to ask you not to get the professional point of view. I would ask it of you if you were lawyers; I would ask it of you if you were merchants; I would ask it of you whatever you expected to be. Do not get the professional point of view. There is nothing narrower or more unserviceable than the professional point of view, to have the attitude toward life that it centers in your profession. It does not. Your profession is only one of the many activities which are meant to keep the world straight, and to keep the energy in its blood and in its muscle. We are all of us in this world, as I understand it, to set forward the affairs of the whole world, though we play a special part in that great function. The Navy goes all over the world, and I think it is to be congratulated upon having that sort of illustration of what the world is and what it contains; and inasmuch as you are going all over the world you ought to be the better able to see the relation that your country bears to the rest of the world.

It ought to be one of your thoughts all the time that you are sample Americans—not merely sample Navy men, not merely sample soldiers, but sample Americans—and that you have the point of view of America with regard to her Navy and her Army; that she is using them as the instruments of civilization, not as the instruments of aggression. The idea of America is to serve humanity, and every time you let the Stars and Stripes free to the wind you ought to realize that that is in itself a message that you are on an errand which other navies have sometimes forgotten; not an errand of conquest, but an errand of service. I always have the same thought when I look at the flag of the United States, for I know something of the history of the struggle of mankind for liberty. When I look at that flag it seems to me as if the white stripes were strips of parchment upon which are written the rights of man, and the red stripes the streams of blood by which those rights have been made good. Then in the little blue firmament in the corner have swung out the stars of the States of the American Union. So it is, as it were, a sort of floating charter that has come down to us from Runnymede, when men said, "We will not have masters; we will be a people, and we will seek our own liberty."

You are not serving a government, gentlemen; you are serving a people. For we who for the time being constitute the Government are merely instruments for a little while in the hands of a great Nation which chooses whom it will to carry out its decrees and who invariably rejects the man who forgets the ideals which it intended him to serve. So that I hope that wherever you go you will have a generous, comprehending love of the people you come into contact with, and will come back and tell us, if you can, what service the United States can render to the remotest parts of the world; tell us where you see men suffering; tell us where you think advice will lift them up; tell us where you think that the counsel of statesmen may better the fortunes of unfortunate men; always having it in mind that you are champions of what is right and fair all 'round for the public welfare, no matter where you are, and that it is that you are ready to fight for and not merely on the drop of a hat or upon some slight punctilio, but that you are champions of your fellow-men, particularly of that great body one hundred million strong whom you represent in the United States.

What do you think is the most lasting impression that those boys down at Vera Cruz are going to leave? They have had to use some force—I pray God it may not be necessary for them to use any more—but do you think that the way they fought is going to be the most lasting impression? Have men not fought ever since the world began? Is there anything new in using force? The new things in the world are the things that are divorced from force. The things that show the moral compulsions of the human conscience, those are the things by which we have been building up civilization, not by force. And the lasting impression that those boys are going to leave is this, that they exercise self-control; that they are ready and diligent to make the place where they went fitter to live in than they found it; that they regarded other people's rights; that they did not strut and bluster, but went quietly, like self-respecting gentlemen, about their legitimate work. And the people of Vera Cruz, who feared the Americans and despised the Americans, are going to get a very different taste in their mouths about the whole thing when the boys of the Navy and the Army come away. Is that not something to be proud of, that you know how to use force like men of conscience and like gentlemen, serving your fellow-men and not trying to overcome them? Like that gallant gentleman who has so long borne the heats and perplexities and distresses of the situation in Vera Cruz—Admiral Fletcher. I mention him, because his service there has been longer and so much of the early perplexities fell upon him. I have been in almost daily communication with Admiral Fletcher, and I have tested his temper. I have tested his discretion. I know that he is a man with a touch of statesmanship about him, and he has grown bigger in my eye each day as I have read his dispatches, for he has sought always to serve the thing he was trying to do in the temper that we all recognize and love to believe is typically American.

I challenge you youngsters to go out with these conceptions, knowing that you are part of the Government and force of the United States and that men will judge us by you. I am not afraid of the verdict. I cannot look in your faces and doubt what it will be, but I want you to take these great engines of force out onto the seas like adventurers enlisted for the elevation of the spirit of the human race. For that is the only distinction that America has. Other nations have been strong, other nations have piled wealth as high as the sky, but they have come into disgrace because they used their force and their wealth for the oppression of mankind and their own aggrandizement; and America will not bring glory to herself, but disgrace, by following the beaten paths of history. We must strike out upon new paths, and we must count upon you gentlemen to be the explorers who will carry this spirit and spread this message all over the seas and in every port of the civilized world.

You see, therefore, why I said that when I faced you I felt there was a special significance. I am not present on an occasion when you are about to scatter on various errands. You are all going on the same errand, and I like to feel bound with you in one common organization for the glory of America. And her glory goes deeper than all the tinsel, goes deeper than the sound of guns and the clash of sabers; it goes down to the very foundations of those things that have made the spirit of men free and happy and content.

# Woodrow Wilson

## WAR MESSAGE TO CONGRESS, APRIL 2, 1917

*It may be many months of fiery trial and sacrifice ahead of us.*
*It is a fearful thing to lead this great peaceful people into war,*
*into the most terrible and disastrous of all wars, civilization itself seeming*
*to be in the balance. But the right is more precious than peace, and we shall fight*
*for the things which we have always carried nearest our hearts—*
*for democracy, for the right of those who submit to authority*
*to have a voice in their own Governments, for the rights and liberties*
*of small nations, for a universal dominion of right*
*by such a concert of free peoples as shall bring peace and safety*
*to all nations and make the world itself at last free.*

President Woodrow Wilson addressing Congress, 1917.

PRESIDENT WOODROW WILSON'S desire to keep America out of World War I was quashed when German submarines violated international law and assaulted merchant and passenger vessels in European waters. In this address to Congress, Wilson frames the war not as a hasty retaliation but as a historic struggle for the values of freedom: "The world must be made safe for democracy. Its peace must be planted upon the tested foundations of political liberty. We have no selfish ends to serve. We desire no conquest, no dominion. We seek no indemnities for ourselves, no material compensation for the sacrifices we shall freely make. We are but one of the champions of the rights of mankind. We shall be satisfied when those rights have been made as secure as the faith and the freedom of nations can make them."

Could anything be more worth fighting for?

I include this speech for another reason. In contrast to contemporary theories that war can be fought quickly and with relative ease, Wilson's speech presents a somber and honest assessment of what must be done to meet the "fiery challenge": the addition of five hundred thousand combatants to the armed forces, universal service, additional forces as necessary, and "well-conceived taxation" to fight the war: "Because," he says, "it seems to me that it would be unwise to base the credits which will now be necessary entirely on money borrowed."

---

**GENTLEMEN OF THE CONGRESS:**

I have called the Congress into extraordinary session because there are serious, very serious, choices of policy to be made, and made immediately, which it was neither right nor constitutionally permissible that I should assume the responsibility of making.

On the third of February last I officially laid before you the extraordinary announcement of the Imperial German Government that on and after the first day of February it was its purpose to put aside all restraints of law or of humanity and use its submarines to sink every vessel that sought to approach either the ports of Great Britain and Ireland or the western coasts of Europe or any of the ports controlled by the enemies of Germany within the Mediterranean. That had seemed to be the object of the German submarine warfare earlier in the war, but since April of last year the Imperial Government had somewhat restrained the commanders of its undersea craft in conformity with its promise then given to us that passenger boats should not be sunk and that due warning would be given to all other vessels which its submarines might seek to destroy when no resistance was offered or escape attempted, and care taken that their crews were given at least a fair chance to save their lives in their open boats. The precautions taken were meager and haphazard enough, as was proved in distressing instance after instance in the progress of the cruel and unmanly business, but a certain degree of restraint was observed. The new policy has swept every restriction aside. Vessels of every kind, whatever their flag, their character, their cargo, their destination, their errand, have been ruthlessly sent to the bottom without warning and without thought of help or mercy for those on board, the vessels of friendly neutrals along with those of belligerents. Even hospital ships and ships carrying relief to the sorely bereaved and stricken people of Belgium, though the latter were provided with safe conduct through the proscribed areas by the German Government itself and were distinguished by unmistakable marks of identity, have been sunk with the same reckless lack of compassion or of principle.

I was for a little while unable to believe that such things would in fact be done by any government that had hitherto subscribed to the humane practices of civilized nations. International law had its origin in the attempt to set up some law which would be respected and observed upon the seas, where no nation had right of dominion and where lay the free highways of the world. By painful stage after stage has that law been built up, with meagre enough results, indeed, after all was accomplished that could be accomplished, but always with a clear view, at least, of what the heart and conscience of mankind demanded. This minimum of right the German Government has swept aside under the plea of retaliation and necessity and because it had no weapons which it could use at sea except these which it is impossible to employ as it is employing them without throwing to the winds all scruples of humanity or of respect for the understandings that were supposed to underlie the intercourse of the world. I am not now thinking of the loss of property involved, immense and serious as that is, but only of the wanton and wholesale destruction of the lives of noncombatants, men, women, and children, engaged in pursuits which have always, even in the darkest periods of modern history, been deemed innocent and legitimate. Property can be paid for; the lives of peaceful and innocent people cannot be. The present German submarine warfare against commerce is a warfare against mankind.

It is a war against all nations. American ships have been sunk, American lives taken, in ways which it has stirred us very deeply to learn of, but the ships and people of other neutral and friendly nations have been sunk and overwhelmed in the waters in the same way. There has been no discrimination. The challenge is to all mankind. Each nation must decide for itself how it will meet it. The choice we make for ourselves must be made with a moderation of counsel and a temperateness of judgment befitting our character and our motives as a nation. We must put excited feeling away. Our motive will not be revenge or the victorious assertion of the physical might of the nation, but only the vindication of right, of human right, of which we are only a single champion.

When I addressed the Congress on the twenty-sixth of February last I thought that it would suffice to assert our neutral rights with arms, our right to use the seas against unlawful interference, our right to keep our people safe against unlawful violence. But armed neutrality, it now appears, is impracticable. Because submarines are in effect outlaws when used as the German submarines have been used against merchant shipping, it is impossible to defend ships against their attacks as the law of nations has assumed that merchantmen would defend themselves against privateers or cruisers, visible craft giving chase upon the open sea. It is common prudence in such circumstances, grim necessity indeed, to endeavor to destroy them before they have shown their own intention. They must be dealt with upon sight, if dealt with at all. The German Government denies the right of neutrals to use arms at all within the areas of the sea which it has proscribed, even in the defense of rights which no modern publicist has ever before questioned their right to defend. The intimation is conveyed that the armed guards which we have placed on our merchant ships will be treated as beyond the pale of law and subject to be dealt with as pirates would be. Armed neutrality is ineffectual enough at best; in such circumstances and in the face of such pretensions it is worse than ineffectual: it is likely only to produce what it was meant to prevent; it is practically certain to draw us into the war without either the rights or the effectiveness of belligerents. There is one choice we cannot make, we are incapable of making: we will not choose the path of submission and suffer the most sacred rights of our Nation and our people to be ignored or violated. The wrongs against which we now array ourselves are no common wrongs; they cut to the very roots of human life.

With a profound sense of the solemn and even tragical character of the step I am taking and of the grave responsibilities which it involves, but in unhesitating obedience to what I deem my constitutional duty, I advise that the Congress declare the recent course of the Imperial German Government to be in fact nothing less than war against the Government and people of the United States; that it formally accept the status of belligerent which has thus been thrust upon it, and that it take immediate steps not only to put the country in a more thorough state of defense but also to exert all its power and employ all its resources to bring the Government of the German Empire to terms and end the war.

What this will involve is clear. It will involve the utmost practicable cooperation in counsel and action with the governments now at war with Germany, and, as incident to that, the extension to those governments of the most liberal financial credit, in order that our resources may so far as possible be added to theirs. It will involve the organization and mobilization of all the material resources of the country to supply the materials of war and serve the incidental needs of the Nation in the most abundant and yet the most economical and efficient way possible. It will involve the immediate full equipment of the navy in all respects but particularly in supplying it with the best means of dealing with the enemy's submarines. It will involve the immediate addition to the armed forces of the United States already provided for by law in case of war at least five hundred thousand men, who should, in my opinion, be chosen upon the principle of universal liability to service, and also the authorization of subsequent additional increments of equal force so soon as they may be needed and can be handled in training. It will involve also, of course, the granting of adequate credits to the Government, sustained, I hope, so far as they can equitably be sustained by the present generation, by well-conceived taxation. . . .

While we do these things, these deeply momentous things, let us be very clear, and make very clear to all the world what our motives and our objects are. My own thought has not been driven from its habitual and normal course by the unhappy events of the last two months, and I do not believe that the thought of the Nation has been altered or clouded by them. I have exactly the same things in mind now that I had in mind when I addressed the Senate on the twenty-second of January last, the same that I had in mind when I addressed the Congress on the third of February and on the twenty-sixth of February. Our object now, as then, is to vindicate the principles of peace and justice in the life of the world as against selfish and autocratic power and to set up amongst the really free and self-governed peoples of the world such a concert of purpose and of action as will henceforth ensure the observance of those principles. Neutrality is no longer feasible or desirable where the peace of the world is involved and the freedom of its peoples, and the menace to that peace and freedom lies in the existence of autocratic governments backed by organized force which is controlled wholly by their will, not by the will of their people. We have seen the last of neutrality in such circumstances. We are at the beginning of an age in which it will be insisted that the same standards of conduct and of responsibility for wrong done shall be observed among nations and their governments that are observed among the individual citizens of civilized states.

We have no quarrel with the German people. We have no feeling towards them but one of sympathy and friendship. It was not upon their impulse that their government acted in entering this war. It was not with their previous knowledge or approval. It was a war determined upon as wars used to be determined upon in the old, unhappy days when peoples were nowhere consulted by their rulers and wars were provoked and waged in the interest of dynasties or of little groups of ambitious men who were accustomed to use their fellow men as pawns and tools. Self-governed nations do not fill their neighbor states with spies or set the course of intrigue to bring about some critical posture of affairs which will give them an opportunity to strike and make conquest. Such designs can be successfully worked out only under cover and where no one has the right to ask questions. Cunningly contrived plans of deception or aggression, carried, it may be, from generation to generation, can be worked out and kept from the light only within the privacy of courts or behind the carefully guarded confidences of a narrow and privileged class. They are happily impossible where public opinion commands and insists upon full information concerning all the nation's affairs.

A steadfast concert for peace can never be maintained except by a partnership of democratic nations. No autocratic government could be trusted to keep faith within it or observe its covenants. It must be a league of honour, a partnership of opinion. Intrigue would eat its vitals away; the plottings of inner circles who could plan what they would and render account to no one would be a corruption seated at its very heart. Only free peoples can hold their purpose and their honour steady to a common end and prefer the interests of mankind to any narrow interest of their own.

Does not every American feel that assurance has been added to our hope for the future peace of the world by the wonderful and heartening things that have been happening within the last few weeks in Russia? Russia was known by those who knew it best to have been always in fact democratic at heart, in all the vital habits of her thought, in all the intimate relationships of her people that spoke their natural instinct, their habitual attitude towards life. The autocracy that crowned the summit of her political structure, long as it had stood and terrible as was the reality of its power, was not in fact Russian in origin, character, or purpose; and now it has been shaken off and the great, generous Russian people have been added in all their naive majesty and might to the forces that are fighting for freedom in the world, for justice, and for peace. Here is a fit partner for a league of honour.

One of the things that has served to convince us that the Prussian autocracy was not and could never be our friend is that from the very outset of the present war it has filled our unsuspecting communities and even our offices of government with spies and set criminal intrigues everywhere afoot against our national unity of counsel, our peace within and without, our industries and our commerce. Indeed it is now evident that its spies were here even before the war began; and it is unhappily not a matter of conjecture but a fact proved in our courts of justice that the intrigues which have more than once come perilously near to disturbing the peace and dislocating the industries of the country have been carried on at the instigation, with the support, and even under the personal direction of official agents of the Imperial Government accredited to the Government of the United States. Even in checking these things and trying to extirpate them we have sought to put the most generous interpretation possible upon them because we knew that their source lay, not in any hostile feeling or purpose of the German people towards us (who were, no doubt, as ignorant of them as we ourselves were), but only in the selfish designs of a Government that did what it pleased and told its people nothing. But they have played their part in serving to convince us at last that that Government entertains no real friendship for us and means to act against our peace and security at its convenience. That it means to stir up enemies against us at our very doors the intercepted note to the German Minister at Mexico City is eloquent evidence.

We are accepting this challenge of hostile purpose because we know that in such a Government, following such methods, we can never have a friend; and that in the presence of its organized power, always lying in wait to accomplish we know not what purpose, there can be no assured security for the democratic Governments of the world. We are now about to accept gauge of battle with this natural foe to liberty and shall, if necessary, spend the whole force of the nation to check and nullify its pretensions and its power. We are glad, now that we see the facts with no veil of false pretense about them to fight thus for the ultimate peace of the world and for the liberation of its peoples, the German peoples included: for the rights of nations great and small and the privilege of men everywhere to choose their way of life and of obedience. The world must be made safe for democracy. Its peace must be planted upon the tested foundations of political liberty. We have no selfish ends to serve. We desire no conquest, no dominion. We seek no indemnities for ourselves, no material compensation for the sacrifices we shall freely make. We are but one of the champions of the rights of mankind. We shall be satisfied when those rights have been made as secure as the faith and the freedom of nations can make them.

Just because we fight without rancor and without selfish object, seeking nothing for ourselves but what we shall wish to share with all free peoples, we shall, I feel confident, conduct our operations as belligerents without passion and ourselves observe with proud punctilio the principles of right and of fair play we profess to be fighting for.

I have said nothing of the governments allied with the Imperial Government of Germany because they have not made war upon us or challenged us to defend our right and our honour. The Austro-Hungarian Government has, indeed, avowed its unqualified endorsement and acceptance of the reckless and lawless submarine warfare adopted now without disguise by the Imperial German Government, and it has therefore not been possible for this Government to receive Count Tarnowski, the Ambassador recently accredited to this Government by the Imperial and Royal Government of Austria-Hungary; but that Government has not actually engaged in warfare against citizens of the United States on the seas, and I take the liberty, for the present at least, of postponing a discussion of our relations with the authorities at Vienna. We enter this war only where we are clearly forced into it because there are no other means of defending our rights.

It will be all the easier for us to conduct ourselves as belligerents in a high spirit of right and fairness because we act without animus, not in enmity towards a people or with the desire to bring any injury or disadvantage upon them, but only in armed opposition to an irresponsible government which has thrown aside all considerations of humanity and of right and is running amuck. We are, let me say again, the sincere friends of the German people, and shall desire nothing so much as the early reestablishment of intimate relations of mutual advantage between us—however hard it may be for them, for the time being, to believe that this is spoken from our hearts. We have borne with their present Government through all these bitter months because of that friendship—exercising a patience and forbearance which would otherwise have been impossible. We shall, happily, still have an opportunity to prove that friendship in our daily attitude and actions towards the millions of men and women of German birth and native sympathy who live amongst us and share our life, and we shall be proud to prove it towards all who are in fact loyal to their neighbors and to the Government in the hour of test. They are, most of them, as true and loyal Americans as if they had never known any other fealty or allegiance. They will be prompt to stand with us in rebuking and restraining the few who may be of a different mind and purpose. If there should be disloyalty, it will be dealt with a firm hand of stern repression; but, if it lifts its head at all, it will lift it only here and there and without countenance except from a lawless and malignant few.

It is a distressing and oppressive duty, gentlemen of the Congress, which I have performed in thus addressing you. There are, it may be, many months of fiery trial and sacrifice ahead of us. It is a fearful thing to lead this great peaceful people into war, into the most terrible and disastrous of all wars, civilization itself seeming to be in the balance. But the right is more precious than peace, and we shall fight for the things which we have always carried nearest our hearts—for democracy, for the right of those who submit to authority to have a voice in their own governments, for the rights and liberties of small nations, for a universal dominion of right by such a concert of free peoples as shall bring peace and safety to all nations and make the world itself at last free. To such a task we can dedicate our lives and our fortunes, everything that we are and everything that we have, with the pride of those who know that the day has come when America is privileged to spend her blood and her might for the principles that gave her birth and happiness and the peace which she has treasured. God helping her, she can do no other.

# Georges Clemenceau

## DEFEND TO THE DEATH, JUNE 4, 1918

*I know of the deeds of a group of lost men,*
*Bretons, surrounded in a wood all night.*
*The next day, still resisting, they sent a carrier pigeon*
*to their corps to say "We are here. We have promised not to yield.*
*We shall fight to the end. If you can come to find us, come;*
*we can hold out half a day longer."*

Photograph by Gaspar-Félix Tournachon (1820–1910).

IN JUNE 1918, Germany was surging against French forces, hoping to cripple them before the United States had fully mobilized. Elements of the French army were retreating and public morale was sinking. The French premier, Georges Clemenceau, had the unenviable task of explaining setbacks and countering increased political opposition in Paris.

Here, Clemenceau delivers to the Chamber of Deputies a speech reminiscent of Pericles in 430 (see "Pericles: Lifting the Morale of Athens"). He refuses to be defensive, stating that the German offensive was predictable. Then Clemenceau issues a stirring reminder that triumph cannot be achieved without sacrifice: "We have an army made up of our children and our brothers—what can we say against it? Their leaders too have come from among us; they too are our brothers, they too are good soldiers. They come back covered with wounds when they are not left on the field of battle. What can you say against them?"

This appeal to patience—particularly by defending the valiant fortitude of men in combat—helped turn the tide of French morale at a critical moment. Within six months, the Allies were victorious.

---

WHEN I ACCEPTED THE PREMIERSHIP offered to me by the President of the Republic I could not ignore the fact that we were at the most critical period of the war. I remember that I told you we should pass together through difficult and exacting times; I remember I spoke of "cruel hours." No one protested when I announced that they would come. They are coming and the only question is whether we can stand them.

When Russia's desertion occurred, when men who believed that it was only necessary to will a democratic peace to obtain it from William II, had given up their country, unwittingly I prefer to think, to the army of the invader, what one of you here could believe that the million German soldiers who were thus liberated would not be turned against us? This and more is what happened. For four years our forces have been wearing themselves out. Our front was guarded by a line of soldiers which was becoming thinner and thinner, without allies who had themselves suffered enormous losses. And at that moment you saw arrive against you a fresh mass of German divisions in good condition when you were far from your best strength.

Is there any one of you who did not realize that under the shock of this enormous mass our lines had to give way at some points? Certainly not, for in all the conversations which I had with members of this assembly, the question asked me was, how much we had to give way.

The recoil was very serious for the English army, which had suffered formidable losses. It was grave and dangerous for the French army. I said dangerous, serious, but nothing more, and there is nothing in that to shake the confidence we should have in our soldiers.

Our men are engaged in the battle, a terrible one. They fought one against five without sleep for three and four days together. These soldiers, these great soldiers, have good and great leaders: worthy of them in every way. I have seen these leaders at work and some of them against whom I will not deny that I was prejudiced, struck me with admiration.

Is that saying that there are nowhere mistakes? I cannot maintain that. I know it too well; my duty is to discover these mistakes and correct them. In this I am supported by two great soldiers—General Foch and General Petain. General Foch enjoys the confidence of our allies to such a degree that yesterday at the conference of Versailles they wished to have their unanimous confidence in him expressed in the communiqué given to the press.

These men are at this moment fighting in the hardest battle of the war, fighting it with a heroism which I can find no phrase worthy to express. And it is we who for a mistake made in such and such a place, or which may not even have been made, demand explanations, on the field of battle of a man worn with fatigue. It is of this man that we demand to know whether on such and such a day he did such and such a thing! Drive me from this place if that is what you ask, for I will not do it.

I came here with the desire to find simple, brief and measured words to express the sentiment of the French people at the front and at the rear, to show the world a state of mind which cannot be analyzed, but which at this moment is the admiration of all civilized people.

I accuse no one. I am the leader of these men and it is my duty to punish them if I consider it of general benefit to do so; but it is also my greater duty to protect them if they have been unjustly attacked.

The army is better than we could ever have expected and when I say "the army" I mean men of all ranks who are under fire. That is one of the elements of our confidence, the main element. Although faith in a cause is an admirable thing, it will not bring victory; men must die for their faith to assure victory and our men are dying. We have an army made up of our children and our brothers—what can we say against it? Their leaders too have come from among us; they too are our brothers, they too are good soldiers. They come back covered with wounds when they are not left on the field of battle. What can you say against them?

We have yielded ground, much more ground than either you or I should have wished. There are men without number who have paid for this with their blood, without reproach. I know of the deeds of a group of lost men, Bretons, surrounded in a wood all night. The next day, still resisting, they sent a carrier pigeon to their corps to say "We are here. We have promised not to yield. We shall fight to the end. If you can come to find us, come; we can hold out half a day longer." These men make and safeguard the country of which you are so proud. They die for the greatest and most noble ideal—to continue a history which shall be the foremost among all the histories of civilized peoples.

Our own duty is very simple, very tame. We run no danger. We are at our posts, you here, I with my cabinet—posts which are not dangerous as are those of the soldiers, but which are nevertheless where the capital interests of the country are decided.

As long as you remain calm, confident in yourself, determined to hold out to the end of this hard struggle, victory is yours. It is yours because our enemies, who are not as intelligent as they are said to be, have only one method—to throw their whole force into the venture and risk everything. They tried it at Verdun and on the Yser, at Dunkirk and at Calais. They were checked—by whom? First by the English and then by the French. After that they appeared in Champagne; they advanced. Do you think it possible to make a war in which you never have to retreat? Our men can only give their lives; but you through patience, firmness and determination can give them what they deserve—victory.

You have before you a government, which, as it told you at the very beginning, never conceived of the possibility of negotiating without victory. You know what you are doing. You can keep us in power or send us away; but as long as you keep us, whatever may happen, you can be sure that the country will be defended to the death and that no force will be spared to obtain success. We will never consent to anything but peace with victory. That is the watchword of our government.

The Germans are once more staking all. The "coup" which they are attempting is to terrorize you, to frighten you so that you will abandon the struggle. One must be ignorant of German tactics to doubt this. Why did they suddenly throw all their forces on the Yser? It was to gain Calais, to separate us from England and force us to surrender. For what was the dreadful march on Paris? To take Paris and through terror force us to surrender. Why are they beginning again to-day? To secure this effect of terror which they have never yet achieved.

The decision is in your hands for the simple reason that it is not a matter of mere reasoning but a question of action. The Americans are coming. The forces of the English and the French, as well as of our enemies, are worn out; but we have allies who are coming as a decisive factor. I have said from the beginning that American cooperation would decide the issue of the war. The point is this: events in Russia have allowed a million of the enemy's men to appear on the Franco-British front. We have allies, whom we did not have in 1870, when we yielded because we were alone. We have allies, who represent the foremost nations of the world, who have pledged themselves to continue the war to the end, to the success which we hold in our grasp, which we are on the point of achieving if we have the necessary tenacity.

I declare, and it must be my last word, that victory depends upon us. The civil forces must rise to the height of their duty; it is not necessary to make this demand of the soldiers. Send me away if I have been an unworthy servant; drive me out, condemn me, but at least take the trouble to formulate criticisms. As for me, I assert that the French people have in all ways done their full duty. Those who have fallen have not fallen in vain, for they have made French history great. It remains for the living to complete the magnificent work of the dead.

# Marshal Ferdinand Foch

## Tribute to Napoléon,
## May 5, 1921

*If our legions have returned victorious through the triumphal arch
which you built, it is because the sword of Austerlitz marked out their direction,
showing how to unite and lead the army that won the victory.*

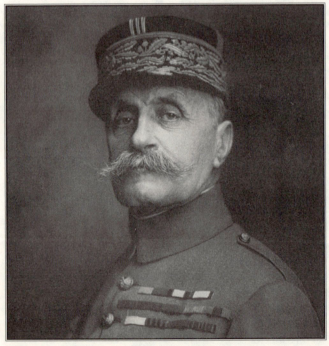

Photograph ca. 1918–20, by Emilie Cambier.

THREE YEARS AFTER WORLD WAR I ENDED, French military leader Ferdinand Foch spoke at the centennial of Napoléon's death in Paris. In this closing portion of Marshal Foch's address, he glorifies Napoléon's military genius and inspires future troops by reminding them of their ultimate obligation: "Decidedly, duty is common to all. Higher than commanding armies victoriously, there is our country to be served for her good as she understands it; there is justice to be respected everywhere. Above war there is peace."

———◆———

IF ONE CONSIDERS THAT Napoléon revealed his powers in 1796 at the age of twenty-seven, it is plain that nature endowed him extraordinarily. These talents he applied unceasingly through the whole length of his prodigious career.

Through them he marks out his way along a resplendent path in the military annals of humanity. He carries his victorious eagles from the Alps to the Pyramids, and from the banks of the Tagus to those of the Moskova, surpassing in their flight the conquests of Alexander, of Hannibal and of Cæsar. Thus he remains the great leader, superior to all others in his prodigious genius, his need of activity, his nature, ardent to excess, which is always favorable to the profits of war but dangerous to the equilibrium of peace.

Thus he lifts the art of war far above all known heights, but this carries him to regions of dizziness. Identifying the greatness of the country with his own, he would rule the destinies of nations with arms, as if one could bring about the prosperity of the people from a succession of victories at grievous sacrifices. As if this people could live by glory instead of by labor. As if the conquered nations, deprived of their independence, would not rise some day to reconquer it, putting an end to a regime of force and presenting armies strong in numbers and invincible in the ardor of outraged justice. As if in a civilized world, moral right should not be greater than a power created entirely by force, however talented that force might be. In attempting this Napoléon himself goes down, not for lack of genius, but because he attempted the impossible, because he undertook with a France exhausted in every way, to bend to his laws a Europe already instructed by its misfortunes, and soon entirely in arms.

Decidedly, duty is common to all. Higher than commanding armies victoriously, there is our country to be served for her good as she understands it; there is justice to be respected everywhere. Above war there is peace.

Assuredly, the most gifted man errs who, in dealing with humanity, depends upon his own insight and intelligence and discards the moral law of society, created by respect for the individual, and those principles of liberty, equality and fraternity, the basis of our civilization, and the essence of Christianity.

Sire, sleep in peace; from the tomb itself you labor continually for France. At every danger to the country, our flags quiver at the passage of the Eagle. If our legions have returned victorious through the triumphal arch which you built, it is because the sword of Austerlitz marked out their direction, showing how to unite and lead the army that won the victory. Your masterly lessons, your determined labors, remain indefeasible examples. In studying them and meditating on them the art of war grows daily greater. It is only in the reverently and thoughtfully gathered rays of your immortal glory that generations of the distant future shall succeed in grasping the science of combat and the management of armies for the sacred cause of the defense of the country.

# Winston Churchill

## VICTORY AT ALL COSTS,
## MAY 13, 1940

*You ask, what is our aim?*
*I can answer in one word: victory,*
*victory at all costs, victory in spite of all terror,*
*victory, however long and hard the road may be;*
*for without victory, there is no survival.*

Photograph taken 1941.

O
N MAY 13, 1940, the new prime minister of Great Britain entered the House of Commons, confronted with political chaos at home and grave threat abroad. The government of Prime Minister Neville Chamberlain had fallen only days before and Holland was about to fall to Hitler's blitzkrieg. The French military was in retreat and officials in Paris were actively considering surrender. Winston Churchill's task that day was to deliver a message that would unite an unstable government and assure a restive nation. After announcing the organization of his government, Churchill describes its mission. In a speech made powerful by its elegant simplicity, Churchill gained the confidence of the House and an entire nation.

———————•◦•———————

ON FRIDAY EVENING last I received His Majesty's Commission to form a new Administration. It was the evident wish and will of Parliament and the nation that this should be conceived on the broadest possible basis and that it should include all parties, both those who supported the late Government and also the parties of the Opposition. I have completed the most important part of this task. A War Cabinet has been formed of five Members, representing, with the Opposition Liberals, the unity of the nation. The three party Leaders have agreed to serve, either in the War Cabinet or in high executive office. The three Fighting Services have been filled. It was necessary that this should be done in one single day, on account of the extreme urgency and rigour of events. A number of other positions, key positions, were filled yesterday, and I am submitting a further list to His Majesty tonight. I hope to complete the appointment of the principal Ministers tomorrow. The appointment of the other Ministers usually takes a little longer, but I trust that, when Parliament meets again, this part of my task will be completed and that the administration will be complete in all respects.

I considered it in the public interest to suggest that the House should be summoned to meet today. Mr. Speaker agreed, and took the necessary steps, in accordance with the powers conferred him by the Resolution of the House. At the end of the proceedings today, the Adjournment of the House will be proposed until Tuesday, 21st May, with, of course, provision for earlier meeting, if need be. The business to be considered during that week will be notified to Members at the earliest opportunity. I now invite the House, by the Motion which stands in my name, to record its approval of the steps taken and to declare its confidence in the new Government.

To form an Administration of this scale and complexity is a serious undertaking in itself, but it must be remembered that we are in the preliminary stage of one of the greatest battles in history, that we are in action at many other points in Norway and in Holland, that we have to be prepared in the Mediterranean, that the air battle is continuous and that many preparations, such as have been indicated by my hon. Friend below the Gangway, have to be made here at home. In this crisis I hope I may be pardoned if I do not address the House at any length today. I hope that any of my friends and colleagues, or former colleagues, who are affected by the political reconstruction, will make allowance, all allowance, for any lack of ceremony with which it has been necessary to act. I would say to the House, as I said to those who have joined this Government: "I have nothing to offer but blood, toil, tears and sweat."

We have before us an ordeal of the most grievous kind. We have before us many, many long months of struggle and of suffering. You ask, what is our policy? I can say: It is to wage war, by sea, land and air, with all our might and with all the strength that God can give us; to wage war against a monstrous tyranny, never surpassed in the dark, lamentable catalogue of human crime. That is our policy. You ask, what is our aim? I can answer in one word: It is victory, victory at all costs, victory in spite of all terror, victory, however long and hard the road may be; for without victory, there is no survival. Let that be realized; no survival for the British Empire, no survival for all that the British Empire has stood for, no survival for the urge and impulse of the ages, that mankind will move forward towards its goal. But I take up my task with buoyancy and hope. I feel sure that our cause will not be suffered to fail among men. At this time I feel entitled to claim the aid of all, and I say, "Come then, let us go forward together with our united strength."

# Winston Churchill

## WE SHALL NEVER SURRENDER,
## JUNE 4, 1940

*We shall go on to the end, we shall fight in France,*
*we shall fight on the seas and oceans,*
*we shall fight with growing confidence and growing strength in the air,*
*we shall defend our Island, whatever the cost may be, we shall fight on the beaches,*
*we shall fight on the landing grounds, we shall fight in the fields*
*and in the streets, we shall fight in the hills; we shall never surrender.*

Photograph taken ca. 1942.

I N THE SOUND-BITE CULTURE in which we live, the inevitable setbacks of war are too often sanitized and simplified—as if our resolve will melt at the slightest exposure to bad news, or our brains will numb with too much detail. This speech by Winston Churchill effectively uses unvarnished facts and a stunning military retreat to demand that the people of Britain stand their ground.

The spring of 1940 was foreboding. In May German forces landed inside Belgium and Holland. By the end of the month Allies had been trapped on a narrow beachhead along the North Sea at Dunkirk, France. "Operation Dynamo" became one of the most audacious evacuations in military history—the sealift to safety of 338,226, between May 26 and June 4.

In this report to Parliament, Churchill provides a detailed recitation of the circumstances that led to the withdrawal; then stirringly describes the heroic efforts to free Allied Forces from probable defeat. But he is clear that this is not to be interpreted as a victory, proclaiming that "wars are not won by evacuations." Then, the prime minister stirs a nation stunned by withdrawal and confronted with threat to stand their ground, concluding "we shall never surrender, and even if, which I do not for a moment believe, this Island or a large part of it were subjugated and starving, then our Empire beyond the seas, armed and guarded by the British Fleet, would carry on the struggle, until, in God's good time, the New World, with all its power and might, steps forth to the rescue and the liberation of the old."

Here are excerpts from Churchill's report to the House of Commons.

———◆———

WHEN, A WEEK AGO TODAY, I asked the House to fix this afternoon as the occasion for a statement, I feared it would be my hard lot to announce the greatest military disaster in our long history. I thought—and some good judges agreed with me—that perhaps twenty thousand or thirty thousand men might be re-embarked. But it certainly seemed that the whole of the French First Army and the whole of the British Expeditionary Force north of the Amiens-Abbeville gap would be broken up in the open field or else would have to capitulate for lack of food and ammunition. These were the hard and heavy tidings for which I called upon the House and the nation to prepare themselves a week ago. The whole root and core and brain of the British Army, on which and around which we were to build, and are to build, the great British Armies in the later years of the war, seemed about to perish upon the field or to be led into an ignominious and starving captivity.

That was the prospect a week ago. But another blow which might well have proved final was yet to fall upon us. The King of the Belgians had called upon us to come to his aid. Had not this Ruler and his Government severed themselves from the Allies, who rescued their country from extinction in the late war, and had they not sought refuge in what was proved to be a fatal neutrality, the French and British Armies might well at the outset have saved not only Belgium but perhaps even Poland. Yet at the last moment, when Belgium was already invaded, King Leopold called upon us to come to his aid, and even at the last moment we came. He and his brave, efficient Army, nearly half a million strong, guarded our left flank and thus kept open our only line of retreat to the sea. Suddenly, without prior consultation, with the least possible notice, without the advice of his Ministers and upon his own personal act, he sent a plenipotentiary to the German Command, surrendered his Army, and exposed our whole flank and means of retreat.

I asked the House a week ago to suspend its judgment because the facts were not clear, but I do not feel that any reason now exists why we should not form our own opinions upon this pitiful episode. The surrender of the Belgian Army compelled the British at the shortest notice to cover a flank to the sea more than thirty miles in length. Otherwise all would have been cut off, and all would have shared the fate to which King Leopold had condemned the finest Army his country had ever formed. So in doing this and in exposing this flank, as anyone who followed the operations on the map will see, contact was lost between the British and two out of the three corps forming the First French Army, who were still farther from the coast than we were, and it seemed impossible that any large number of Allied troops could reach the coast.

The enemy attacked on all sides with great strength and fierceness, and their main power, the power of their far more numerous Air Force, was thrown into the battle or else concentrated upon Dunkirk and the beaches. Pressing in upon the narrow exit, both from the east and from the west, the enemy began to fire with cannon upon the beaches by which alone the shipping could approach or depart. They sowed magnetic mines in the channels and seas; they sent repeated waves of hostile aircraft, sometimes more than a hundred strong in one formation, to cast their bombs upon the single pier that remained, and upon the sand dunes upon which the troops had their eyes for shelter. Their U-boats, one of which was sunk, and their motor launches took their toll of the vast traffic which now began. For four or five days an intense struggle reigned. All their armored divisions—or what was left of them— together with great masses of infantry and artillery, hurled themselves in vain upon the ever-narrowing, ever-contracting appendix within which the British and French Armies fought.

Meanwhile, the Royal Navy, with the willing help of countless merchant seamen, strained every nerve to embark the British and Allied troops; two hundred and twenty light warships and six hundred and fifty other vessels were engaged. They had to operate upon the difficult coast, often in adverse weather, under an almost ceaseless hail of bombs and an increasing concentration of artillery fire. Nor were the seas, as I have said, themselves free from mines and torpedoes. It was in conditions such as these that our men carried on, with little or no rest, for days and nights on end, making trip after trip across the dangerous waters, bringing with them always men whom they had rescued. The numbers they have brought back are the measure of their devotion and their courage. The hospital ships, which brought off many thousands of British and French wounded, being so plainly marked were a special target for Nazi bombs; but the men and women on board them never faltered in their duty.

Meanwhile, the Royal Air Force, which had already been intervening in the battle, so far as its range would allow, from home bases, now used part of its main metropolitan fighter strength, and struck at the German bombers and at the fighters which in large numbers protected them. This struggle was protracted and fierce. Suddenly the scene has cleared, the crash and thunder has for the moment—but only for the moment—died away. A miracle of deliverance, achieved by valor, by perseverance, by perfect discipline, by faultless service, by resource, by skill, by unconquerable fidelity, is manifest to us all. The enemy was hurled back by the retreating British and French troops. He was so roughly handled that he did not hurry their departure seriously. The Royal Air Force engaged the main strength of the German Air Force, and inflicted upon them losses of at least four to one; and the Navy, using nearly one thousand ships of all kinds, carried over three hundred and thirty five thousand men, French and British, out of the jaws of death and shame, to their native land and to the tasks which lie immediately ahead. We must be very careful not to assign to this deliverance the attributes of a victory. Wars are not won by evacuations. But there was a victory inside this deliverance, which should be noted. It was gained by the Air Force. Many of our soldiers coming back have not seen the Air Force at work; they saw only the bombers which escaped its protective attack. They underrate its achievements. I have heard much talk of this; that is why I go out of my way to say this. I will tell you about it.

This was a great trial of strength between the British and German Air Forces. Can you conceive a greater objective for the Germans in the air than to make evacuation from these beaches impossible, and to sink all these ships which were displayed, almost to the extent of thousands? Could there have been an objective of greater military importance and significance for the whole purpose of the war than this? They tried hard, and they were beaten back; they were frustrated in their task. We got the Army away; and they have paid fourfold for any losses which they have inflicted. Very large formations of German aeroplanes—and we know that they are a very brave race—have turned on several occasions from the attack of one-quarter of their number of the Royal Air Force, and have dispersed in different directions. Twelve airplanes have been hunted by two. One aeroplane was driven into the water and cast away by the mere charge of a British aeroplane, which had no more ammunition. All of our types—the Hurricane, the Spitfire and the new Defiant—and all our pilots have been vindicated as superior to what they have at present to face.

When we consider how much greater would be our advantage in defending the air above this Island against an overseas attack, I must say that I find in these facts a sure basis upon which practical and reassuring thoughts may rest. I will pay my tribute to these young airmen. The great French Army was very largely, for the time being, cast back and disturbed by the onrush of a few thousands of armored vehicles. May it not also be that the cause of civilization itself will be defended by the skill and devotion of a few thousand airmen? There never has been, I suppose, in all the world, in all the history of war, such an opportunity for youth. The Knights of the Round Table, the Crusaders, all fall back into the past—not only distant but prosaic; these young men, going forth every morn to guard their native land and all that we stand for, holding in their hands these instruments of colossal and shattering power, of whom it may be said that

> *Every morn brought forth a noble chance*
> *And every chance brought forth a noble knight*

deserve our gratitude, as do all the brave men who, in so many ways and on so many occasions, are ready, and continue ready to give life and all for their native land.

I return to the Army. In the long series of very fierce battles, now on this front, now on that, fighting on three fronts at once, battles fought by two or three divisions against an equal or somewhat larger number of the enemy, and fought fiercely on some of the old grounds that so many of us knew so well—in these battles our losses in men have exceeded thirty thousand killed, wounded and missing. I take occasion to express the sympathy of the House to all who have suffered bereavement or who are still anxious. The President of the Board of Trade is not here today. His son has been killed, and many in the House have felt the pangs of affliction in the sharpest form. But I will say this about the missing: We have had a large number of wounded come home safely to this country, but I would say about the missing that there may be very many reported missing who will come back home, some day, in one way or another. In the confusion of this fight it is inevitable that many have been left in positions where honor required no further resistance from them.

Against this loss of over thirty thousand men, we can set a far heavier loss certainly inflicted upon the enemy. But our losses in material are enormous. We have perhaps lost one-third of the men we lost in the opening days of the battle of 21st March, 1918, but we have lost nearly as many guns—nearly one thousand—and all our transport, all the armored vehicles that were with the Army in the north. This loss will impose a further delay on the expansion of our military strength. That expansion had not been proceeding as far as we had hoped. The best of all we had to give had gone to the British Expeditionary Force, and although they had not the numbers of tanks and some articles of equipment which were desirable, they were a very well and finely equipped Army. They had the first fruits of all that our industry had to give, and that is gone. And now here is this further delay. How long it will be, how long it will last, depends upon the exertions which we make in this Island. An effort the like of which has never been seen in our records is now being made. Work is proceeding everywhere, night and day, Sundays and weekdays. Capital and Labor have cast aside their interests, rights, and customs and put them into the common stock. Already the flow of munitions has leaped forward. There is no reason why we should not in a few months overtake the sudden and serious loss that has come upon us, without retarding the development of our general program.

Nevertheless, our thankfulness at the escape of our Army and so many men, whose loved ones have passed through an agonizing week, must not blind us to the fact that what has happened in France and Belgium is a colossal military disaster. The French Army has been weakened, the Belgian Army has been lost, a large part of those fortified lines upon which so much faith had been reposed is gone, many valuable mining districts and factories have passed into the enemy's possession, the whole of the Channel ports are in his hands, with all the tragic consequences that follow from that, and we must expect another blow to be struck almost immediately at us or at France. We are told that Herr Hitler has a plan for invading the British Isles. This has often been thought of before. When Napoléon lay at Boulogne for a year with his flat-bottomed boats and his Grand Army, he was told by someone. "There are bitter weeds in England." There are certainly a great many more of them since the British Expeditionary Force returned.

The whole question of home defense against invasion is, of course, powerfully affected by the fact that we have for the time being in this Island incomparably more powerful military forces than we have ever had at any moment in this war or the last. But this will not continue. We shall not be content with a defensive war. We have our duty to our Ally. We have to reconstitute and build up the British Expeditionary Force once again, under its gallant Commander-in-Chief, Lord Gort. All this is in train; but in the interval we must put our defenses in this Island into such a high state of organization that the fewest possible numbers will be required to give effective security and that the largest possible potential of offensive effort may be realized. On this we are now engaged. It will be very convenient, if it be the desire of the House, to enter upon this subject in a secret Session. Not that the government would necessarily be able to reveal in very great detail military secrets, but we like to have our discussions free, without the restraint imposed by the fact that they will be read the next day by the enemy; and the Government would benefit by views freely expressed in all parts of the House by Members with their knowledge of so many different parts of the country. I understand that some request is to be made upon this subject, which will be readily acceded to by His Majesty's Government.

We have found it necessary to take measures of increasing stringency, not only against enemy aliens and suspicious characters of other nationalities, but also against British subjects who may become a danger or a nuisance should the war be transported to the United Kingdom. I know there are a great many people affected by the orders which we have made who are the passionate enemies of Nazi Germany. I am very sorry for them, but we cannot, at the present time and under the present stress, draw all the distinctions which we should like to do. If parachute landings were attempted and fierce fighting attendant upon them followed, these unfortunate people would be far better out of the way, for their own sakes as well as for ours. There is, however, another class, for which I feel not the slightest sympathy. Parliament has given us the powers to put down Fifth Column activities with a strong hand, and we shall use those powers subject to the supervision and correction of the House, without the slightest hesitation until we are satisfied, and more than satisfied, that this malignancy in our midst has been effectively stamped out.

Turning once again, and this time more generally, to the question of invasion, I would observe that there has never been a period in all these long centuries of which we boast when an absolute guarantee against invasion, still less against serious raids, could have been given to our people. In the days of Napoléon the same wind which would have carried his transports across the Channel might have driven away the blockading fleet. There was always the chance, and it is that chance which has excited and befooled the imaginations of many Continental tyrants. Many are the tales that are told. We are assured that novel methods will be adopted, and when we see the originality of malice, the ingenuity of aggression, which our enemy displays, we may certainly prepare ourselves for every kind of novel stratagem and every kind of brutal and treacherous maneuver. I think that no idea is so outlandish that it should not be considered and viewed with a searching, but at the same time, I hope, with a steady eye. We must never forget the solid assurances of sea power and those which belong to air power if it can be locally exercised.

I have, myself, full confidence that if all do their duty, if nothing is neglected, and if the best arrangements are made, as they are being made, we shall prove ourselves once again able to defend our Island home, to ride out the storm of war, and to outlive the menace of tyranny, if necessary for years, if necessary alone. At any rate, that is what we are going to try to do. That is the resolve of His Majesty's Government—every man of them. That is the will of Parliament and the nation. The British Empire and the French Republic, linked together in their cause and in their need, will defend to the death their native soil, aiding each other like good comrades to the utmost of their strength. Even though large tracts of Europe and many old and famous States have fallen or may fall into the grip of the Gestapo and all the odious apparatus of Nazi rule, we shall not flag or fail. We shall go on to the end, we shall fight in France, we shall fight on the seas and oceans, we shall fight with growing confidence and growing strength in the air, we shall defend our Island, whatever the cost may be, we shall fight on the beaches, we shall fight on the landing grounds, we shall fight in the fields and in the streets, we shall fight in the hills; we shall never surrender, and even if, which I do not for a moment believe, this Island or a large part of it were subjugated and starving, then our Empire beyond the seas, armed and guarded by the British Fleet, would carry on the struggle, until, in God's good time, the New World, with all its power and might, steps forth to the rescue and the liberation of the old.

# Henry Stimson

## ASKING FOR SACRIFICE,
## MAY 6, 1941

*Unless we on our side are ready to sacrifice and, if need be,
die for the conviction that the freedom of America must be saved,
it will not be saved.*

Photograph taken August 8, 1929.

SEVEN MONTHS BEFORE the Japanese attack on Pearl Harbor and the U.S. entry into World War II, Secretary of War Henry Stimson sought to rouse the American people from a comfortable slumber. In this radio address, Stimson warned that America's confidence in natural ocean borders should not lull it into complacency and challenged the nation to sacrifice for the principle of freedom: "Today a small group of evil leaders have taught the young men of Germany that the freedom of other men and nations must be destroyed. Today these young men are ready to die for that perverted conviction. Unless we on our side are ready to sacrifice and, if need be, die for the conviction that the freedom of America must be saved, it will not be saved. Only by a readiness for the same sacrifice can that freedom be preserved."

---

THE PEOPLE OF THE UNITED STATES have been greatly blessed by the geographical conditions of their homeland. Two broad oceans lie to the east and west of us, while north and south of us are only friendly nations of whose intentions and power we have no fear. Thus the instinct of our people in regard to their ocean defense is a sound instinct. There is great possibility of protection in the fact that we have the Atlantic Ocean between us and Europe, and the Pacific Ocean between us and Asia. So long as those oceans are under our own or of friendly control, their broad waters constitute an insuperable barrier to any armies which may be built up by would-be aggressor governments. But that condition of friendly control is imperative. If it should be lost, the oceans over night would become easy channels for the path of attack against us.

The development of modern air power greatly intensifies this necessity of friendly control of the oceans. It now makes it necessary for us to command not only the reaches of ocean adjacent to our own shores but the entire reach of the oceans surrounding the western continent; for, if hostile nations possessing powerful armies and air power can once make a landing on the shores of our weaker neighbor nations either north or south of us, our immunity is gone. It would then become a comparatively simple matter for them to establish air bases within striking distance of the great industrial cities which now fill our country. And the only way in which we could prevent this would be the intolerable method of ourselves maintaining armies large enough to command the areas of our continent for thousands of miles beyond our own borders. Such a condition would transform the good neighbor relations which now prevail throughout the American republics, into the same abhorrent system of forceful domination which we are seeking to keep out of the hemisphere.

In short, to the nations of America, friendly control of the surrounding oceans is a condition of the reign of freedom and mutual independence which now prevails in that continent.

For over one hundred years the control of the Atlantic Ocean has been exercised by the British fleet. By the Washington Treaty of 1922 Great Britain voluntarily consented to parity between her fleet and ours and thus admitted us to an equal share in that control. The significant feature to us of this century-old condition has been that a country speaking our language, possessing our traditions of individual and legal freedom, and inhabited by a population from which considerably more than 50 percent of our own population is descended, has been accepted by us as a dominant factor in the ocean defense upon which our safety and mode of life depend. During that century we have accommodated our whole method of life to that situation. We have maintained no large standing armies. We have built populous cities upon our seacoast which are easily vulnerable to attack from the Atlantic Ocean. We have in short adopted a mode of national life which is dependent upon the continuance of a sea power of which we ourselves feel in no apprehension.

Today that situation is gravely threatened. The British Isles, which have been a fortress against any despotic approach to our shores through the northern reaches of the Atlantic, are threatened both by attacks from the air and blockade from the sea. If their government should fall either from starvation or from attack, the British fleet, if it survived at all, would have no adequate base for its continued operations. If the British Isles should fall, all of the great shipyards of Britain would pass into the hands of the aggressor nations and their maritime shipbuilding capacity, thus augmented, would become six or seven times as large as our own. Under such conditions our own fleet would be quite unable to protect the western hemisphere from the overwhelming sea power which would then confront it. Even today its tonnage is exceeded by the combined tonnage of the Axis powers and, with the enormous preponderance in building capacity which they would then have, command of the entire seas surrounding us would in time inevitably pass into their hands.

The unrestricted submarine warfare which Germany is carrying on in the North Atlantic, sinking ships without warning and without the possibility of saving the lives of their crews, is not a legal blockade under the rules of marine warfare. It has never been recognized as lawful by the United States. America's spokesmen at international conferences have again and again condemned it as a form of piracy. It was expressly the violation of law and humanity involved in unrestricted submarine warfare which in 1917 caused the President and Congress to take up arms in defense of the freedom of the seas. Today Germany by these same illegal means is not only seeking to frighten our commerce and our vessels from the Atlantic; she has extended even into the western hemisphere a zone into which she has forbidden us to enter. Hitler has not only torn up all the rules of international law but he is expanding his lawless activities into our hemisphere.

Our government is acting with care and prudence. But our own self-defense requires that limits should be put to lawless aggression on the ocean.

I am not one of those who think that the priceless freedom of our country can be saved without sacrifice. It can not. That has not been the way by which during millions of years humanity has slowly and painfully toiled upwards towards a better and more humane civilization. The men who suffered at Valley Forge and won at Yorktown gave more than money to the cause of freedom.

Today a small group of evil leaders have taught the young men of Germany that the freedom of other men and nations must be destroyed. Today these young men are ready to die for that perverted conviction. Unless we on our side are ready to sacrifice and, if need be, die for the conviction that the freedom of America must be saved, it will not be saved. Only by a readiness for the same sacrifice can that freedom be preserved.

# Harold Ickes

## IMPLORING AMERICANS TO FIGHT, MAY 18, 1941

*Here in America we have something so worth living for that it is worth dying for!*

Harold Ickes as he leaves the White House, 1938.

**D**ESPITE THE GRAVE THREATS presented by Adolf Hitler, many Americans were skeptical of direct U.S. involvement in the war in Europe. During an "I Am an American" Day meeting in New York City, Secretary of the Interior Harold Ickes attempted to inspire Americans to march forward and assist Great Britain.

Ickes begins by decrying the doubts that have crept into the American discourse. He paints a bleak but vivid picture of the consequences of a British defeat: "If Britain should be defeated, then the totalitarian undertaker will prepare to hang crepe on the door of our own independence." He argues that the United States would then become an "armed camp" surrounded by permanent threat.

Finally, Ickes exhorts America to prepare for battle: "We Americans must gird spiritually for the battle. We must dispel the fog of uncertainty and vacillation. We must greet with raucous laughter the corroding arguments of our appeasers and fascists. They doubt democracy. We affirm it triumphantly so that all the world may hear."

---

**I** WANT TO ASK A FEW SIMPLE QUESTIONS. And then I shall answer them.

What has happened to our vaunted idealism? Why have some of us been behaving like scared chickens? Where is the million-throated, democratic voice of America?

For years it has been dinned into us that we are a weak nation; that we are an inefficient people; that we are simple-minded. For years we have been told that we are beaten, decayed, and that no part of the world belongs to us any longer.

Some amongst us have fallen for this carefully pickled tripe. Some amongst us have fallen for this calculated poison. Some amongst us have begun to preach that the "wave of the future" has passed over us and left us a wet, dead fish.

They shout—from public platforms in printed pages, through the microphones—that it is futile to oppose the "wave of the future." They cry that we Americans, we free Americans nourished on Magna Carta and the Declaration of Independence, hold moth-eaten ideas. They exclaim that there is no room for free men in the world anymore and that only the slaves will inherit the earth. America—the America of Washington and Jefferson and Lincoln and Walt Whitman—they say, is waiting for the undertaker and all the hopes and aspirations that have gone into the making of America are dead too.

However, my fellow citizens, this is not the real point of the story. The real point—the shameful point—is that many of us are listening to them and some of us almost believe them.

I say that it is time for the great American people to raise its voice and cry out in mighty triumph what it is to be an American. And why it is that only Americans, with the aid of our brave allies—yes, let's call them "allies"—the British, can and will build the only future worth having. I mean a future, not of concentration camps, not of physical torture and mental straitjackets, not of sawdust bread or of sawdust Caesars—I mean a future when free men will live free lives in dignity and in security.

This tide of the future, the democratic future, is ours. It is ours if we show ourselves worthy of our culture and of our heritage.

But make no mistake about it; the tide of the democratic future is not like the ocean tide—regular, relentless, and inevitable. Nothing in human affairs is mechanical or inevitable. Nor are Americans mechanical. They are very human indeed.

What constitutes an American? Not color nor race nor religion. Not the pedigree of his family nor the place of his birth. Not the coincidence of his citizenship. Not his social status nor his bank account. Not his trade nor his profession. An American is one who loves justice and believes in the dignity of man. An American is one who will fight for his freedom and that of his neighbor. An American is one who will sacrifice property, ease and security in order that he and his children may retain the rights of free men. An American is one in whose heart is engraved the immortal second sentence of the Declaration of Independence.

Americans have always known how to fight for their rights and their way of life. Americans are not afraid to fight. They fight joyously in a just cause.

We Americans know that freedom, like peace, is indivisible. We cannot retain our liberty if three-fourths of the world is enslaved. Brutality, injustice and slavery, if practiced as dictators would have them, universally and systematically, in the long run would destroy us as surely as a fire raging in our nearby neighbor's house would burn ours if we didn't help to put out his.

If we are to retain our own freedom, we must do everything within our power to aid Britain. We must also do everything to restore to the conquered peoples their freedom. This means the Germans too.

Such a program, if you stop to think, is selfishness on our part. It is the sort of enlightened selfishness that makes the wheels of history go around. It is the sort of enlightened selfishness that wins victories.

Do you know why? Because we cannot live in the world alone, without friends and without allies. If Britain should be defeated, then the totalitarian undertaker will prepare to hang crepe on the door of our own independence.

Perhaps you wonder how this could come about? Perhaps you have heard "them"—the wavers of the future—cry, with calculated malice, that even if Britain were defeated we could live alone and defend ourselves single-handed, even against the whole world.

I tell you that this is a cold-blooded lie.

We would be alone in the world, facing an unscrupulous military-economic bloc that would dominate all of Europe, all of Africa, most of Asia, and perhaps even Russia and South America. Even to do that, we would have to spend most of our national income on tanks and guns and planes and ships. Nor would this be all. We would have to live perpetually as an armed camp, maintaining a huge standing army, a gigantic air force, two vast navies. And we could not do this without endangering our freedom, our democracy, our way of life.

Perhaps such is the America "they"—the wavers of the future—foresee. Perhaps such is the America that a certain aviator, with his contempt for democracy, would prefer. Perhaps such is the America that a certain Senator desires. Perhaps such is the America that a certain mail order executive longs for.

But a perpetually militarized, isolated and impoverished America is not the America that our fathers came here to build.

It is not the America that has been the dream and the hope of countless generations in all parts of the world.

It is not the America that one hundred and thirty million of us would care to live in.

The continued security of our country demands that we aid the enslaved millions of Europe—yes, even of Germany—to win back their liberty and independence. I am convinced that if we do not embark upon such a program we will lose our own freedom.

We should be clear on this point. What is convulsing the world today is not merely another old-fashioned war. It is a counterrevolution against our ideas and ideals, against our sense of justice and our human values.

Three systems today compete for world domination. Communism, fascism, and democracy are struggling for social-economic-political world control. As the conflict sharpens, it becomes clear that the other two, fascism and communism, are merging into one. They have one common enemy, democracy. They have one common goal, the destruction of democracy.

This is why this war is not an ordinary war. It is not a conflict for markets or territories. It is a desperate struggle for the possession of the souls of men.

This is why the British are not fighting for themselves alone. They are fighting to preserve freedom for mankind. For the moment, the battleground is the British Isles. But they are fighting our war; they are the first soldiers in trenches that are also our front-line trenches.

In this world war of ideas and of loyalties we believers in democracy must do two things. We must unite our forces to form one great democratic international. We must offer a clear program to freedom-loving peoples throughout the world.

Freedom-loving men and women in every land must organize and tighten their ranks. The masses everywhere must be helped to fight their oppressors and conquerors.

We, free, democratic Americans are in a position to help. We know that the spirit of freedom never dies. We know that men have fought and bled for freedom since time immemorial. We realize that the liberty-loving German people are only temporarily enslaved. We do not doubt that the Italian people are looking forward to the appearance of another Garibaldi. We know how the Poles have for centuries maintained a heroic resistance against tyranny. We remember the brave struggle of the Hungarians under Kossuth and other leaders. We recall the heroic figure of Masaryk and the gallant fight for freedom of the Czech people. The story of the Yugoslavs', especially the Serbs' blows for liberty and independence is a saga of extraordinary heroism. The Greeks will stand again at Thermopylae, as they have in the past. The annals of our American sister-republics, too, are glorious with freedom-inspiring exploits. The noble figure of Simon Bolivar, the great South American liberator, has naturally been compared with that of George Washington.

No, liberty never dies. The Genghis Khans come and go. The Attilas come and go. The Hitlers flash and sputter out. But freedom endures.

Destroy a whole generation of those who have known how to walk with heads erect in God's free air, and the next generation will rise against the oppressors and restore freedom. Today in Europe, the Nazi Attila may gloat that he has destroyed democracy. He is wrong. In small farmhouses all over Central Europe, in the shops of Germany and Italy, on the docks of Holland and Belgium, freedom still lives in the hearts of men. It will endure like a hardy tree gone into the wintertime, awaiting the spring.

And, like spring, spreading from the South into Scandinavia, the democratic revolution will come. And men with democratic hearts will experience comradeship across artificial boundaries.

These men and women, hundreds of millions of them, now in bondage or threatened with slavery, are our comrades and our allies. They are only waiting for our leadership and our encouragement, for the spark that we can supply.

These hundreds of millions, of liberty-loving people, now oppressed, constitute the greatest sixth column in history. They have the will to destroy the Nazi gangsters.

We have always helped in struggles for human freedom. And we will help again. But our hundreds of millions of liberty-loving allies would despair if we did not provide aid and encouragement. The quicker we help them the sooner this dreadful revolution will be over. We cannot, we must not, we dare not delay much longer.

The fight for Britain is in its crucial stages. We must give the British everything we have. And by everything, I mean everything needed to beat the life out of our common enemy.

The second step must be to aid and encourage our friends and allies everywhere. And by everywhere I mean Europe and Asia and Africa and America.

And finally, the most important of all, we Americans must gird spiritually for the battle. We must dispel the fog of uncertainty and vacillation. We must greet with raucous laughter the corroding arguments of our appeasers and fascists. They doubt democracy. We affirm it triumphantly so that all the world may hear:

Here in America we have something so worth living for that it is worth dying for! The so-called "wave of the future" is but the slimy backwash of the past. We have not heaved from our necks the tyrant's crushing heel, only to stretch our necks out again for its weight. Not only will we fight for democracy, we will make it more worth fighting for. Under our free institutions, we will work for the good of mankind, including Hitler's victims in Germany, so that all may have plenty and security.

We American democrats know that when good will prevails among men there will be a world of plenty and a world of security.

In the words of Winston Churchill, "Are we downhearted?" No, we are not! But someone is downhearted! Witness the terrified flight of Hess, Hitler's Number Three Man. And listen to this—listen carefully:

"The British nation can be counted upon to carry through to victory any struggle that it once enters upon no matter how long such a struggle may last or however great the sacrifices that may be necessary or whatever the means that have to be employed; and all this even though the actual military equipment at hand may be utterly inadequate when compared with that of other nations."

Do you know who wrote that? Adolf Hitler in *Mein Kampf.* And do you know who took down that dictation? Rudolf Hess.

We will help to make Hitler's prophecy come true. We will help brave England drive back the hordes from Hell who besiege her and then we will join for the destruction of savage and blood-thirsty dictators everywhere. But we must be firm and decisive. We must know our will and make it felt. And we must hurry.

# Vyacheslav Molotov

## RESPONDING TO GERMANY'S INVASION, JUNE 22, 1941

*The Red Army and our whole people will again wage victorious war for the fatherland, for our country, for honor, for liberty.*

Photograph taken ca. 1955.

O N AUGUST **23, 1939**, Berlin and Moscow signed a nonaggression pact. Less than two years later, Hitler violated the pact with Operation Barbarossa—the invasion of the USSR.

In this address, Soviet Foreign Minister Vyacheslav Molotov attempted to fortify his nation by reminding them of their own history in repelling attack: "This is not the first time that our people have had to deal with an attack of an arrogant foe. At the time of Napoléon's invasion of Russia our people's reply was war for the fatherland, and Napoléon suffered defeat and met his doom. It will be the same with Hitler, who in his arrogance has proclaimed a new crusade against our country."

Although Operation Barbarossa failed in seizing Moscow, it did leave Germany in control of vast areas of the Soviet Union.

* * *

CITIZENS OF THE SOVIET UNION:

The Soviet Government and its head, Comrade Stalin, have authorized me to make the following statement:

Today at 4 o'clock AM, without any claims having been presented to the Soviet Union, without a declaration of war, German troops attacked our country, attacked our borders at many points and bombed from their airplanes our cities; Zhitomir, Kiev, Sevastopol, Kaunas and some others, killing and wounding over two hundred persons.

There were also enemy air raids and artillery shelling from Rumanian and Finnish territory.

This unheard of attack upon our country is perfidy unparalleled in the history of civilized nations. The attack on our country was perpetrated despite the fact that a treaty of non-aggression had been signed between the USSR and Germany and that the Soviet Government most faithfully abided by all provisions of this treaty.

The attack upon our country was perpetrated despite the fact that during the entire period of operation of this treaty, the German Government could not find grounds for a single complaint against the USSR as regards observance of this treaty.

Entire responsibility for this predatory attack upon the Soviet Union falls fully and completely upon the German Fascist rulers.

At 5:30 AM—that is, after the attack had already been perpetrated, Von der Schulenburg, the German Ambassador in Moscow, on behalf of his government made the statement to me as People's Commissar of Foreign

Affairs to the effect that the German Government had decided to launch war against the USSR in connection with the concentration of Red Army units near the eastern German frontier.

In reply to this I stated on behalf of the Soviet Government that, until the very last moment, the German Government had not presented any claims to the Soviet Government, that Germany attacked the USSR despite the peaceable position of the Soviet Union, and that for this reason Fascist Germany is the aggressor.

On instruction of the government of the Soviet Union I also stated that at no point had our troops or our air force committed a violation of the frontier and therefore the statement made this morning by the Rumanian radio to the effect that Soviet aircraft allegedly had fired on Rumanian airdromes is a sheer lie and provocation.

Likewise a lie and provocation is the whole declaration made today by Hitler, who is trying belatedly to concoct accusations charging the Soviet Union with failure to observe the Soviet-German pact.

Now that the attack on the Soviet Union has already been committed, the Soviet Government has ordered our troops to repulse the predatory assault and to drive German troops from the territory of our country.

This war has been forced upon us, not by the German people, not by German workers, peasants and intellectuals, whose sufferings we well understand, but by the clique of bloodthirsty Fascist rulers of Germany who have enslaved Frenchmen, Czechs, Poles, Serbians, Norway, Belgium, Denmark, Holland, Greece and other nations.

The government of the Soviet Union expresses its unshakable confidence that our valiant army and navy and brave falcons of the Soviet Air Force will acquit themselves with honor in performing their duty to the fatherland and to the Soviet people, and will inflict a crushing blow upon the aggressor.

This is not the first time that our people have had to deal with an attack of an arrogant foe. At the time of Napoléon's invasion of Russia our people's reply was war for the fatherland, and Napoléon suffered defeat and met his doom.

It will be the same with Hitler, who in his arrogance has proclaimed a new crusade against our country. The Red Army and our whole people will again wage victorious war for the fatherland, for our country, for honor, for liberty.

The government of the Soviet Union expresses the firm conviction that the whole population of our country, all workers, peasants and intellectuals, men and women, will conscientiously perform their duties and do their work. Our entire people must now stand solid and united as never before.

Each one of us must demand of himself and of others discipline, organization and self-denial worthy of real Soviet patriots, in order to provide for all the needs of the Red Army, Navy and Air Force, to insure victory over the enemy.

The government calls upon you, citizens of the Soviet Union, to rally still more closely around our glorious Bolshevist party, around our Soviet Government, around our great leader and comrade, Stalin. Ours is a righteous cause. The enemy shall be defeated. Victory will be ours.

# Josef Stalin

## DEFEND EVERY INCH,
## JULY 3, 1941

*The Red Army, Red Navy and all citizens of the Soviet Union
must defend every inch of Soviet soil, must fight to the last drop of blood
for our towns and villages, must display the daring initiative
and intelligence that are inherent in our people.*

Soviet propaganda photo.

L ESS THAN TWO WEEKS after Germany's June 22nd invasion of the Soviet Union, Josef Stalin was compelled to explain to his people how the stunning attack occurred and to mobilize them to recover from the invasion and resist even greater threats.

Stalin's radio address begins by acknowledging the enormity of the situation: "How could it have happened that our glorious Red Army surrendered a number of our cities and districts to fascist armies? Is it really true that German fascist troops are invincible, as is ceaselessly trumpeted by the boastful fascist propagandists?"

His response draws from the rich heritage of the Russian people to inspire them against a clear and present danger: "Of course not! History shows that there are no invincible armies and never have been. Napoléon's army was considered invincible but it was beaten successively by Russian, English and German armies. Kaiser Wilhelm's German Army in the period of the first imperialist war was also considered invincible, but it was beaten several times by the Russian and Anglo-French forces and was finally smashed by the Anglo-French forces. The same must be said of Hitler's German fascist army today."

However, Stalin acknowledges the Russian people cannot rely on history alone to defeat an implacable enemy. He asks: "What is required to put an end to the danger hovering over our country, and what measures must be taken to smash the enemy? Above all, it is essential that our people, the Soviet people, should understand the full immensity of the danger that threatens our country and should abandon all complacency, all heedlessness, all those moods of peaceful constructive work which were so natural before the war, but which are fatal today when war has fundamentally changed everything."

Here, as reprinted in *Soviet Russia Today* in August 1941, is Josef Stalin's appeal to the Russian people to defend every inch of Soviet soil.

---

COMRADES! CITIZENS! BROTHERS AND SISTERS! MEN OF OUR ARMY AND NAVY! I AM ADDRESSING YOU, MY FRIENDS!

The perfidious military attack on our Fatherland, begun on June 22nd by Hitler Germany, is continuing.

In spite of the heroic resistance of the Red Army, and although the enemy's finest divisions and finest air force units have already been smashed and have met their doom on the field of battle, the enemy continues to push forward, hurling fresh forces into the attack.

Hitler's troops have succeeded in capturing Lithuania, a considerable part of Latvia, the western part of Byelo-Russia, part of Western Ukraine. The fascist air force is extending the range of operations of its bombers, and is bombing Murmansk, Orsha, Mogilev, Smolensk, Kiev, Odessa and Sebastopol.

A grave danger hangs over our country.

How could it have happened that our glorious Red Army surrendered a number of our cities and districts to fascist armies? Is it really true that German fascist troops are invincible, as is ceaselessly trumpeted by the boastful fascist propagandists? Of course not!

History shows that there are no invincible armies and never have been. Napoléon's army was considered invincible but it was beaten successively by Russian, English and German armies. Kaiser Wilhelm's German Army in the period of the first imperialist war was also considered invincible, but it was beaten several times by the Russian and Anglo-French forces and was finally smashed by the Anglo-French forces.

The same must be said of Hitler's German fascist army today. This army had not yet met with serious resistance on the continent of Europe. Only on our territory has it met serious resistance. And if, as a result of this resistance, the finest divisions of Hitler's German fascist army have been defeated by our Red Army, it means that this army too can be smashed and will be smashed, as were the armies of Napoléon and Wilhelm.

As to part of our territory having nevertheless been seized by Germany fascist troops, this is chiefly due to the fact that the war of fascist Germany on the USSR began under conditions favorable for the German forces and unfavorable for Soviet forces. The fact of the matter is that the troops of Germany, as a country at war, were already fully mobilized, and the one hundred and seventy divisions hurled by Germany against the USSR and brought up to the Soviet frontiers, were in a state of complete readiness, only awaiting the signal to move into action, whereas Soviet troops had still to effect mobilization and move up to the frontier.

Of no little importance in this respect is the fact that fascist Germany suddenly and treacherously violated the non-aggression pact she concluded in 1939 with the USSR, disregarding the fact that she would be regarded as the aggressor by the whole world.

Naturally, our peace-loving country, not wishing to take the initiative of breaking the pact, could not resort to perfidy.

It may be asked: How could the Soviet Government have consented to conclude a non-aggression pact with such treacherous fiends as Hitler and Ribbentrop? Was this not an error on the part of the Soviet Government? Of course not!

Non-aggression pacts are pacts of peace between States. It was such a pact that Germany proposed to us in 1939. Could the Soviet Government have declined such a proposal? I think that not a single peace-loving state could decline a peace treaty with a neighboring state, even though the latter was headed by such fiends and cannibals as Hitler and Ribbentrop. But that, of course, only on one indispensable condition—namely, that this peace treaty does not infringe either directly or indirectly on the territorial integrity, independence and honor of the peace-loving State.

As is well known, the non-aggression pact between Germany and the USSR is precisely such a pact.

What did we gain by concluding the non-aggression pact with Germany? We secured our country peace for a year and a half, and the opportunity of preparing its forces to repulse Fascist Germany should she risk an attack on our country despite the Pact.

This was a definite advantage for us and a disadvantage for Fascist Germany.

What has fascist Germany gained and what has she lost by treacherously tearing up the pact and attacking the USSR?

She has gained a certain advantageous position for her troops for a short period, but she has lost politically by exposing herself in the eyes of the entire world as a bloodthirsty aggressor.

There can be no doubt that this short-lived military gain for Germany is only an episode, while the tremendous political gain of the USSR is a serious lasting factor that is bound to form the basis for development of decisive military successes of the Red Army in the war with Fascist Germany.

That is why our whole valiant Red Army, our whole valiant Navy, all our falcons of the air, all the peoples of our country, all the finest men and women of Europe, America and Asia, finally all the finest men and women of Germany—condemn the treacherous acts of German Fascists and sympathize with the Soviet Government, approve the conduct of the Soviet Government, and see that ours is a just cause, that the enemy will be defeated, that we are bound to win.

By virtue of this war which has been forced upon us, our country has come to death grips with its most malicious and most perfidious enemy—German fascism.

Our troops are fighting heroically against an enemy armed to the teeth with tanks and aircraft. Overcoming innumerable difficulties, the Red Army and Red Navy are self-sacrificingly disputing every inch of Soviet soil. The main forces of the Red Army are coming into action armed with thousands of tanks and airplanes. Men of the Red Army are displaying unexampled valor. Our resistance to the enemy is growing in strength and power. Side by side with the Red Army, the entire Soviet people are rising in defense of our native land.

What is required to put an end to the danger hovering over our country, and what measures must be taken to smash the enemy?

Above all, it is essential that our people, the Soviet people, should understand the full immensity of the danger that threatens our country and should abandon all complacency, all heedlessness, all those moods of peaceful constructive work which were so natural before the war, but which are fatal today when war has fundamentally changed everything.

The enemy is cruel and implacable. He is out to seize our lands, watered with our sweat, to seize our grain and oil secured by our labor. He is out to restore the rule of landlords, to restore Tsarism, to destroy national culture and the national state existence of the Russians, Ukrainians, Byelo-Russians, Lithuanians, Letts, Esthonians, Uzbeks, Tatars, Moldavians, Georgians, Armenians, Azerbaidzhanians and the other free people of the Soviet Union, to Germanize them, to convert them into the slaves of German princes and barons.

Thus the issue is one of life or death for the Soviet State, for the peoples of the U.S.S.R. The issue is whether the peoples of the Soviet Union shall remain free or fall into slavery.

The Soviet people must realize this and abandon all heedlessness, they must mobilize themselves and reorganize all their work on new, wartime bases, when there can be no mercy to the enemy.

Further, there must be no room in our ranks for whimperers and cowards, for panic-mongers and deserters. Our people must know no fear in fight and must selflessly join our patriotic war of liberation, our war against the fascist enslavers.

Lenin, the great founder of our State, used to say that the chief virtue of the Bolshevik must be courage, valor, fearlessness in struggle, readiness to fight, together with the people, against the enemies of our country.

This splendid virtue of the Bolshevik must become the virtue of the millions of the Red Army, of the Red Navy, of all peoples of the Soviet Union.

All our work must be immediately reconstructed on a war footing, everything must be subordinated to the interests of the front and the task of organizing the demolition of the enemy.

The people of the Soviet Union now see that there is no taming of German fascism in its savage fury and hatred of our country which has ensured all working people labor in freedom and prosperity.

The peoples of the Soviet Union must rise against the enemy and defend their rights and their land. The Red Army, Red Navy and all citizens of the Soviet Union must defend every inch of Soviet soil, must fight to the last drop of blood for our towns and villages, must display the daring initiative and intelligence that are inherent in our people.

We must organize all-round assistance for the Red Army, ensure powerful reinforcements for its ranks and the supply of everything it requires, we must organize the rapid transport of troops and military freight and extensive aid to the wounded.

We must strengthen the Red Army's rear, subordinating all our work to this cause. All our industries must be got to work with greater intensity to produce more rifles, machineguns, artillery, bullets, shells, airplanes; we must organize the guarding of factories, power stations, telephonic and telegraphic communications and arrange effective air raid precautions in all localities.

We must wage a ruthless fight against all disorganizers of the rear, deserters, panic-mongers, rumor-mongers; we must exterminate spies, diversionists and enemy parachutists, rendering rapid aid in all this to our destroyer battalions. We must bear in mind that the enemy is crafty, unscrupulous, experienced in deception and the dissemination of false rumors.

We must reckon with all this and not fall victim to provocation. All who by their panic-mongering and cowardice hinder the work of defense, no matter who they are, must be immediately haled before the military tribunal.

In case of forced retreat of Red Army units, all rolling stock must be evacuated; the enemy must not be left a single engine, a single railway car, not a single pound of grain or a gallon of fuel.

Collective farmers must drive off all their cattle, and turn over their grain to the safekeeping of State authorities for transportation to the rear. All valuable property, including non-ferrous metals, grain and fuel which cannot be withdrawn, must without fail be destroyed. In areas occupied by the enemy, guerrilla units, mounted and on foot, must be formed, diversionist groups must be organized to combat the enemy troops, to foment guerrilla warfare everywhere, to blow up bridges and roads, damage telephone and telegraph lines, set fire to forests, stores, transports.

In the occupied regions conditions must be made unbearable for the enemy and all his accomplices. They must be hounded and annihilated at every step, and all their measures frustrated.

This war with Fascist Germany cannot be considered an ordinary war. It is not only a war between two armies, it is also a great war of the entire Soviet people against the German fascist forces.

The aim of this national war in defense of our country against the fascist oppressors is not only elimination of the danger hanging over our country, but also aid to all European peoples groaning under the yoke of German fascism.

In this war of liberation we shall not be alone.

In this great war we shall have loyal allies in the peoples of Europe and America, including the German people who are enslaved by the Hitlerite despots.

Our war for the freedom of our country will merge with the struggle of the peoples of Europe and America for their independence, for democratic liberties.

It will be a united front of peoples standing for freedom and against enslavement and threats of enslavement by Hitler's Fascist armies.

In this connection the historic utterance of the British Prime Minister Churchill regarding aid to the Soviet Union and the declaration of the United States Government signifying its readiness to render aid to our country, which can only evoke a feeling of gratitude in the hearts of the peoples of the Soviet Union, are fully comprehensible and symptomatic.

Comrades, our forces are numberless. The overweening enemy will soon learn this to his cost. Side by side with the Red Army many thousands of workers, collective farmers, intellectuals are rising to fight the enemy aggressor. The masses of our people will rise up in their millions. The working people of Moscow and Leningrad have already commenced to form vast popular levies in support of the Red Army. Such popular levies must be raised in every city which is in danger of enemy invasion, all working people must be roused to defend our freedom, our honor, our country—in our patriotic war against German Fascism.

In order to ensure the rapid mobilization of all forces of the peoples of the U.S.S.R. and to repulse the enemy who treacherously attacked our country, a State Committee of Defense has been formed in whose hands the entire power of the State has been vested.

The State Committee of Defense has entered upon its functions and calls upon all people to rally around the Party of Lenin-Stalin and around the Soviet Government, so as to self-denyingly support the Red Army and Navy, demolish the enemy and secure victory.

All our forces for support of our heroic Red Army and our glorious Red Navy!

All forces of the people—for the demolition of the enemy!

Forward, to our victory!

# Winston Churchill

## WE CAN TAKE IT AGAIN,
## JULY 14, 1941

*If the lull is to end, if the storm is to renew itself,*
*we will be ready, will not flinch, we can take it again.*

Churchill at a conference in Quebec.

THE LUFTWAFFE'S DEVASTATING RAIDS on Great Britain receded in the spring of 1941, leaving the British to dig out from immense destruction. In this tribute to rescue workers, Winston Churchill lifts the morale of an entire population by challenging them not to retreat into their grief but by continuing to defy evil: "If tonight our people were asked to cast their vote whether a convention should be entered into to stop the bombing of cities, the overwhelming majority would cry, 'No, we will mete out to them the measure, and more than the measure, that they have meted out to us.' The people with one voice would say: 'You have committed every crime under the sun. Where you have been the least resisted there you have been the most brutal. It was you who began the indiscriminate bombing. We will have no truce or parley with you, or the grisly gang who work your wicked will. You do your worst—and we will do our best.' Perhaps it may be our turn soon; perhaps it may be our turn now.

———◆•◆•◆———

THE IMPRESSIVE AND INSPIRING SPECTACLE we have witnessed displays the vigour and efficiency of the civil defense forces. They have grown up in the stress of emergency. They have been shaped and tempered by the fire of the enemy, and we saw them all, in their many grades and classes—the wardens, the rescue and first-aid parties, the casualty services, the decontamination squads, the fire services, the report and control centre staffs, the highways and public utility services, the messengers, the police. No one could but feel how great a people, how great a nation we have the honor to belong to. How complex, sensitive, and resilient is the society we have evolved over the centuries, and how capable of withstanding the most unexpected strain.

I must, however, admit that when the storm broke in September, I was for several weeks very anxious about the result. Sometimes the gas failed; sometimes the electricity. There were grievous complaints about the shelters and about conditions in them. Water was cut off, railways were cut or broken, large districts were destroyed, thousands were killed, and many more thousands were wounded. But there was one thing about which there was never any doubt. The courage, the unconquerable grit and stamina of our people, showed itself from the very outset. Without that all would have failed. Upon that rock, all stood unshakable. All the public services were carried on, and all the intricate arrangements, far-reaching details, involving the daily lives of so many millions, were carried out, improvised, elaborated, and perfected in the very teeth of the cruel and devastating storm.

We have to ask ourselves this question: Will the bombing attacks come back again? We have proceeded on the assumption that they will. Many new arrangements are being contrived as a result of the hard experience through which we have passed and the many mistakes which no doubt we have made—for success is the result of making many mistakes and learning from experience. If the lull is to end, if the storm is to renew itself, we will be ready, will not flinch, we can take it again.

We ask no favors of the enemy. We seek from them no compunction. On the contrary, if tonight our people were asked to cast their vote whether a convention should be entered into to stop the bombing of cities, the overwhelming majority would cry, "No, we will mete out to them the measure, and more than the measure, that they have meted out to us." The people with one voice would say: "You have committed every crime under the sun. Where you have been the least resisted there you have been the most brutal. It was you who began the indiscriminate bombing. We will have no truce or parley with you, or the grisly gang who work your wicked will. You do your worst—and we will do our best." Perhaps it may be our turn soon; perhaps it may be our turn now.

We live in a terrible epoch of the human story, but we believe there is a broad and sure justice running through its theme. It is time that the enemy should be made to suffer in their own homelands something of the torment they have let loose upon their neighbors and upon the world. We believe it to be in our power to keep this process going, on a steadily rising tide, month after month, year after year, until they are either extirpated by us or, better still, torn to pieces by their own people.

It is for this reason that I must ask you to be prepared for vehement counteraction by the enemy. Our methods of dealing with them have steadily improved. They no longer relish their trips to our shores. I do not know why they do not come, but it is certainly not because they have begun to love us more. It may be because they are saving up, but even if that be so, the very fact that they have to save up should give us confidence by revealing the truth of our steady advance from an almost unarmed position to superiority. But all engaged in our defense forces must prepare themselves for further heavy assaults. Your organization, your vigilance, your devotion to duty, your zeal for the cause must be raised to the highest intensity.

We do not expect to hit without being hit back, and we intend with every week that passes to hit harder. Prepare yourselves, then, my friends and comrades, for this renewal of your exertions. We shall never turn from our purpose, however somber the road, however grievous the cost, because we know that out of this time of trial and tribulation will be born a new freedom and glory for all mankind.

# Franklin D. Roosevelt

## 9/11 ADDRESS,
## SEPTEMBER 11, 1941

*The American people have faced other grave crises in their history—*
*with American courage, with American resolution.*
*They will do no less today.*

Photograph taken December 27, 1933.

ARLY IN THE MORNING OF SEPTEMBER 11, 2001, just as I entered an elevator in the U.S. Capitol, my office sent me this e-mail: "A plane has crashed into the World Trade Center. It is likely deliberate." That message profoundly changed the nature of my time in Congress as it profoundly changed our country.

It is a strange irony of history that exactly sixty years before—on September 11, 1941—President Franklin D. Roosevelt prepared the American people for the wrenching challenges that would come with World War II. Although the United States had not yet entered the war, a German attack on a U.S. destroyer on September 4 prompted this White House radio address by Roosevelt a week later.

I have been called on to speak many times about the challenges confronting the United States in a post-9/11 world. This fireside chat, given sixty years before the terrorist attacks on our nation, has provided comfort by reminding me that if we could rally then and defeat the evil of Nazism, we can rally today and defeat the evil of terrorism.*

---

**MY FELLOW AMERICANS:**

The Navy Department of the United States has reported to me that on the morning of September fourth the United States destroyer GREER, proceeding in full daylight towards Iceland, had reached a point southeast of Greenland. She was carrying American mail to Iceland. She was flying the American flag. Her identity as an American ship was unmistakable.

She was then and there attacked by a submarine. Germany admits that it was a German submarine. The submarine deliberately fired a torpedo at the GREER, followed later by another torpedo attack. In spite of what Hitler's propaganda bureau has invented, and in spite of what any American obstructionist organization may prefer to believe, I tell you the blunt fact that the German submarine fired first upon this American destroyer without warning, and with deliberate design to sink her.

Our destroyer, at the time, was in waters which the Government of the United States had declared to be waters of self-defense—surrounding outposts of American protection in the Atlantic.

In the North of the Atlantic, outposts have been established by us in Iceland, in Greenland, in Labrador and in Newfoundland. Through these waters there pass many ships of many flags. They bear food and other supplies to civilians; and they bear material of war, for which the people of the United

---

*Parenthetical additions throughout speech are in the original.

States are spending billions of dollars, and which, by Congressional action, they have declared to be essential for the defense of (their) our own land.

THE UNITED STATES DESTROYER, when attacked, was proceeding on a legitimate mission.

If the destroyer was visible to the submarine when the torpedo was fired, then the attack was a deliberate attempt by the Nazis to sink a clearly identified American warship. On the other hand, if the submarine was beneath the surface of the sea and, with the aid of its listening devices, fired in the direction of the sound of the American destroyer without even taking the trouble to learn its identity—as the official German communiqué would indicate—then the attack was even more outrageous. For it indicates a policy of indiscriminate violence against any vessel sailing the seas—belligerent or non-belligerent.

This was piracy—piracy legally and morally. It was not the first nor the last act of piracy which the Nazi Government has committed against the American flag in this war. For attack has followed attack.

A few months ago an American flag merchant ship, the ROBIN MOOR, was sunk by a Nazi submarine in the middle of the South Atlantic, under circumstances violating long-established international law and violating every principle of humanity. The passengers and the crew were forced into open boats hundreds of miles from land, in direct violation of international agreements signed by nearly all nations including the Government of Germany. No apology, no allegation of mistake, no offer of reparations has come from the Nazi Government.

In July, 1941, nearly two months ago an American battleship in North American waters was followed by a submarine which for a long time sought to maneuver itself into a position of attack upon the battleship. The periscope of the submarine was clearly seen. No British or American submarines were within hundreds of miles of this spot at the time, so the nationality of the submarine is clear.

Five days ago a United States Navy ship on patrol picked up three survivors of an American-owned ship operating under the flag of our sister Republic of Panama—the S.S. SESSA. On August seventeenth, she had been first torpedoed without warning, and then shelled, near Greenland, while carrying civilian supplies to Iceland. It is feared that the other members of her crew have been drowned. In view of the established presence of German submarines in this vicinity, there can be no reasonable doubt as to the identity of the flag of the attacker.

Five days ago, another United States merchant ship, the STEEL SEAFARER, was sunk by a German aircraft in the Red Sea two hundred and twenty miles south of Suez. She was bound for an Egyptian port.

So four of the vessels sunk or attacked flew the American flag and were clearly identifiable. Two of these ships were warships of the American Navy. In the fifth case, the vessel sunk clearly carried the flag of our sister Republic of Panama.

In the face of all this, we Americans are keeping our feet on the ground. Our type of democratic civilization has outgrown the thought of feeling compelled to fight some other nation by reason of any single piratical attack on one of our ships. We are not becoming hysterical or losing our sense of proportion. Therefore, what I am thinking and saying tonight does not relate to any isolated episode.

Instead, we Americans are taking a long-range point of view in regard to certain fundamentals (and)—a point of view in regard to a series of events on land and on sea which must be considered as a whole—as a part of a world pattern.

It would be unworthy of a great nation to exaggerate an isolated incident, or to become inflamed by some one act of violence. But it would be inexcusable folly to minimize such incidents in the face of evidence which makes it clear that the incident is not isolated, but is part of a general plan.

The important truth is that these acts of international lawlessness are a manifestation of a design (which)—a design that has been made clear to the American people for a long time. It is the Nazi design to abolish the freedom of the seas, and to acquire absolute control and domination of (the) these seas for themselves.

For with control of the seas in their own hands, the way can obviously become clear for their next step—domination of the United States (and the)—domination of the Western Hemisphere by force of arms. Under Nazi control of the seas, no merchant ship of the United States or of any other American Republic would be free to carry on any peaceful commerce, except by the condescending grace of this foreign and tyrannical power. The Atlantic Ocean which has been, and which should always be, a free and friendly highway for us would then become a deadly menace to the commerce of the United States, to the coasts of the United States, and even to the inland cities of the United States.

The Hitler Government, in defiance of the laws of the sea, (and) in defiance of the recognized rights of all other nations, has presumed to declare, on paper, that great areas of the seas—even including a vast expanse lying in the Western Hemisphere—are to be closed, and that no ships may enter them for any purpose, except at peril of being sunk. Actually they are sinking ships at will and without warning in widely separated areas both within and far outside of these far-flung pretended zones.

This Nazi attempt to seize control of the oceans is but a counterpart of the Nazi plots now being carried on throughout the Western Hemisphere—all designed toward the same end. For Hitler's advance guards—not only his avowed agents but also his dupes among us—have sought to make ready for him footholds, (and) bridgeheads in the New World, to be used as soon as he has gained control of the oceans.

His intrigues, his plots, his machinations, his sabotage in this New World are all known to the Government of the United States. Conspiracy has followed conspiracy. For example, last year a plot to seize the Government of Uruguay was smashed by the prompt action of that country, which was supported in full by her American neighbors. A like plot was then hatching in Argentina, and that government has carefully and wisely blocked it at every point. More recently, an endeavor was made to subvert the government of Bolivia. And within the past few weeks the discovery was made of secret air-landing fields in Colombia, within easy range of the Panama Canal. I could multiply instances upon instance.

To be ultimately successful in world mastery, Hitler knows that he must get control of the seas. He must first destroy the bridge of ships which we are building across the Atlantic and over which we shall continue to roll the implements of war to help destroy him, (and) to destroy all his works in the end. He must wipe out our patrol on sea and in the air if he is to do it. He must silence the British Navy.

I think it must be explained (again and) over and over again to people who like to think of the United States Navy as an invincible protection, that this can be true only if the British Navy survives. And that, my friends, is simple arithmetic.

For if the world outside of the Americas falls under Axis domination, the shipbuilding facilities which the Axis powers would then possess in all of Europe, in the British Isles and in the Far East would be much greater than all the shipbuilding facilities and potentialities of all of the Americas—not only greater, but two or three times greater, enough to win. Even if the United States threw all its resources into such a situation, seeking to double and even redouble the size of our Navy, the Axis powers, in control of the rest of the world, would have the manpower and the physical resources to out build us several times over.

It is time for all Americans, Americans of all the Americas to stop being deluded by the romantic notion that the Americas can go on living happily and peacefully in a Nazi-dominated world.

Generation after generation, America has battled for the general policy of the freedom of the seas. And that policy is a very simple one, but a basic, a fundamental one. It means that no nation has the right to make the broad oceans of the world at great distances from the actual theatre of land war, unsafe for the commerce of others.

That has been our policy, proved time and (time) again, in all of our history. Our policy has applied from (time immemorial) the earliest days of the Republic—and still applies—not merely to the Atlantic but to the Pacific and to all other oceans as well.

Unrestricted submarine warfare in 1941 constitutes defiance—an act of aggression—against that historic American policy.

It is now clear that Hitler has begun his campaign to control the seas by ruthless force and by wiping out every vestige of international law, (and) every vestige of humanity.

His intention has been made clear. The American people can have no further illusions about it.

No tender whisperings of appeasers that Hitler is not interested in the Western Hemisphere, no soporific lullabies that a wide ocean protects us from him—can long have any effect on the hard-headed, far-sighted and realistic American people.

Because of these episodes, because of the movements and operations of German warships, and because of the clear, repeated proof that the present government of Germany has no respect for treaties or for international law, that it has no decent attitude toward neutral nations or human life—we Americans are now face to face not with abstract theories but with cruel, relentless facts.

This attack on the GREER was no localized military operation in the North Atlantic. This was no mere episode in a struggle between two nations. This was one determined step towards creating a permanent world system based on force, on terror and on murder.

And I am sure that even now the Nazis are waiting, waiting to see whether the United States will by silence give them the green light to go ahead on this path of destruction.

The Nazi danger to our Western world has long ceased to be a mere possibility. The danger is here now—not only from a military enemy but from an enemy of all law, all liberty, all morality, all religion.

There has now come a time when you and I must see the cold inexorable necessity of saying to these inhuman, unrestrained seekers of world conquest and permanent world domination by the sword: "You seek to throw our children and our children's children into your form of terrorism and slavery. You have now attacked our own safety. You shall go no further."

Normal practices of diplomacy—note writing—are of no possible use in dealing with international outlaws who sink our ships and kill our citizens.

One peaceful nation after another has met disaster because each refused to look the Nazi danger squarely in the eye until it had actually had them by the throat.

The United States will not make that fatal mistake.

No act of violence, (or) no act of intimidation will keep us from maintaining intact two bulwarks of American defense: First, our line of supply of material to the enemies of Hitler; and second, the freedom of our shipping on the high seas.

No matter what it takes, no matter what it costs, we will keep open the line of legitimate commerce in these defensive water of ours.

We have sought no shooting war with Hitler. We do not seek it now. But neither do we want peace so much, that we are willing to pay for it by permitting him to attack our naval and merchant ships while they are on legitimate business.

I assume that the German leaders are not deeply concerned, tonight or any other time, by what we Americans or the American Government say or publish about them. We cannot bring about the downfall of Nazism by the use of long-range invective.

But when you see a rattlesnake poised to strike, you do not wait until he has struck before you crush him.

These Nazi submarines and raiders are the rattlesnakes of the Atlantic. They are a menace to the free pathways of the high seas. They are a challenge to our own sovereignty. They hammer at our most precious rights when they attack ships of the American flag—symbols of our independence, our freedom, our very life.

It is clear to all Americans that the time has come when the Americas themselves must now be defended. A continuation of attacks in our own waters or in waters that could be used for further and greater attacks on us, will inevitably weaken our American ability to repel Hitlerism.

Do not let us (split hairs) be hair-splitters. Let us not ask ourselves whether the Americas should begin to defend themselves after the (fifth) first attack, or the (tenth) fifth attack, or the tenth attack, or the twentieth attack.

The time for active defense is now.

Do not let us split hairs. Let us not say: "We will only defend ourselves if the torpedo succeeds in getting home, or if the crew and the passengers are drowned."

This is the time for prevention of attack.

If submarines or raiders attack in distant waters, they can attack equally well within sight of our own shores. Their very presence in any waters which America deems vital to its defense constitutes an attack.

In the waters which we deem necessary for our defense, American naval vessels and American planes will no longer wait until Axis submarines lurking under the water, or Axis raiders on the surface of the sea, strike their deadly blow—first.

Upon our naval and air patrol—now operating in large number over a vast expanse of the Atlantic Ocean—falls the duty of maintaining the American policy of freedom of the seas—now. That means, very simply, (and) very clearly, that our patrolling vessels and planes will protect all merchant ships—not only American ships but ships of any flag—engaged in commerce in our defensive waters. They will protect them from submarines; they will protect them from surface raiders.

This situation is not new. The second President of the United States, John Adams, ordered the United States Navy to clean out European privateers and European ships of war which were infesting the Caribbean and South American waters, destroying American commerce.

The third President of the United States, Thomas Jefferson, ordered the United States Navy to end the attacks being made upon American and other ships by the corsairs of the nations of North Africa.

My obligation as President is historic; it is clear. Yes, it is inescapable.

It is no act of war on our part when we decide to protect the seas (which) that are vital to American defense. The aggression is not ours. Ours is solely defense.

But let this warning be clear. From now on, if German or Italian vessels of war enter the waters, the protection of which is necessary for American defense, they do so at their own peril.

The orders which I have given as Commander-in-Chief (to) of the United States Army and Navy are to carry out that policy—at once.

The sole responsibility rests upon Germany. There will be no shooting unless Germany continues to seek it.

That is my obvious duty in this crisis. That is the clear right of this sovereign nation. (That) This is the only step possible, if we would keep tight the wall of defense which we are pledged to maintain around this Western Hemisphere.

I have no illusions about the gravity of this step. I have not taken it hurriedly or lightly. It is the result of months and months of constant thought and anxiety and prayer. In the protection of your nation and mine it cannot be avoided.

The American people have faced other grave crises in their history—with American courage, with American resolution. They will do no less today.

They know the actualities of the attacks upon us. They know the necessities of a bold defense against these attacks. They know that the times call for clear heads and fearless hearts.

And with that inner strength that comes to a free people conscious of their duty, (and) conscious of the righteousness of what they do, they will—with Divine help and guidance—stand their ground against this latest assault upon their democracy, their sovereignty, and their freedom.

# Winston Churchill

## ON REFUSING TO "GIVE IN,"
## OCTOBER 29, 1941

*Never give in, never give in, never, never, never, never. . . .*

Churchill arrives for the start of the Potsdam Conference.

IN LATE OCTOBER 1941, Winston Churchill visited his alma mater, the Harrow School. He reminded the students of the dire situation during his last visit: "Our country stood in the gap. There was no flinching and no thought of giving in; and by what seemed almost a miracle to those outside these Islands, though we ourselves never doubted it, we now find ourselves in a position where I say that we can be sure that we have only to persevere to conquer."

The lesson of the ten intervening months, Churchill famously proclaimed to the students, is: "never give in, never give in, never, never, never, never—in nothing, great or small, large or petty—never give in except to convictions of honor and good sense. Never yield to force; never yield to the apparently overwhelming might of the enemy."

The speech may have been to a group of students. But it resonated with millions of people fighting for freedom around the world.

---

ALMOST A YEAR HAS PASSED since I came down here at your Head Master's kind invitation in order to cheer myself and cheer the hearts of a few of my friends by singing some of our own songs. The ten months that have passed have seen very terrible catastrophic events in the world—ups and downs, misfortunes—but can anyone sitting here this afternoon, this October afternoon, not feel deeply thankful for what has happened in the time that has passed and for the very great improvement in the position of our country and of our home? Why, when I was here last time we were quite alone, desperately alone, and we had been so for five or six months. We were poorly armed. We are not so poorly armed today; but then we were very poorly armed. We had the unmeasured menace of the enemy and their air attack still beating upon us, and you yourselves had had experience of this attack; and I expect you are beginning to feel impatient that there has been this long lull with nothing particular turning up!

But we must learn to be equally good at what is short and sharp and what is long and tough. It is generally said that the British are often better at the last. They do not expect to move from crisis to crisis; they do not always expect that each day will bring up some noble chance of war; but when they very slowly make up their minds that the thing has to be done and the job put through and finished, then, even if it takes months—if it takes years—they do it.

Another lesson I think we may take, just throwing our minds back to our meeting here ten months ago and now, is that appearances are often very deceptive, and as Kipling well says, we must "meet with Triumph and Disaster. And treat those two impostors just the same."

You cannot tell from appearances how things will go. Sometimes imagination makes things out far worse than they are; yet without imagination not much can be done. Those people who are imaginative see many more dangers than perhaps exist; certainly many more than will happen; but then they must also pray to be given that extra courage to carry this far-reaching imagination. But for everyone, surely, what we have gone through in this period—I am addressing myself to the School—surely from this period of ten months this is the lesson: never give in, never give in, never, never, never, never—in nothing, great or small, large or petty—never give in except to convictions of honour and good sense. Never yield to force; never yield to the apparently overwhelming might of the enemy. We stood all alone a year ago, and to many countries it seemed that our account was closed, we were finished. All this tradition of ours, our songs, our School history, this part of the history of this country, were gone and finished and liquidated.

Very different is the mood today. Britain, other nations thought, had drawn a sponge across her slate. But instead our country stood in the gap. There was no flinching and no thought of giving in; and by what seemed almost a miracle to those outside these Islands, though we ourselves never doubted it, we now find ourselves in a position where I say that we can be sure that we have only to persevere to conquer.

You sang here a verse of a School Song: you sang that extra verse written in my honor, which I was very greatly complimented by and which you have repeated today. But there is one word in it I want to alter—I wanted to do so last year, but I did not venture to. It is the line: "Not less we praise in darker days."

I have obtained the Head Master's permission to alter darker to sterner. "Not less we praise in sterner days."

Do not let us speak of darker days: let us speak rather of sterner days. These are not dark days; these are great days—the greatest days our country has ever lived; and we must all thank God that we have been allowed, each of us according to our stations, to play a part in making these days memorable in the history of our race.

# Franklin D. Roosevelt

## DECLARING WAR ON JAPAN,
## DECEMBER 8, 1941

*With confidence in our armed forces—with the unbounding determination of our people—we will gain the inevitable triumph—so help us God.*

President Roosevelt signing the declaration of war against Japan, 1941.

O N SEPTEMBER 14, 2001, I voted to authorize the use of force in Afghanistan to respond to the horrific attacks on the World Trade Center and the Pentagon. Only a few feet from where I cast my vote—and sixty years before—Franklin Delano Roosevelt summoned America into war with Japan in response to the attack on Pearl Harbor.

Not unlike Churchill, Roosevelt girds his nation for the immense hardships ahead. The enemy is not trivialized; the challenge will be difficult; the goal is set high: "No matter how long it may take us to overcome this premeditated invasion, the American people in the righteous might will win through to absolute victory." Roosevelt concludes with a plain acknowledgement of the gravity of the moment and a stirring sense of what will be required to meet the threat: "Hostilities exist. There is no blinking at the act that our people, our territory, and our interests are in grave danger. With confidence in our armed forces—with the unbounding determination of our people—we will gain the inevitable triumph—so help us God."

---

MR. VICE-PRESIDENT, MR. SPEAKER, AND MEMBERS OF THE SENATE AND HOUSE OF REPRESENTATIVES:

Yesterday, December 7, 1941—a date which will live in infamy—the United States of America was suddenly and deliberately attacked by naval and air forces of the Empire of Japan.

The United States was at peace with that nation and, at the solicitation of Japan, was still in conversation with the government and its emperor looking toward the maintenance of peace in the Pacific. Indeed, one hour after Japanese air squadrons had commenced bombing in Oahu, the Japanese ambassador to the United States and his colleagues delivered to the Secretary of State a formal reply to a recent American message. While this reply stated that it seemed useless to continue the existing diplomatic negotiations, it contained no threat or hint of war or armed attack.

It will be recorded that the distance of Hawaii from Japan makes it obvious that the attack was deliberately planned many days or even weeks ago. During the intervening time, the Japanese government has deliberately sought to deceive the United States by false statements and expressions of hope for continued peace.

The attack yesterday on the Hawaiian Islands has caused severe damage to American naval and military forces. Very many American lives have been lost. In addition, American ships have been reported torpedoed on the high seas between San Francisco and Honolulu.

Yesterday, the Japanese government also launched an attack against Malaya.

Last night, Japanese forces attacked Hong Kong.

Last night, Japanese forces attacked Guam.

Last night, Japanese forces attacked the Philippine Islands.

Last night, the Japanese attacked Wake Island.

This morning, the Japanese attacked Midway Island.

Japan has, therefore, undertaken a surprise offensive extending throughout the Pacific area. The facts of yesterday speak for themselves. The people of the United States have already formed their opinions and well understand the implications to the very life and safety of our nation.

As Commander in Chief of the Army and Navy, I have directed that all measures be taken for our defense.

Always will we remember the character of the onslaught against us.

No matter how long it may take us to overcome this premeditated invasion, the American people in the righteous might will win through to absolute victory.

I believe I interpret the will of the Congress and of the people when I assert that we will not only defend ourselves to the uttermost, but will make very certain that this form of treachery shall never endanger us again.

Hostilities exist. There is no blinking at the act that our people, our territory, and our interests are in grave danger.

With confidence in our armed forces—with the unbounding determination of our people—we will gain the inevitable triumph—so help us God.

I ask that the Congress declare that since the unprovoked and dastardly attack by Japan on Sunday, December 7, a state of war has existed between the United States and the Japanese empire.

# Franklin D. Roosevelt

## ON PREPARING AMERICA FOR WAR, DECEMBER 9, 1941

*And in the dark hours of this day—through dark days
that may be yet to come—we will know that the vast majority
of the members of the human race are on our side.
Many of them are fighting with us. All of them are praying for us.
But, in representing our cause, we represent theirs as well—
our hope and their hope for liberty under God.*

President Roosevelt at Arlington National Cemetery.

I BELIEVE THAT TWO OF THE WORST INVENTIONS in modern society are the television clicker and the reality television show. Combined, both allow us to sit back in the comfort of our homes and view war as a form of entertainment. When it becomes too hard, too grizzly, we click to another channel. When the reality becomes too painful, we switch to a sitcom. The result: the fantasy mixes with the reality. Today, war is about kinetic operations—but also about public relations. Wars are fought on the battlefield, and then instantly interpreted in battlefield "media centers"; they are condensed in sound-bite analysis between commercials on television news interviews. They are not debated carefully in Congress; they become verbal equivalents of partisan machine-gun volleys. Hardships are trivialized. Complexities are reduced to the policy equivalent of an E-ZPass. Bad news, difficult concepts, are too frequently spoon-fed to the American people as if they suffer from a national case of attention deficit disorder and a physiological inability to sacrifice.

This fireside speech by Franklin Roosevelt—two days after the attack on Pearl Harbor—is the antidote. It takes the time to detail a historic record of aggression by the Axis powers. It imposes the burden for victory on every American. It acknowledges that "so far the war has been all bad," and the casualties will be high.

It promises hardship and demands patience. And it inspires men and women with this reference to sacrifice: "I was about to add that ahead there lies sacrifice for all of us. But it is not correct to use that word. The United States does not consider it a sacrifice to do all one can, to give one's best to our nation, when the nation is fighting for its existence and its future life. It is not a sacrifice for any man, old or young, to be in the Army or the Navy of the United States. Rather it is a privilege. It is not a sacrifice for the industrialist or the wage earner, the farmer or the shopkeeper, the trainmen or the doctor, to pay more taxes, to buy more bonds, to forego extra profits, to work longer or harder at the task for which he is best fitted. Rather it is a privilege. It is not a sacrifice to do without many things to which we are accustomed if the national defense calls for doing without it."

⁘

## MY FELLOW AMERICANS:

The sudden criminal attacks perpetrated by the Japanese in the Pacific provide the climax of a decade of international immorality.

Powerful and resourceful gangsters have banded together to make war upon the whole human race. Their challenge has now been flung at the United States of America. The Japanese have treacherously violated the long-standing peace between us. Many American soldiers and sailors have been killed by enemy action. American ships have been sunk; American airplanes have been destroyed.

The Congress and the people of the United States have accepted that challenge.

Together with other free peoples, we are now fighting to maintain our right to live among our world neighbors in freedom, in common decency, without fear of assault.

I have prepared the full record of our past relations with Japan, and it will be submitted to the Congress. It begins with the visit of Commodore Parry to Japan eighty-eight years ago. It ends with the visit of two Japanese emissaries to the Secretary of State last Sunday, an hour after Japanese forces had loosed their bombs and machine guns against our flag, our forces and our citizens.

I can say with utmost confidence that no Americans today or a thousand years hence, need feel anything but pride in our patience and in our efforts through all the years toward achieving a peace in the Pacific which would be fair and honorable to every nation, large or small. And no honest person, today or a thousand years hence, will be able to suppress a sense of indignation and horror at the treachery committed by the military dictators of Japan, under the very shadow of the flag of peace borne by their special envoys in our midst.

The course that Japan has followed for the past ten years in Asia has paralleled the course of Hitler and Mussolini in Europe and in Africa. Today, it has become far more than a parallel. It is actual collaboration so well calculated that all the continents of the world, and all the oceans, are now considered by the Axis strategists as one gigantic battlefield.

In 1931, ten years ago, Japan invaded Manchukuo—without warning.

In 1935, Italy invaded Ethiopia—without warning. In 1938, Hitler occupied Austria—without warning.

In 1939, Hitler invaded Czechoslovakia—without warning. Later in '39, Hitler invaded Poland—without warning. In 1940, Hitler invaded Norway, Denmark, the Netherlands, Belgium and Luxembourg—without warning.

In 1940, Italy attacked France and later Greece—without warning. And this year, in 1941, the Axis Powers attacked Yugoslavia and Greece and they dominated the Balkans—without warning. In 1941, also, Hitler invaded Russia—without warning. And now Japan has attacked Malaya and Thailand—and the United States—without warning.

It is all of one pattern.

We are now in this war. We are all in it—all the way. Every single man, woman and child is a partner in the most tremendous undertaking of our

American history. We must share together the bad news and the good news, the defeats and the victories—the changing fortunes of war.

So far, the news has been all bad. We have suffered a serious setback in Hawaii. Our forces in the Philippines, which include the brave people of that Commonwealth, are taking punishment, but are defending themselves vigorously. The reports from Guam and Wake and Midway Islands are still confused, but we must be prepared for the announcement that all these three outposts have been seized.

The casualty lists of these first few days will undoubtedly be large. I deeply feel the anxiety of all of the families of the men in our armed forces and the relatives of people in cities which have been bombed. I can only give them my solemn promise that they will get news just as quickly as possible.

This Government will put its trust in the stamina of the American people, and will give the facts to the public just as soon as two conditions have been fulfilled: first, that the information has been definitely and officially confirmed; and, second, that the release of the information at the time it is received will not prove valuable to the enemy directly or indirectly.

Most earnestly I urge my countrymen to reject all rumors. These ugly little hints of complete disaster fly thick and fast in wartime. They have to be examined and appraised.

As an example, I can tell you frankly that until further surveys are made, I have not sufficient information to state the exact damage which has been done to our naval vessels at Pearl Harbor. Admittedly the damage is serious. But no one can say how serious, until we know how much of this damage can be repaired and how quickly the necessary repairs can be made.

I cite as another example a statement made on Sunday night that a Japanese carrier had been located and sunk off the Canal Zone. And when you hear statements that are attributed to what they call an "authoritative source," you can be reasonably sure from now on that under these war circumstances the "authoritative source" is not any person in authority.

Many rumors and reports which we now hear originate, of course, with enemy sources. For instance, today the Japanese are claiming that as a result of their one action against Hawaii they have gained naval supremacy in the Pacific. This is an old trick of propaganda which has been used innumerable times by the Nazis. The purposes of such fantastic claims are, of course, to spread fear and confusion among us, and to goad us into revealing military information which our enemies are desperately anxious to obtain.

Our Government will not be caught in this obvious trap—and neither will the people of the United States.

It must be remembered by each and every one of us that our free and rapid communication these days must be greatly restricted in wartime. It is not possible to receive full and speedy and accurate reports from distant areas of combat. This is particularly true where naval operations are concerned. For in these days of the marvels of the radio it is often impossible for the Commanders of various units to report their activities by radio at all, for the very simple reason that this information would become available to the enemy and would disclose their position and their plan of defense or attack.

Of necessity there will be delays in officially confirming or denying reports of operations, but we will not hide facts from the country if we know the facts and if the enemy will not be aided by their disclosure.

To all newspapers and radio stations—all those who reach the eyes and ears of the American people—I say this: You have a most grave responsibility to the nation now and for the duration of this war.

If you feel that your Government is not disclosing enough of the truth, you have every right to say so. But in the absence of all the facts, as revealed by official sources, you have no right in the ethics of patriotism to deal out unconfirmed reports in such a way as to make people believe that they are gospel truth.

Every citizen, in every walk of life, shares this same responsibility. The lives of our soldiers and sailors—the whole future of this nation—depend upon the manner in which each and every one of us fulfills his obligation to our country.

Now a word about the recent past and the future. A year and a half has elapsed since the fall of France, when the whole world first realized the mechanized might which the Axis nations had been building up for so many years. America has used that year and a half to great advantage. Knowing that the attack might reach us in all too short a time, we immediately began greatly to increase our industrial strength and our capacity to meet the demands of modern warfare.

Precious months were gained by sending vast quantities of our war material to the nations of the world still able to resist Axis aggression. Our policy rested on the fundamental truth that the defense of any country resisting Hitler or Japan was in the long run the defense of our own country. That policy has been justified. It has given us time, invaluable time, to build our American assembly lines of production.

Assembly lines are now in operation. Others are being rushed to completion. A steady stream of tanks and planes, of guns and ships and shells and equipment—that is what these eighteen months have given us.

But it is all only a beginning of what still has to be done. We must be set to face a long war against crafty and powerful bandits. The attack at Pearl Harbor can be repeated at any one of many points, points in both oceans and along both our coastlines and against all the rest of the Hemisphere.

It will not only be a long war, it will be a hard war. That is the basis on which we now lay all our plans. That is the yardstick by which we measure what we shall need and demand; money, materials, doubled and quadrupled production—ever-increasing. The production must be not only for our own Army and Navy and air forces. It must reinforce the other armies and navies and air forces fighting the Nazis and the warlords of Japan throughout the Americas and throughout the world.

I have been working today on the subject of production. Your Government has decided on two broad policies.

The first is to speed up all existing production by working on a seven-day week basis in every war industry, including the production of essential raw materials.

The second policy, now being put into form, is to rush additions to the capacity of production by building more new plants, by adding to old plants, and by using the many smaller plants for war needs.

Over the hard road of the past months, we have at times met obstacles and difficulties, divisions and disputes, indifference and callousness. That is now all past—and, I am sure, forgotten.

The fact is that the country now has an organization in Washington built around men and women who are recognized experts in their own fields. I think the country knows that the people who are actually responsible in each and every one of these many fields are pulling together with a teamwork that has never before been excelled.

On the road ahead there lies hard work—grueling work—day and night, every hour and every minute.

I was about to add that ahead there lies sacrifice for all of us.

But it is not correct to use that word. The United States does not consider it a sacrifice to do all one can, to give one's best to our nation, when the nation is fighting for its existence and its future life.

It is not a sacrifice for any man, old or young, to be in the Army or the Navy of the United States. Rather it is a privilege.

It is not a sacrifice for the industrialist or the wage earner, the farmer or the shopkeeper, the trainmen or the doctor, to pay more taxes, to buy more bonds, to forego extra profits, to work longer or harder at the task for which he is best fitted. Rather it is a privilege.

It is not a sacrifice to do without many things to which we are accustomed if the national defense calls for doing without it.

A review this morning leads me to the conclusion that at present we shall not have to curtail the normal use of articles of food. There is enough food today for all of us and enough left over to send to those who are fighting on the same side with us.

But there will be a clear and definite shortage of metals for many kinds of civilian use, for the very good reason that in our increased program we shall need for war purposes more than half of that portion of the principal metals which during the past year have gone into articles for civilian use. Yes, we shall have to give up many things entirely.

And I am sure that the people in every part of the nation are prepared in their individual living to win this war. I am sure that they will cheerfully help to pay a large part of its financial cost while it goes on. I am sure they will cheerfully give up those material things that they are asked to give up.

And I am sure that they will retain all those great spiritual things without which we cannot win through.

I repeat that the United States can accept no result save victory, final and complete. Not only must the shame of Japanese treachery be wiped out, but the sources of international brutality, wherever they exist, must be absolutely and finally broken.

In my Message to the Congress yesterday I said that we "will make very certain that this form of treachery shall never endanger us again." In order to achieve that certainty, we must begin the great task that is before us by abandoning once and for all the illusion that we can ever again isolate ourselves from the rest of humanity.

In these past few years—and, most violently, in the past three days—we have learned a terrible lesson.

It is our obligation to our dead—it is our sacred obligation to their children and to our children—that we must never forget what we have learned.

And what we have learned is this:

There is no such thing as security for any nation—or any individual—in a world ruled by the principles of gangsterism.

There is no such thing as impregnable defense against powerful aggressors who sneak up in the dark and strike without warning.

We have learned that our ocean-girt hemisphere is not immune from severe attack—that we cannot measure our safety in terms of miles on any map any more.

We may acknowledge that our enemies have performed a brilliant feat of deception, perfectly timed and executed with great skill. It was a thoroughly dishonorable deed, but we must face the fact that modern warfare as conducted in the Nazi manner is a dirty business. We don't like it—we didn't want to get in it—but we are in it and we're going to fight it with everything we've got.

I do not think any American has any doubt of our ability to administer proper punishment to the perpetrators of these crimes.

Your Government knows that for weeks Germany has been telling Japan that if Japan did not attack the United States, Japan would not share in dividing the spoils with Germany when peace came. She was promised by Germany that if she came in she would receive the complete and perpetual control of the whole of the Pacific area—and that means not only the Ear East, but also all of the Islands in the Pacific, and also a stranglehold on the west coast of North, Central and South America.

We know also that Germany and Japan are conducting their military and naval operations in accordance with a joint plan. That plan considers all peoples and nations which are not helping the Axis powers as common enemies of each and every one of the Axis powers.

That is their simple and obvious grand strategy. And that is why the American people must realize that it can be matched only with similar grand strategy. We must realize for example that Japanese successes against the United States in the Pacific are helpful to German operations in Libya; that any German success against the Caucasus is inevitably an assistance to Japan in her operations against the Dutch East Indies; that a German attack against Algiers or Morocco opens the way to a German attack against South America and the Canal.

On the other side of the picture, we must learn also to know that guerilla warfare against the Germans in, let us say Serbia or Norway, helps us; that a successful Russian offensive against the Germans helps us; and that British successes on land or sea in any part of the world strengthen our hands.

Remember always that Germany and Italy, regardless of any formal declaration of war, consider themselves at war with the United States at this moment just as much as they consider themselves at war with Britain or Russia. And Germany puts all the other Republics of the Americas into the same category of enemies. The people of our sister Republics of this Hemisphere can be honored by that fact.

The true goal we seek is far above and beyond the ugly field of battle. When we resort to force, as now we must, we are determined that this force shall be directed toward ultimate good as well as against immediate evil. We Americans are not destroyers—we are builders.

We are now in the midst of a war, not for conquest, not for vengeance, but for a world in which this nation, and all that this nation represents, will be safe for our children. We expect to eliminate the danger from Japan, but it would serve us ill if we accomplished that and found that the rest of the world was dominated by Hitler and Mussolini.

So we are going to win the war and we are going to win the peace that follows.

And in the dark hours of this day—through dark days that may be yet to come—we will know that the vast majority of the members of the human race are on our side. Many of them are fighting with us. All of them are praying for us. But, in representing our cause, we represent theirs as well—our hope and their hope for liberty under God.

# Josef Stalin

## DEMANDING COURAGE,
## JULY 28, 1942

*It is time to stop the retreat. Not a single step back!*

Secretary-general of the Communist Party of Soviet Russia, ca. 1942.

I N THE EXPLOSIVE HEAT OF BATTLE or in the dark and silent moments of approaching threat, words become critical tools in achieving strategic and tactical goals. They push troops to march into hell; they turn troops sharply away from retreat; they compel troops simply to hold their ground. Like weapons, words are chosen carefully to achieve a specific objective. In some cases, they motivate by offering spiritualism. (Moses promising, "the Lord your God Himself marches with you.") In other cases, they inspire by stoking the embers of pride. (Napoléon proclaiming, "Men will say, as they point you out, 'He belonged to the army of Italy.'") And in the case of Josef Stalin's Order Number 227, words use the great power of fear to compel his forces to cease their retreat from advancing German forces.

Stalin begins bluntly, expressing disappointment with the Red Army for retreating from German forces.

"From now on," he states, "the iron law of discipline for every officer, soldier, political officer should be—not a single step back without order from higher command. Company, battalion, regiment and division commanders, as well as the commissars and political officers of corresponding ranks who retreat without order from above, are traitors of the Motherland."

Stalin's order ends with a series of disciplinary actions intended to stop further retreats, including court-martial and the transfer of uncooperative battalions to "more difficult sections of a Front, thus giving them an opportunity to redeem their crimes against the Motherland by blood."

After reading this speech, see General Sir Bernard Montgomery's speech to the Eighth Army for a considerably different tone to the same objective: no retreat.

---

T HE ENEMY FEEDS MORE AND MORE resources to the front, and, paying no attention to losses, moves on, penetrates deeper into the Soviet Union, captures new areas, devastates and plunders our cities and villages, rapes, kills and robs the Soviet people. The fighting goes on in Voronezh area, at Don, in the Southern Russia, at the gates of the North Caucasus. The German invaders are driving towards Stalingrad, towards Volga, and want to capture Kuban and the North Caucasus with their oil and bread riches at any price. The enemy has already captured Voroshilovgrad, Starobelsk, Rossosh, Kupyansk, Valuiki, Novocherkassk, Rostov on Don, half of Voronezh. Some units of the South front, following the panic-mongers, have abandoned Rostov and Novocherkassk without serious resistance and without order from Moscow, thus covering their banners with shame.

The people of our country, who treat the Red Army with love and respect, are now starting to be disappointed with it, lose faith in the Red Army, and many of them curse the Army for its fleeing to the east and leaving the population under German yoke.

Some unwise people at the front comfort themselves with arguments that we can continue the retreat to the east, as we have vast territories, a lot of soil, many people, and that we will always have abundance of bread. By these arguments they try to justify their shameful behavior at the front. But all these arguments are fully false, faked and working for our enemies.

Every commander, every soldier and political officer have to realize that our resources are not infinite. The territory of the Soviet Union is not a wilderness, but people—workers, peasants, intelligentsia, our fathers and mothers, wives, brothers, children. Territory of USSR that has been captured by the enemy and which enemy is longing to capture is bread and other resources for the army and the civilians, iron and fuel for the industries, factories and plants that supply the military with hardware and ammo; this is also railroads. With loss of Ukraine, Belorussia, the Baltics, Donetsk basin and other areas we have lost vast territories; that means that we have lost many people, bread, metals, factories, and plants. We no longer have superiority over enemy in human resources and in bread supply. Continuation of retreat means to destroy us and also our Motherland. Every new piece of territory that we leave to the enemy will strengthen our enemy and weaken us, our defences, our Motherland.

This is why we have to eradicate the conversations that we can retreat without ending, that we have a lot of territory, that our country is great and rich, that we have a lot of population and we will always have enough bread. These conversations are false and harmful, as they weaken us and strengthen the enemy, for if we do not stop retreating, we will be left without bread, without fuel, without metals, without raw materials, without factories and plants, without railways.

The conclusion is that it is time to stop the retreat. Not a single step back! This should be our slogan from now.

We need to protect every strongpoint, every meter of Soviet soil stubbornly, till the last droplet of blood, grab every piece of our soil and defend it as long as it is possible. Our Motherland is going through hard times. We have to stop, and then throw back and destroy the enemy, whatever it might cost us. The Germans are not as strong as the panic-mongers say. They are stretching their strength to the limit. To withstand their blow now means to ensure victory in the future.

Can we stand and throw the enemy back toward west? Yes, we can, as our plants and factories in the rear areas are working perfectly and are supplying our army with more and more tanks, planes, artillery and mortars. So what do we lack? We lack order and discipline in companies, regiments and divisions, in tank units, in the Air Force squadrons. This is our major drawback. We have to introduce the strictest order and strong discipline in our army, if we want to save the situation and defend our Motherland.

We can no longer tolerate commanders, commissars, and political officers, whose units leave their defences at will. We can no longer tolerate the fact that the commanders, commissars and political officers allow several cowards to run the show at the battlefield, that the panic-mongers carry away other soldiers in their retreat and open the way to the enemy. Panic-mongers and cowards are to be exterminated at the site.

From now on the iron law of discipline for every officer, soldier, political officer should be—not a single step back without order from higher command. Company, battalion, regiment and division commanders, as well as the commissars and political officers of corresponding ranks who retreat without order from above, are traitors of the Motherland. They should be treated as traitors of the Motherland. This is the call of our Motherland.

To fulfill this order means to defend our country, to save our Motherland, to destroy and overcome the hated enemy.

After their winter retreat under pressure of the Red Army, when morale and discipline fell in the German troops, the Germans took some strict measures that led to pretty good results. They have formed one hundred penal companies that were comprised of soldiers who broke discipline due to cowardice or instability; they have deployed them at the most dangerous sections of the front and have ordered them to redeem their sins by blood. Further on, they have formed around ten penal battalions comprised of officers who had broken discipline due to cowardice and instability, deprived them of their decorations and put them at even more dangerous sections of the front and ordered them to redeem their sins by blood. And finally, the Germans have formed special guards units and deployed them behind unstable divisions and ordered them to execute panic-mongers at the site if they tried to leave their defensive positions without order or if they tried to surrender. As we know, these measures were effective, and now the German troops fight better than they fought in winter. What we have here is that the German troops have good discipline, although they do not have an uplifted mission of protection of the Motherland, and only have one goal—to conquer a strange land. Our troops, having defence of defiled Motherland as their mission, do not have this discipline and thus suffer defeat.

Shouldn't we learn this lesson from our enemy, as our ancestors learned from their enemies in the past and overcame their enemies? I think that we should.

## THE SUPREME COMMAND OF
## THE RED ARMY ORDERS:

1. The military Councils of the fronts and first of all front commanders should:

a) In all circumstances decisively eradicate retreat attitude in the troops and with an iron hand prevent propaganda that we can and should continue the retreat to the east, and this retreat will not be harmful to us;

b) In all circumstances remove from offices and send to Stavka for court-martial those army commanders who allowed their troops to retreat at will, without authorization by the Front command;

c) Form within each Front 1 to 3 (depending on the situation) penal battalions (800 personnel), where commanding, senior commanders and political officers of corresponding ranks from all services, who have broken discipline due to cowardice or instability, should be sent. These battalions should be put on the more difficult sections of a Front, thus giving them an opportunity to redeem their crimes against the Motherland by blood.

2. The Military Councils of armies and first of all army commanders should:

a) In all circumstances remove from offices corps and army commanders and commissars, who have allowed their troops to retreat at will without authorization by the army command, and send them to the Military Councils of the Fronts for court-martial;

b) Form 3 to 5 well-armed guards (barrage) units (zagradotryads), deploy them in the rear of unstable divisions and oblige them to execute panic-mongers and cowards at site in case of panic and chaotic retreat, thus giving faithful soldiers a chance to do their duty before the Motherland;

c) Form 5 to 10 (depending on the situation) penal companies, where soldiers and NCOs, who have broken discipline due to cowardice or instability, should be sent. These units should be deployed at the most difficult sectors of the front, thus giving their soldiers an opportunity to redeem their crimes against the Motherland by blood.

3. Corps and division commanders and commissars should:

a) In all circumstances remove from offices regiment and battalion commanders and commissars who allowed their troops to retreat at will without authorization from divisional or corps command, deprive them of their military decorations and send them to the Military Councils of fronts for court-martial;

b) Provide all possible help and support to the guards (barrage) units (zagradotryads) of the army in their work of strengthening discipline and order in the units. This order is to be read aloud in all companies, troops, batteries, squadrons, teams and staffs.

# General Sir Bernard Montgomery

## No Retreat,
## August 13, 1942

*I have ordered that all plans and instructions
dealing with further withdrawal are to be burned, and at once.
We will stand and fight here. If we can't stay here alive,
then let us stay here dead.*

Photograph taken ca. 1942.

T HEY WERE DEMORALIZED AND IN DISARRAY. They had ceded large swaths of North Africa to Rommel's army. They were confident about only one thing: an attack on them was imminent, and so was yet another retreat.

That is the environment that General Bernard Montgomery inherited when Churchill chose him to command the Eighth Army in August 1942. His introductory remarks to his troops reflect the wisdom of a leader who understands the importance of morale and unit cohesion in securing victory. Almost immediately he unpeels the layers of doubt that have burdened the Eighth Army. "I have only been here a few hours. But from what I have seen and heard since I arrived I am prepared to say, here and now, that I have confidence in you. We will then work together as a team; and together we will gain the confidence of this great army and go forward to final victory in Africa." Then he goes on to announce that he has ordered that all plans for further withdrawal be burned.

After sharing his plan to fortify the army, Montgomery leaves his troops with a final note of confidence: "The great point to remember is that we are going to finish with this chap Rommel once and for all. It will be quite easy. There is no doubt about it. He is definitely a nuisance. Therefore we will hit him a crack and finish with him."

Montgomery's speech worked. When Rommel attacked, the Eighth Army stood its ground. Three months later, it was Rommel's Afrika Korps that was retreating in North Africa.

◆◆◆

I WANT TO FIRST OF ALL TO INTRODUCE MYSELF to you. You do not know me. I do not know you. But we have got to work together; therefore we must understand each other, and we must have confidence each in the other. I have only been here a few hours. But from what I have seen and heard since I arrived I am prepared to say, here and now, that I have confidence in you. We will then work together as a team; and together we will gain the confidence of this great army and go forward to final victory in Africa.

I believe that one of the first duties of a commander is to create what I call atmosphere, and in that atmosphere his staff, subordinate commanders, and troops will live and work and fight.

I do no like the general atmosphere I find here. It is an atmosphere of doubt, of looking back to select the next place to which to withdraw, of loss of confidence in our ability to defeat Rommel, of desperate defense measures by reserves in preparing positions in Cairo and the Delta.

All that must cease.

Let us have a new atmosphere.

The defense of Egypt lies here at Alamein and on the Ruweisat Ridge. What is the use of digging trenches in the Delta? It is quite useless; if we lose this position we lose Egypt; all the fighting troops now in the Delta must come here at once, and will.

Here we will stand and fight; there will be no further withdrawal. I have ordered that all plans and instructions dealing with further withdrawal are to be burned, and at once. We will stand and fight here. If we can't stay here alive, then let us stay here dead.

I want to impress on everyone that the bad times are over. Fresh divisions from the UK are now arriving in Egypt, together with ample reinforcements for our present divisions. We have three hundred to four hundred new Sherman tanks coming and these are actually being unloaded at Suez now. Our mandate from the prime minister is to destroy the Axis forces in North Africa; I have seen it, written on half a sheet of notepaper. And it will be done. If anyone here thinks it can't be done, let him go at once; I don't want any doubters in this party. It can be done, and it will be done; beyond any possibility of doubt.

Now I understand that Rommel is expected to attack at any moment. Excellent. Let him attack.

I would sooner it didn't come for a week, just give me time to sort things out. If we have two weeks to prepare we will be sitting pretty. Rommel can attack as soon as he likes after that, and I hope he does.

Meanwhile, we ourselves will start to plan a great offensive; it will be the beginning of a campaign which will hit Rommel and his army for six right out of Africa.

But first we must create a reserve corps, mobile and strong in armor, which we will train out of line. Rommel has always had such a force in his Africa Corps, which is never used to hold the line but which is always in reserve, available for striking blows. Therein has been his great strength. We will create such a corps ourselves, a British Panzer Corps; it will consist of two armored divisions and one motorized division; I gave orders yesterday for it to begin to form, back in the Delta.

I have no intention of launching our great attack until we are completely ready; there will be pressure from many quarters to attack soon; I will not attack until we are ready, and you can rest assured on that point.

Meanwhile, if Rommel attacks while we are preparing, let him do so with pleasure; we will merely continue with our own preparations and we will attack when we are ready, and not before.

I want to tell you that I always work on the Chief of Staff system. I have nominated Brigadier de Guingand as Chief of Staff English Army. I will issue orders through him. Whatever he says will be taken as coming from me and will be acted on at once. I understand there has been a great deal of bellyaching out here. By bellyaching I mean inventing poor reasons for not doing what one has been told to do.

All this is to stop at once.

I will tolerate no bellyaching.

If anyone objects to doing what he is told, then he can get out of it; and at once. I want that made very clear right down through the Eighth Army.

I have little more to say just at present. And some of you may think it is quite enough and may wonder if I am mad.

I assure you I am quite sane.

I understand there are people who often think I am slightly mad; so often that I now regard it as rather a compliment.

All I have to say to that is that if I am slightly mad, there are a large number of people I could name who are raving lunatics!

What I have done is to get over to you the "atmosphere" in which we will now work and fight; you must see that that atmosphere permeates right through the Eighth Army to the most junior private soldier. All the soldiers must know what is wanted; when they see it coming to pass there will be a surge of confidence throughout the army.

I ask you to give me your confidence and to have faith that what I have said will come to pass.

There is much work to be done.

The orders I have given about no further withdrawal will mean a complete change in the layout of our dispositions; also, we must begin to prepare for our great offensive.

The first thing to do is to move our HQ to a decent place where we can live in reasonable comfort and where the army staff can all be together and side by side with the HQ of the Desert Air Force. This is a frightful place here, depressing, unhealthy, and a rendezvous for every fly in Africa; we shall do no good work here. Let us get over there by the sea where it is fresh and healthy. If officers are to do good work they must have decent messes, and be comfortable. So off we go on the new line.

The Chief of Staff will be issuing orders on many points very shortly, and I am always available to be consulted by the senior officers of the staff. The great point to remember is that we are going to finish with this chap Rommel once and for all. It will be quite easy. There is no doubt about it.

He is definitely a nuisance. Therefore we will hit him a crack and finish with him.

# General George Patton

## EXHORTING THE THIRD ARMY,
## SPRING 1944

*I don't want to get any messages saying, "I am holding my position."*
*We are not holding a goddamned thing. Let the Germans do that.*
*We are advancing constantly and we are not interested*
*in holding onto anything, except the enemy's balls.*

Patton as lieutenant general, March 30, 1943.

I N **62 BCE**, Catiline urged that "if Fortune be unjust to your valor, take care not to lose lives unavenged; take care not to be taken and butchered like cattle, rather than, fighting like men, to leave to your enemies a bloody and mournful victory." In his 1944 speech to the Third Army, Gen. George Patton urged a similar goal in blunter terms: "You've got to spill their blood, or they will spill yours. Rip them up the belly. Shoot them in the guts. When shells are hitting all around you and you wipe the dirt off your face and realize that instead of dirt it's the blood and guts of what once was your best friend beside you, you'll know what to do!"

Napoléon, in 1805, proclaimed: "It will be enough for one of you to say, 'I was at the battle of Austerlitz'; and for all your fellow citizens to explain, 'There is a brave man.'" In his Third Army speech, Patton said, "You may be thankful that twenty years from now when you are sitting by the fireplace with your grandson on your knee and he asks you what you did in the great World War II, you won't have to cough, shift him to the other knee and say, 'Well, your Granddaddy shoveled shit in Louisiana.' No, Sir, you can look him straight in the eye and say, 'Son, your Granddaddy rode with the Great Third Army and a Son-of-a-Goddamned-Bitch named George Patton.'"

In World War I, Georges Clemenceau inspired his audiences with the heroic tale of "a group of lost men, Bretons, surrounded in a wood all night. The next day, still resisting, they sent a carrier pigeon to their corps to say, 'We are here. We have promised not to yield. We shall fight to the end. If you can come to find us, come; we can hold out half a day longer.'" In this speech, Patton tells a similar story, with a touch of humor: "One of the bravest men that I ever saw was a fellow on top of a telegraph pole in the midst of a furious fire fight in Tunisia. I stopped and asked what the hell he was doing up there at a time like that. He answered, 'Fixing the wire, Sir.' I asked, 'Isn't that a little unhealthy right about now?' He answered, 'Yes Sir, but the goddamned wire has to be fixed.' I asked, 'Don't those planes strafing the road bother you?' And he answered, 'No, Sir, but you sure as hell do!'"

Here, based on written accounts of the speech, is Patton's attempt to motivate the Third Army to sweep across Europe in the spring of 1944. Above all, it helps explain why Patton was called "Old Blood and Guts."

---

MEN, THIS STUFF THAT SOME SOURCES sling around about America wanting to stay out of this war, not wanting to fight, is a crock of bullshit. Americans love to fight, traditionally. All real Americans love the sting and clash of battle. Americans love a winner. Americans will not tolerate a loser.

Americans despise cowards. Americans play to win. That's why Americans have never lost nor will ever lose a war.

You are not all going to die. Only two percent of you right here today would die in a major battle. Death must not be feared. Death, in time, comes to all men. And every man is scared in his first battle. If he says he's not, he's a goddamn liar. Some men are cowards but they fight the same as the brave men or they get the hell slammed out of them watching men fight who are just as scared as they are. Remember that the enemy is just as frightened as you are, and probably more so. They are not supermen.

The real hero is the man who fights even though he's scared. Some men get over their fright in a minute under fire, others take an hour, for some it takes days, but a real man will never let his fear of death overpower his honor, his sense of duty to his country and to his manhood.

All through your Army careers, you men have bitched about what you call "chicken shit drilling." That, like everything else in this army, has a definite purpose. That purpose is alertness. Alertness must be bred into every soldier. A man must be alert at all times if he expects to stay alive. If you're not alert, sometime, a German son-of-an-asshole-bitch is going to sneak up behind you and beat you to death with a sock-full of shit! There are four hundred neatly marked graves somewhere in Sicily, all because one man went to sleep on the job. But they are German graves, because we caught the bastard asleep.

An Army is a team. It lives, sleeps, eats, and fights as a team. This individual heroic stuff is pure horseshit. The bilious bastards who write that kind of stuff for the *Saturday Evening Post* don't know any more about real fighting under fire than they know about fucking! We have the finest food, the finest equipment, the best spirit, and the best men in the world. Why, by God, I actually pity those poor sons-of-bitches we're going up against.

My men don't surrender, and I don't want to hear of any soldier under my command being captured unless he has been hit. Even if you are hit, you can still fight back. The kind of man that I want in my command is just like the lieutenant in Libya, who, with a Luger against his chest, jerked off his helmet, swept the gun aside with one hand, and busted the hell out of the Kraut with his helmet. Then he jumped on the gun and went out and killed another German before they knew what the hell was coming off. And, all of that time, this man had a bullet through a lung. There was a real man!

Every single man in this Army plays a vital role. Every man is a vital link in the great chain. What if every truck driver suddenly decided that he didn't like the whine of those shells overhead, turned yellow, and jumped headlong into a ditch? The cowardly bastard could say, "Hell, they won't miss me, just one man in thousands." But, what if every man thought that way? Where in the hell would we be now? What would our country, our loved ones, our homes, even the world, be like? No, goddamnit, Americans don't think like that. Every man does his job, serves the whole. Ordnance men are needed to supply the guns and machinery of war to keep us rolling. Quartermasters are needed to bring up food and clothes because where we are going there isn't a hell of a lot to steal. Every last man on KP has a job to do, even the one who heats our water to keep us from getting the "G.I. Shits." Each man must not think only of himself, but also of his buddy fighting beside him.

One of the bravest men that I ever saw was a fellow on top of a telegraph pole in the midst of a furious firefight in Tunisia. I stopped and asked what the hell he was doing up there at a time like that. He answered, "Fixing the wire, Sir." I asked, "Isn't that a little unhealthy right about now?" He answered, "Yes Sir, but the goddamned wire has to be fixed." I asked, "Don't those planes strafing the road bother you?" And he answered, "No, Sir, but you sure as hell do!"

Now, there was a real man. A real soldier. There was a man who devoted all he had to his duty, no matter how seemingly insignificant his duty might appear at the time, no matter how great the odds. And you should have seen those trucks on the road to Tunisia. Those drivers were magnificent. All day and all night they rolled over those son-of-a-bitching roads, never stopping, never faltering from their course, with shells bursting all around them all of the time. We got through on good old American guts. Many of those men drove for over forty consecutive hours. These men weren't combat men, but they were soldiers with a job to do. They did it, and in one hell of a way they did it. They were part of a team. Without team effort, without them, the fight would have been lost. All of the links in the chain pulled together and the chain became unbreakable.

Remember, men, you men don't know that I'm here. No mention of that fact is to be made in any letters. The world is not supposed to know what the hell happened to me. I'm not supposed to be commanding this army. I'm not even supposed to be here in England. Let the first bastards to find out be the goddamned Germans. We want to get the hell over there, the quicker we clean up this mess, the quicker we can take a little jaunt against the purplepissing Japs and clean out their nest, too. Before the goddamned Marines get all of the credit.

Sure, we want to go home. We want this war over with. The quickest way to get it over with is to go get the bastards who started it. The quicker they are whipped, the quicker we can go home. The shortest way home is through Berlin and Tokyo. And when we get to Berlin, I am personally going to shoot that paper hanging son-of-a-bitch Hitler. Just like I'd shoot a snake!

When a man is lying in a shell hole, if he just stays there all day, a German will get to him eventually. The hell with that idea. The hell with taking it. My men don't dig foxholes. I don't want them to. Foxholes only slow up an offensive. Keep moving. And don't give the enemy time to dig one either. We'll win this war, but we'll win it only by fighting and by showing the Germans that we've got more guts than they have; or ever will have.

War is a bloody, killing business. You've got to spill their blood, or they will spill yours. Rip them up the belly. Shoot them in the guts. When shells are hitting all around you and you wipe the dirt off your face and realize that instead of dirt it's the blood and guts of what once was your best friend beside you, you'll know what to do!

I don't want to get any messages saying, "I am holding my position." We are not holding a goddamned thing. Let the Germans do that. We are advancing constantly and we are not interested in holding onto anything, except the enemy's balls. We are going to twist his balls and kick the living shit out of him all of the time. Our basic plan of operation is to advance and to keep on advancing regardless of whether we have to go over, under, or through the enemy.

From time to time there will be some complaints that we are pushing our people too hard. I don't give a good Goddamn about such complaints. I believe in the old and sound rule that an ounce of sweat will save a gallon of blood. The harder we push, the more Germans we will kill. The more Germans we kill, the fewer of our men will be killed. Pushing means fewer casualties. I want you all to remember that.

There is one great thing that you men will all be able to say after this war is over and you are home once again. You may be thankful that twenty years from now when you are sitting by the fireplace with your grandson on your knee and he asks you what you did in the great World War II, you won't have to cough, shift him to the other knee and say, "Well, your Granddaddy shoveled shit in Louisiana." No, Sir, you can look him straight in the eye and say, "Son, your Granddaddy rode with the Great Third Army and a Son-of-a-Goddamned-Bitch named George Patton."

That is all.

# General Dwight D. Eisenhower

## ORDERING THE NORMANDY INVASION, JUNE 6, 1944

*We will accept nothing less than full victory.*

Photograph taken November 19, 1947.

EVERY GENERATIONAL THREAT IN OUR HISTORY has been defeated by the fortitude of men and women willing to storm beaches, to take hills, to sweep across deserts. To soar into skies on planes and even drop from the skies with paratroops. To refuse the hindrance of any boundary in the pursuit of freedom.

The beaches of Normandy were indeed a formidable barrier for the Allied Expeditionary Forces. Today, the images of the June 6, 1944, invasion of Normandy remain fresh in our minds. Courageous soldiers plunging from landing crafts into cold, gray waters; struggling onto the beach against the fierce rain of German gunners; some dropping, others plodding forward. All in one of the most audacious invasions in military history, in the decisive Western European battle of World War II.

There were grave doubts among the planners of the invasion. In his D-day Order, Gen. Dwight Eisenhower sought to imbue his forces with the monumental confidence that would be required to control the human instinct for self-preservation. To keep moving toward danger, without looking back.

Here, in these brief words, Eisenhower gives voice to the eternal command that propelled men and women forward into grave danger despite great doubt. Here, Eisenhower orders: "Charge!"

---

SOLDIERS, SAILORS AND AIRMEN of the Allied Expeditionary Forces! You are about to embark upon the Great Crusade, toward which we have striven these many months. The eyes of the world are upon you. The hopes and prayers of liberty-loving people everywhere march with you. In company with our brave Allies and brothers-in-arms on other Fronts, you will bring about the destruction of the German war machine, the elimination of Nazi tyranny over oppressed peoples of Europe, and security for ourselves in a free world.

Your task will not be an easy one. Your enemy is well trained, well equipped and battle-hardened. He will fight savagely.

But this is the year 1944! Much has happened since the Nazi triumphs of 1940–41. The United Nations have inflicted upon the Germans great defeats, in open battle, man-to-man. Our air offensive has seriously reduced their strength in the air and their capacity to wage war on the ground. Our Home Fronts have given us an overwhelming superiority in weapons and munitions of war, and placed at our disposal great reserves of trained fighting men. The tide has turned! The free men of the world are marching together to victory!

I have full confidence in your courage, devotion to duty, and skill in battle. We will accept nothing less than full victory.

Good Luck! And let us all beseech the blessing of Almighty God upon this great and noble undertaking.

# PART 4

# BEAR ANY BURDEN

*Let every nation know, whether it wishes us well or ill,
that we shall pay any price, bear any burden, meet any hardship,
support any friend, oppose any foe to assure the survival
and the success of liberty.*

—JOHN F. KENNEDY, 1961

# Harry S. Truman

## CALLING AMERICA TO THE COLD WAR,
## MARCH 12, 1947

*The free peoples of the world look to us for support in maintaining their freedoms.*
*If we falter in our leadership, we may endanger the peace of the world.*
*And we shall surely endanger the welfare of this nation.*

Photograph taken November 1945.

THE TRAUMA OF WORLD WAR II was still fresh, the wounds un-healed, when Harry Truman stepped into the well of the House of Representatives and summoned the American people to a new challenge: the Cold War. The Truman Doctrine—announced to a Joint Session of Congress on March 12, 1947—may have been precipitated by a communist insurgency in Greece and potential instability in Turkey. Yet, it was the basis for a generational commitment against totalitarianism and oppression.

Truman outlines in detail the risks of instability in Greece, Turkey, and elsewhere, and he reminds Congress of a condition that continues to plague us sixty years later. "The seeds of totalitarian regimes are nurtured by misery and want. They spread and grow in the evil soil of poverty and strife. They reach their full growth when the hope of a people for a better life has died. We must keep that hope alive."

As a Truman Democrat—one who believes in the use of both hard and soft power to protect our vital interests—I think often of Truman's words as well as actions when I am on the floor of the House. Soon after his speech, Truman announced the Marshal Plan, organized NATO, and supported a robust and effective United Nations. Today, we face new generational threats that require the same organizing principles articulated by Harry Truman. For me, his words are a rallying cry.

Here is the closing excerpt of President Truman's speech to the House—words as relevant and necessary in meeting today's challenges as they were sixty years ago.

———•◦•———

ONE OF THE PRIMARY OBJECTIVES of the foreign policy of the United States is the creation of conditions in which we and other nations will be able to work out a way of life free from coercion. This was a fundamental issue in the war with Germany and Japan. Our victory was won over countries which sought to impose their will, and their way of life, upon other nations.

To ensure the peaceful development of nations, free from coercion, the United States has taken a leading part in establishing the United Nations. The United Nations is designed to make possible lasting freedom and independence for all its members. We shall not realize our objectives, however, unless we are willing to help free peoples to maintain their free institutions and their national integrity against aggressive movements that seek to impose upon them totalitarian regimes. This is no more than a frank recognition that totalitarian regimes imposed upon free peoples, by direct or indirect aggression, undermine the foundations of international peace, and hence the security of the United States.

The peoples of a number of countries of the world have recently had totalitarian regimes forced upon them against their will. The Government of the United States has made frequent protests against coercion and intimidation in violation of the Yalta agreement in Poland, Rumania, and Bulgaria. I must also state that in a number of other countries there have been similar developments.

At the present moment in world history nearly every nation must choose between alternative ways of life. The choice is too often not a free one. One way of life is based upon the will of the majority, and is distinguished by free institutions, representative government, free elections, guarantees of individual liberty, freedom of speech and religion, and freedom from political oppression. The second way of life is based upon the will of a minority forcibly imposed upon the majority. It relies upon terror and oppression, a controlled press and radio, fixed elections, and the suppression of personal freedoms.

I believe that it must be the policy of the United States to support free peoples who are resisting attempted subjugation by armed minorities or by outside pressures.

I believe that we must assist free peoples to work out their own destinies in their own way.

I believe that our help should be primarily through economic and financial aid which is essential to economic stability and orderly political processes.

The world is not static, and the status quo is not sacred. But we cannot allow changes in the status quo in violation of the Charter of the United Nations by such methods as coercion, or by such subterfuges as political infiltration. In helping free and independent nations to maintain their freedom, the United States will be giving effect to the principles of the Charter of the United Nations.

It is necessary only to glance at a map to realize that the survival and integrity of the Greek nation are of grave importance in a much wider situation. If Greece should fall under the control of an armed minority, the effect upon its neighbor, Turkey, would be immediate and serious. Confusion and disorder might well spread throughout the entire Middle East. Moreover, the disappearance of Greece as an independent state would have a profound effect upon those countries in Europe whose peoples are struggling against great difficulties to maintain their freedoms and their independence while they repair the damages of war.

It would be an unspeakable tragedy if these countries, which have struggled so long against overwhelming odds, should lose that victory for which they sacrificed so much. Collapse of free institutions and loss of independence would be disastrous not only for them but for the world. Discouragement and possibly failure would quickly be the lot of neighboring peoples striving to maintain their freedom and independence.

Should we fail to aid Greece and Turkey in this fateful hour, the effect will be far-reaching to the West as well as to the East.

We must take immediate and resolute action. I therefore ask the Congress to provide authority for assistance to Greece and Turkey in the amount of four hundred million dollars for the period ending June 30, 1948. In requesting these funds, I have taken into consideration the maximum amount of relief assistance which would be furnished to Greece out of the three hundred million dollars which I recently requested that the Congress authorize for the prevention of starvation and suffering in countries devastated by the war.

In addition to funds, I ask the Congress to authorize the detail of American civilian and military personnel to Greece and Turkey, at the request of those countries, to assist in the tasks of reconstruction, and for the purpose of supervising the use of such financial and material assistance as may be furnished. I recommend that authority also be provided for the instruction and training of selected Greek and Turkish personnel. Finally, I ask that the Congress provide authority which will permit the speediest and most effective use, in terms of needed commodities, supplies, and equipment, of such funds as may be authorized. If further funds, or further authority, should be needed for the purposes indicated in this message, I shall not hesitate to bring the situation before the Congress. On this subject the Executive and Legislative branches of the Government must work together.

This is a serious course upon which we embark. I would not recommend it except that the alternative is much more serious. The United States contributed three hundred forty one billion dollars toward winning World War II. This is an investment in world freedom and world peace. The assistance that I am recommending for Greece and Turkey amounts to little more than one-tenth of one percent of this investment. It is only common sense that we should safeguard this investment and make sure that it was not in vain. The seeds of totalitarian regimes are nurtured by misery and want. They spread and grow in the evil soil of poverty and strife. They reach their full growth when the hope of a people for a better life has died.

We must keep that hope alive.

The free peoples of the world look to us for support in maintaining their freedoms. If we falter in our leadership, we may endanger the peace of the world. And we shall surely endanger the welfare of this nation.

Great responsibilities have been placed upon us by the swift movement of events.

I am confident that the Congress will face these responsibilities squarely.

# Menachem Begin

## Preparing Israel for an Arab Attack, May 14, 1948

*We shall go on our way into battle....*
*And we shall be accompanied by the spirit of millions of our martyrs,*
*our ancestors tortured and burned for their faith, our murdered fathers*
*and butchered mothers, our murdered brothers and strangled children.*
*And in this battle we shall break the enemy and bring salvation to our people,*
*tried in the furnace of persecution, thirsting only for freedom,*
*for righteousness, and for justice.*

Photograph from 1978.

THE HORRORS OF THE HOLOCAUST still lingered in November 1947, when the United Nations passed a partition plan creating a Jewish State as well as a new, autonomous Arab State. While the plan was rejected by Arab nations, Israel proclaimed its statehood on May 14, 1948. That very night, the new nation faced an imminent threat. Arab armies massed against an untested and numerically inferior Israeli military. It seemed to many that the Jewish State would be extinguished in its very first days. In that climate, Menachem Begin—who had led the underground resistance group Irgun—took to the radio. He helped unify Israel by announcing that Irgun would no longer operate underground and would respect the rule of law in the new Israeli State. And he rallied the Israeli people to prepare to resist the overwhelming Arab military power gathering at their new borders.

After assessing the severity of threat and exhorting people to arms, the Polish-born Holocaust survivor speaks in terms evocative of Winston Churchill: "But in addition to these arms, each and every one of us has need of another weapon, a spiritual weapon, the weapon of unflinching endurance in face of attacks from the air; in face of grievous casualties; in face of local disasters and temporary defeats; unflinching resistance to threats and cajolery."

Begin weaves his speech with references to the battles Jews had fought to secure the Promised Land throughout their painful history. Reaching his crescendo, Begin evokes the words of Moses, who thousands of years before prepared the Jewish people to battle in that very place: "Be brave of spirit and ready for more trials. We shall withstand them. The Lord of Hosts will help us; he will sustain the bravery of the Hebrew youth, the bravery of the Hebrew mothers who, like Hannah, offer their sons on the altar of God."

Against superior numbers, the Israeli military held their ground, saved their State, and thirty years later, Menachem Begin became prime minister of Israel.

━━━━◆━━━━

AFTER MANY YEARS of underground warfare, years of persecution and moral and physical suffering, the rebels against the oppressor stand before you, with a blessing of thanks on their lips and a prayer in their hearts. The blessing is the age-old blessing with which our fathers and our forefathers have always greeted holy days. It was with this blessing that they used to taste any fruit for the first time in the season. Today is truly a holiday, a holy day, and a new fruit is visible before our very eyes. The Hebrew revolt of 1944–48 has been blessed with success—the first Hebrew revolt since the Hasmonean insurrection that has ended in victory. The rule of oppression in our country has been beaten, uprooted; it has crumbled and been dispersed. The state of Israel has arisen in bloody battle. The highway for the mass return to Zion has been cast up.

The foundation has been laid—but only the foundation—for true independence. One phase of the battle for freedom, for the return of the whole people of Israel to its homeland, for the restoration of the whole land of Israel to its God-covenanted owners, has ended. But only one phase.

The state of Israel has arisen. And it has arisen "Only Thus"; through blood, through fire, with an outstretched hand and a mighty arm, with sufferings and with sacrifices. It could not have been otherwise. And yet, even before our state is able to set up its normal national institutions, it is compelled to fight—or to continue to fight satanic enemies and bloodthirsty mercenaries, on land, in the air, and on the sea. In these circumstances, the warning sounded by the philosopher-president Thomáš Masaryk to the Czechoslovak nation when it attained its freedom, after three hundred years of slavery, has a special significance for us.

In 1918, when Masaryk stepped out into the Wilson railway station in Prague, he warned his cheering countrymen, "It is difficult to set up a state; it is even more difficult to keep it going." In truth, it has been difficult for us to set up our state. Tens of generations, and millions of wanderers, from one land of massacre to another, were needed; it was necessary that there be exile, burning at the stake and torture in the dungeons; we had to suffer agonizing disillusionments; we needed the warnings—though they often went unheeded—of prophets and of seers; we needed the sweat and toil of generations of pioneers and builders; we had to have an uprising of rebels to crush the enemy; we had to have the gallows, the banishments beyond seas, the prisons, and the cages in the deserts—all this was necessary that we might reach the present stage where six hundred thousand Jews are in the homeland, where the direct rule of oppression has been driven out, and Hebrew independence declared in part at least of the country, the whole of which is ours.

It has been difficult to create our state. But it will be still more difficult to keep it going. We are surrounded by enemies who long for our destruction. And that same oppressor, who has been defeated by us directly, is trying indirectly to make us surrender with the aid of mercenaries from the south, the north, and the east. Our one-day-old state is set up in the midst of the flames of battle. And the first pillar of our state must therefore be victory, total victory, in the war which is raging all over the country. For this victory, without which we shall have neither freedom nor life, we need arms—weapons of all sorts, in order to strike the enemies, in order to disperse the invaders, in order to free the entire length and breadth of the country from its would-be destroyers.

But in addition to these arms, each and every one of us has need of another weapon, a spiritual weapon, the weapon of unflinching endurance in the face of attacks from the air; in the face of grievous casualties; in the face of local disasters and temporary defeats; unflinching resistance to threats and cajolery.

If, within the coming days and weeks, we can put on this whole armor of an undying nation in resurrection, we shall in the meantime receive the blessed arms with which to drive off the enemy and bring freedom and peace to our nation and country.

But, even after emerging victorious from this campaign—and victorious we shall be—we shall still have to exert superhuman efforts in order to remain independent, in order to free our country. First of all it will be necessary to increase and strengthen the fighting arm of Israel, without which there can be no freedom and no survival for our homeland.

We shall need a wise foreign policy in order to free our country and maintain our state. We must turn our declaration of independence into a reality. And we must grasp this fact: that so long as even one British or any other foreign soldier treads the soil of our country, our sovereign independence remains nothing but an aspiration, an aspiration for whose fulfillment we must be ready to fight not only on the battlefront but also in the international arena. Secondly, we must establish and maintain the principle of reciprocity in our relations with the nations of the world. There must be no self-denigration. There must be no surrender, and no favoritism. There must be reciprocity. Enmity for enmity. Aid for aid. Friendship must be repaid with friendship.

We must foster friendship and understanding between us and every nation, great or small, strong or weak, near or far, which recognizes our independence, which aids our national regeneration, and which is interested, even as we are, in international justice and peace among nations.

Of no less importance is our internal policy. The first pillar of this policy is the return to Zion. Ships! For heaven's sake, let us have ships! Let us not be poisoned with inertia. Let us not talk empty words about absorptive capacity. Let us not make restrictions for the sake of so-called order. Quickly! Quickly! Our nation has no time! Bring in hundreds of thousands. We are now in the midst of a war of survival; and our tomorrow and theirs depends on the quickest concentration of our nation's exiles.

And within our homeland: justice must be the supreme ruler, the ruler over all rulers. There must be no tyranny. The ministers and officials must be the servants of the nation and not their masters. There must be no exploitation. There must be no man within our country—be he citizen or foreigner—compelled to go hungry, to want for a roof over his head, or to lack elementary education. "Remember, ye were strangers in the land of Egypt"—this supreme rule must continually light our way in our relations with the strangers within our gates. "Righteousness, Righteousness shalt thou pursue!" Righteousness must be the guiding principle in our relations amongst ourselves.

The Irgun Zvai Leumi is leaving the underground inside the boundaries of the Hebrew independent state. We went underground, we arose in the underground under the rule of oppression, in order to strike at oppression to overthrow it. And right well have we struck. Now, for the time being, we have Hebrew rule in part of our homeland. And as in this part there will be Hebrew law—and that is the only rightful law in this country—there is no need for a Hebrew underground. In the state of Israel we shall be soldiers and builders. And we shall respect its government, for it is our government.

The state of Israel has arisen, but we must remember that our country is not yet liberated. The battle continues, and you see now that the words of your Irgun fighters were not vain words: it is Hebrew arms which decide the boundaries of the Hebrew state. So it is now in this battle; so it will be in the future. Our God-given country is a unity. The attempt to dissect it is not only a crime but a blasphemy and an abortion. Whoever does not recognize our natural right to our entire homeland, does not recognize our right to any part of it. And we shall never forgo this natural right. We shall continue to foster the aspiration of full independence.

Citizens of the Hebrew state, soldiers of Israel, we are in the midst of battles. Difficult days lie ahead of us. We cannot buy peace from our enemies with appeasement. There is only one kind of peace that can be bought—the peace of the graveyard, the peace of Treblinka. Be brave of spirit and ready for more trials. We shall withstand them. The Lord of Hosts will help us; he will sustain the bravery of the Hebrew youth, the bravery of the Hebrew mothers who, like Hannah, offer their sons on the altar of God.

And you, brothers of our fighting family, do you remember how we started? With what we started? You were alone and persecuted, rejected, despised, and numbered with the transgressors. But you fought on with deep faith and did not retreat; you were tortured but you did not surrender; you were cast into prison but you did not yield; you were exiled from your country but your spirit was not crushed; you were driven to the gallows but went forth with a song. You have written a glorious page in history. You will not recall past grievances; you will ask for no reward.

But for the time being let us think of the battle, for only the outcome of the battle will decide our faith and future. We shall go on our way into battle, soldiers of the Lord of Hosts, inspired by the spirit of our ancient heroes, from the conquerors of Canaan to the Rebels of Judah. We shall be accompanied by the spirit of those who revived our nation. Zeev Benjamin Herzi, Max Nordau, Joseph Trumpeldor, and the father of resurrected Hebrew heroism, Zeev Jabotinsky. We shall be accompanied by the spirit of David Raziel, greatest of the Hebrew commanders of our day; and by Dov Gruner, one of the greatest of Hebrew soldiers. We shall be accompanied into battle by the spirit of the heroes of the gallows, the conquerors of death. And we shall be accompanied by the spirit of millions of our martyrs, our ancestors tortured and burned for their faith, our murdered fathers and butchered mothers, our murdered brothers and strangled children. And in this battle we shall break the enemy and bring salvation to our people, tried in the furnace of persecution, thirsting only for freedom, for righteousness, and for justice.

# John F. Kennedy

## WHAT YOU CAN DO FOR YOUR COUNTRY, JANUARY 20, 1961

*Let every nation know,*
*whether it wishes us well or ill,*
*that we shall pay any price, bear any burden,*
*meet any hardship,*
*support any friend, oppose any foe*
*to assure the survival and the success of liberty.*

Photograph by Fabian Bachrach, 1961.

THE COLD WAR RAGED. Proxy battles threatened to flare around the world. At home, the American consciousness was just beginning to grasp the injustice of segregation and the devastation of poverty. And on a bitterly cold day in January 1961, the new president of the United States roused his nation to accept these burdens.

Kennedy's inaugural address is best known for the proclamation: "And so, my fellow Americans: ask not what your country can do for you—ask what you can do for your country." But the speech in its entirety is a forceful, elegant appeal for Americans to enlist in battling all forms of evil. Less than twenty years after the end of World War II, Kennedy declared, "Now the trumpet summons us again, not as a call to bear arms, though arms we need—not as a call to battle, though embattled we are—but a call to bear the burden of a long twilight struggle, year in and year out, 'rejoicing in hope, patient in tribulation'—a struggle against the common enemies of man: tyranny, poverty, disease and war itself."

Just before reciting the more famous words from his inaugural, Kennedy inspired Americans by reminding them of their special place: "In the long history of the world, only a few generations have been granted the role of defending freedom in its hour of maximum danger. I do not shrink from this responsibility—I welcome it. I do not believe that any of us would exchange places with any other people or any other generation. The energy, the faith, the devotion which we bring to this endeavor will light our country and all who serve it—and the glow from that fire can truly light the world."

---

VICE PRESIDENT JOHNSON, MR. SPEAKER, MR. CHIEF JUSTICE, PRESIDENT EISENHOWER, VICE PRESIDENT NIXON, PRESIDENT TRUMAN, REVEREND CLERGY, FELLOW CITIZENS:

We observe today not a victory of party but a celebration of freedom—symbolizing an end as well as a beginning—signifying renewal as well as change. For I have sworn before you and Almighty God the same solemn oath our forebears prescribed nearly a century and three quarters ago.

The world is very different now. For man holds in his mortal hands the power to abolish all forms of human poverty and all forms of human life. And yet the same revolutionary beliefs for which our forebears fought are still at issue around the globe—the belief that the rights of man come not from the generosity of the state but from the hand of God.

We dare not forget today that we are the heirs of that first revolution. Let the word go forth from this time and place, to friend and foe alike, that the torch has been passed to a new generation of Americans—born in this century, tempered by war, disciplined by a hard and bitter peace, proud of our ancient heritage—and unwilling to witness or permit the slow undoing of those human rights to which this nation has always been committed, and to which we are committed today at home and around the world.

Let every nation know, whether it wishes us well or ill, that we shall pay any price, bear any burden, meet any hardship, support any friend, oppose any foe to assure the survival and the success of liberty.

This much we pledge—and more.

To those old allies whose cultural and spiritual origins we share, we pledge the loyalty of faithful friends. United, there is little we cannot do in a host of cooperative ventures. Divided, there is little we can do—for we dare not meet a powerful challenge at odds and split asunder.

To those new states whom we welcome to the ranks of the free, we pledge our word that one form of colonial control shall not have passed away merely to be replaced by a far more iron tyranny. We shall not always expect to find them supporting our view. But we shall always hope to find them strongly supporting their own freedom—and to remember that, in the past, those who foolishly sought power by riding the back of the tiger ended up inside.

To those peoples in the huts and villages of half the globe struggling to break the bonds of mass misery, we pledge our best efforts to help them help themselves, for whatever period is required—not because the communists may be doing it, not because we seek their votes, but because it is right. If a free society cannot help the many who are poor, it cannot save the few who are rich.

To our sister republics south of our border, we offer a special pledge—to convert our good words into good deeds—in a new alliance for progress—to assist free men and free governments in casting off the chains of poverty. But this peaceful revolution of hope cannot become the prey of hostile powers. Let all our neighbors know that we shall join with them to oppose aggression or subversion anywhere in the Americas. And let every other power know that this Hemisphere intends to remain the master of its own house.

To that world assembly of sovereign states, the United Nations, our last best hope in an age where the instruments of war have far outpaced the instruments of peace, we renew our pledge of support—to prevent it from becoming merely a forum for invective—to strengthen its shield of the new and the weak—and to enlarge the area in which its writ may run.

Finally, to those nations who would make themselves our adversary, we offer not a pledge but a request: that both sides begin anew the quest for peace, before the dark powers of destruction unleashed by science engulf all humanity in planned or accidental self-destruction.

We dare not tempt them with weakness. For only when our arms are sufficient beyond doubt can we be certain beyond doubt that they will never be employed.

But neither can two great and powerful groups of nations take comfort from our present course—both sides overburdened by the cost of modern weapons, both rightly alarmed by the steady spread of the deadly atom, yet both racing to alter that uncertain balance of terror that stays the hand of mankind's final war.

So let us begin anew—remembering on both sides that civility is not a sign of weakness, and sincerity is always subject to proof. Let us never negotiate out of fear. But let us never fear to negotiate.

Let both sides explore what problems unite us instead of belaboring those problems which divide us.

Let both sides, for the first time, formulate serious and precise proposals for the inspection and control of arms—and bring the absolute power to destroy other nations under the absolute control of all nations.

Let both sides seek to invoke the wonders of science instead of its terrors. Together let us explore the stars, conquer the deserts, eradicate disease, tap the ocean depths and encourage the arts and commerce.

Let both sides unite to heed in all corners of the earth the command of Isaiah—to "undo the heavy burdens (and) let the oppressed go free."

And if a beachhead of cooperation may push back the jungle of suspicion, let both sides join in creating a new endeavor, not a new balance of power, but a new world of law, where the strong are just and the weak secure and the peace preserved.

All this will not be finished in the first one hundred days. Nor will it be finished in the first one thousand days, nor in the life of this Administration, nor even perhaps in our lifetime on this planet. But let us begin.

In your hands, my fellow citizens, more than mine, will rest the final success or failure of our course. Since this country was founded, each generation of Americans has been summoned to give testimony to its national loyalty. The graves of young Americans who answered the call to service surround the globe.

Now the trumpet summons us again—not as a call to bear arms, though arms we need—not as a call to battle, though embattled we are—but a call to bear the burden of a long twilight struggle, year in and year out, "rejoicing in hope, patient in tribulation"—a struggle against the common enemies of man: tyranny, poverty, disease and war itself.

Can we forge against these enemies a grand and global alliance, North and South, East and West, that can assure a more fruitful life for all mankind? Will you join in that historic effort?

In the long history of the world, only a few generations have been granted the role of defending freedom in its hour of maximum danger. I do not shrink from this responsibility—I welcome it. I do not believe that any of us would exchange places with any other people or any other generation. The energy, the faith, the devotion which we bring to this endeavor will light our country and all who serve it—and the glow from that fire can truly light the world.

And so, my fellow Americans: ask not what your country can do for you— ask what you can do for your country.

My fellow citizens of the world: ask not what America will do for you, but what together we can do for the freedom of man.

Finally, whether you are citizens of America or citizens of the world, ask of us here the same high standards of strength and sacrifice which we ask of you. With a good conscience our only sure reward, with history the final judge of our deeds, let us go forth to lead the land we love, asking His blessing and His help, but knowing that here on earth God's work must truly be our own.

# General Douglas MacArthur

## DUTY, HONOR, COUNTRY,
## MAY 12, 1962

*I do not know the dignity of their birth,*
*but I do know the glory of their death.*
*They died unquestioning, uncomplaining, with faith in their hearts,*
*and on their lips the hope that we would go on to victory.*

General MacArthur surveying the beachhead on Leyte Island, 1944.

G EN. DOUGLAS MACARTHUR'S SPEECH to the cadets of West
Point may not answer the question "why do we fight." However, it
profoundly describes "who we are."

An army devoid of values is simply a killing machine. Great armies are not
known for their firepower, but for their willpower. Not for their hardware, but
for their software—the qualities of character, leadership, ingenuity. It is not difficult to follow an operating manual on how to fire a weapon in battle. The real
achievement is fighting with the ingrained qualities of "duty, honor, country."

Nearly twenty four hundred years earlier, at a funeral for fallen soldiers,
Pericles declared: "In the fighting, they thought it more honorable to stand
their ground and suffer death than to give in and save their lives."

Here, MacArthur proclaims: "I do not know the dignity of their birth, but
I do know the glory of their death."

GENERAL WESTMORELAND, GENERAL GROVE, DISTINGUISHED GUESTS,
AND GENTLEMEN OF THE CORPS!

As I was leaving the hotel this morning, a doorman asked me, "Where are
you bound for, General?" And when I replied, "West Point," he remarked,
"Beautiful place. Have you ever been there before?"

No human being could fail to be deeply moved by such a tribute as this.
Coming from a profession I have served so long, and a people I have loved so
well, it fills me with an emotion I cannot express. But this award is not intended primarily to honor a personality, but to symbolize a great moral code—the
code of conduct and chivalry of those who guard this beloved land of culture
and ancient descent. That is the animation of this medallion. For all eyes and
for all time, it is an expression of the ethics of the American soldier. That I
should be integrated in this way with so noble an ideal arouses a sense of pride
and yet of humility which will be with me always.

Duty-Honor-Country. Those three hallowed words reverently dictate
what you ought to be, what you can be, what you will be. They are your rallying points: to build courage when courage seems to fail; to regain faith when
there seems to be little cause for faith; to create hope when hope becomes
forlorn. Unhappily, I possess neither that eloquence of diction, that poetry
of imagination, nor that brilliance of metaphor to tell you all that they mean.
The unbelievers will say they are but words, but a slogan, but a flamboyant
phrase. Every pedant, every demagogue, every cynic, every hypocrite, every
troublemaker, and I am sorry to say, some others of an entirely different character, will try to downgrade them even to the extent of mockery and ridicule.

But these are some of the things they do. They build your basic character. They mold you for your future roles as the custodians of the nation's defense. They make you strong enough to know when you are weak, and brave enough to face yourself when you are afraid. They teach you to be proud and unbending in honest failure, but humble and gentle in success; not to substitute words for actions, not to seek the path of comfort, but to face the stress and spur of difficulty and challenge; to learn to stand up in the storm but to have compassion on those who fall; to master yourself before you seek to master others; to have a heart that is clean, a goal that is high; to learn to laugh, yet never forget how to weep; to reach into the future yet never neglect the past; to be serious yet never to take yourself too seriously; to be modest so that you will remember the simplicity of true greatness, the open mind of true wisdom, the meekness of true strength. They give you a temper of the will, a quality of the imagination, a vigor of the emotions, a freshness of the deep springs of life, a temperamental predominance of courage over timidity, of an appetite for adventure over love of ease. They create in your heart the sense of wonder, the unfailing hope of what next, and the joy and inspiration of life. They teach you in this way to be an officer and a gentleman.

And what sort of soldiers are those you are to lead? Are they reliable? Are they brave? Are they capable of victory? Their story is known to all of you. It is the story of the American man-at-arms. My estimate of him was formed on the battlefield many, many years ago, and has never changed. I regarded him then as I regard him now—as one of the world's noblest figures, not only as one of the finest military characters, but also as one of the most stainless. His name and fame are the birthright of every American citizen. In his youth and strength, his love and loyalty, he gave all that mortality can give. He needs no eulogy from me or from any other man. He has written his own history and written it in red on his enemy's breast. But when I think of his patience under adversity, of his courage under fire, and of his modesty in victory, I am filled with an emotion of admiration I cannot put into words. He belongs to history as furnishing one of the greatest examples of successful patriotism. He belongs to posterity as the instructor of future generations in the principles of liberty and freedom. He belongs to the present, to us, by his virtues and by his achievements. In twenty campaigns, on a hundred battlefields, around a thousand campfires, I have witnessed that enduring fortitude, that patriotic self-abnegation, and that invincible determination which have carved his statue in the hearts of his people. From one end of the world to the other he has drained deep the chalice of courage.

As I listened to those songs in memory's eye I could see those staggering columns of the First World War, bending under soggy packs, on many a weary march from dripping dusk to drizzling dawn, slogging ankle-deep through the mire of shell-shocked roads, to form grimly for the attack, blue-lipped, covered with sludge and mud, chilled by the wind and rain, driving home to their objective, and for many, to the judgment seat of God. I do not know the dignity of their birth, but I do know the glory of their death. They died unquestioning, uncomplaining, with faith in their hearts, and on their lips the hope that we would go on to victory.

And 20 years after, on the other side of the globe, again the filth of murky foxholes, the stench of ghostly trenches, the slime of dripping dugouts; those boiling suns of relentless heat, those torrential rains of devastating storms; the loneliness and utter desolation of jungle trails; the bitterness of long separation from those they loved and cherished; the deadly pestilence of tropical disease; the horror of stricken areas of war; their resolute and determined defense, their swift and sure attack, their indomitable purpose, their complete and decisive victory—always victory. Always through the bloody haze of their last reverberating shot, the vision of gaunt, ghastly men reverently following your password of Duty-Honor-Country.

The code which those words perpetuate embraces the highest moral laws and will stand the test of any ethics or philosophies ever promulgated for the uplift of mankind. Its requirements are for the things that are right, and its restraints are from the things that are wrong.

The soldier, above all other men, is required to practice the greatest act of religious training—sacrifice. In battle and in the face of danger and death, he discloses those divine attributes which his Maker gave when he created man in his own image. No physical courage and no brute instinct can take the place of the Divine help which alone can sustain him. However horrible the incidents of war may be, the soldier who is called upon to offer and to give his life for his country is the noblest development of mankind.

You now face a new world—a world of change. The thrust into outer space of the satellite, spheres, and missiles mark the beginning of another epoch in the long story of mankind. In the five or more billions of years the scientists tell us it has taken to form the earth, in the three or more billion years of development of the human race, there has never been a more abrupt or staggering evolution. We deal now not with things of this world alone, but with the illimitable distances and as yet unfathomed mysteries of the universe. We are reaching out for a new and boundless frontier. We speak in strange terms: of harnessing the cosmic energy; of making winds and tides work for us; of creating unheard synthetic materials to supplement or even replace our old standard basics; to purify sea water for our drink; of mining ocean floors for new fields of wealth and food; of disease preventatives to expand life into the hundreds of years; of controlling the weather for a more equitable distribution of heat and cold, of rain and shine; of space ships to the moon; of the primary target in war, no longer limited to the armed forces of an enemy, but instead to include his civil populations; of ultimate conflict between a united human race and the sinister forces of some other planetary galaxy; of such dreams and fantasies as to make life the most exciting of all time.

And through all this welter of change and development, your mission remains fixed, determined, inviolable: it is to win our wars. Everything else in your professional career is but corollary to this vital dedication. All other public purposes, all other public projects, all other public needs, great or small, will find others for their accomplishment. But you are the ones who are trained to fight. Yours is the profession of arms, the will to win, the sure knowledge that in war there is no substitute for victory; that if you lose, the nation will be destroyed; that the very obsession of your public service must be Duty-Honor-Country. Others will debate the controversial issues, national and international, which divide men's minds; but serene, calm, aloof, you stand as the Nation's war-guardian, as its lifeguard from the raging tides of international conflict, as its gladiator in the arena of battle. For a century and a half you have defended, guarded, and protected its hallowed traditions of liberty and freedom, of right and justice. Let civilian voices argue the merits or demerits of our processes of government; whether our strength is being sapped by deficit financing, indulged in too long, by federal paternalism grown too mighty, by power groups grown too arrogant, by politics grown too corrupt, by crime grown too rampant, by morals grown too low, by taxes grown too high, by extremists grown too violent; whether our personal liberties are as thorough and complete as they should be. These great national problems are not for your professional participation or military solution. Your guidepost stands out like a ten-fold beacon in the night Duty-Honor-Country.

You are the leaven which binds together the entire fabric of our national system of defense. From your ranks come the great captains who hold the nation's destiny in their hands the moment the war tocsin sounds. The Long Gray Line has never failed us. Were you to do so, a million ghosts in olive drab, in brown khaki, in blue and gray, would rise from their white crosses thundering those magic words Duty-Honor-Country.

This does not mean that you are warmongers. On the contrary, the soldier, above all other people, prays for peace, for he must suffer and bear the deepest wounds and scars of war. But always in our ears ring the ominous words of Plato, that wisest of all philosophers: "Only the dead have seen the end of war."

The shadows are lengthening for me. The twilight is here. My days of old have vanished, tone and tint. They have gone glimmering through the dreams of things that were. Their memory is one of wondrous beauty, watered by tears, and coaxed and caressed by the smiles of yesterday. I listen vainly, but with thirsty ears, for the witching melody of faint bugles blowing reveille, of far drums beating the long roll. In my dreams I hear again the crash of guns, the rattle of musketry, the strange, mournful mutter of the battlefield.

But in the evening of my memory, always I come back to West Point. Always there echoes and re-echoes Duty-Honor-Country.

Today marks my final roll call with you, but I want you to know that when I cross the river my last conscious thoughts will be of The Corps, and The Corps, and The Corps. I bid you farewell.

# John F. Kennedy

## CHALLENGING AMERICA TO REACH THE MOON,
## SEPTEMBER 12, 1962

*We choose to go to the moon in this decade and do the other things,
not because they are easy, but because they are hard.*

President Kennedy in the Oval Office, 1963.

LTHOUGH THIS IS NOT A MILITARY SPEECH, I include it because it mobilized our nation to commit ourselves to conquer the most implacable foe: the great expanse of Space. In 1962, President John F. Kennedy looked at the moon and commanded: "Charge!"

A generation earlier, FDR had summoned Americans into World War II, demanding that we mobilize and manufacture, research and develop, serve, sacrifice, and build. We stormed Normandy, leapt over hills, ran through France, freed France; raced through Europe, liberated concentration camps, freed Europe; raced to the Pacific and defeated fascism. Then, we came home, peered at the moon and said, "We can go there too."

Yet, we experienced an early setback. In 1957 the Soviets leapfrogged us in the Space Race by launching Sputnik. An early battle of the Cold War— primacy above the earth—was lost. Five years later, John F. Kennedy visited Rice University in Houston and challenged America to enlist in the battle— announcing that we would land Americans on the moon within eight years.

The task seemed prohibitive. But this speech inspired the American people to put their doubts aside. It did not minimize the difficulty involved in achieving triumph: "We choose to go to the moon in this decade and do the other things, not because they are easy, but because they are hard, because that goal will serve to organize and measure the best of our energies and skills, because that challenge is one that we are willing to accept, one we are unwilling to postpone, and one which we intend to win, and the others, too."

The battle for the moon required transforming our economy, marshalling the resources of millions of people, and mobilizing men and women with the sheer courage to venture into the unknown. The battle required that we defeat two enemies: the physical barrier imposed by gravity, and the intellectual gravity we impose on ourselves. Only by unleashing the second were we able to break through the first. And it was this speech by John F. Kennedy that truly ignited a nation:

———•◦•———

PRESIDENT PITZER, MR. VICE PRESIDENT, GOVERNOR, CONGRESSMAN THOMAS, SENATOR WILEY, AND CONGRESSMAN MILLER, MR. WEBB, MR. BELL, SCIENTISTS, DISTINGUISHED GUESTS, AND LADIES AND GENTLEMEN:

I appreciate your president having made me an honorary visiting professor, and I will assure you that my first lecture will be very brief.

I am delighted to be here and I'm particularly delighted to be here on this occasion.

We meet at a college noted for knowledge, in a city noted for progress, in a State noted for strength, and we stand in need of all three, for we meet in an hour of change and challenge, in a decade of hope and fear, in an age of both knowledge and ignorance. The greater our knowledge increases, the greater our ignorance unfolds.

Despite the striking fact that most of the scientists that the world has ever known are alive and working today, despite the fact that this Nation's own scientific manpower is doubling every 12 years in a rate of growth more than three times that of our population as a whole, despite that, the vast stretches of the unknown and the unanswered and the unfinished still far outstrip our collective comprehension.

No man can fully grasp how far and how fast we have come, but condense, if you will, the 50,000 years of man's recorded history in a time span of but a half century. Stated in these terms, we know very little about the first 40 years, except at the end of them advanced man had learned to use the skins of animals to cover them. Then about 10 years ago, under this standard, man emerged from his caves to construct other kinds of shelter. Only five years ago man learned to write and use a cart with wheels. Christianity began less than two years ago. The printing press came this year, and then less than two months ago, during this whole 50-year span of human history, the steam engine provided a new source of power.

Newton explored the meaning of gravity. Last month electric lights and telephones and automobiles and airplanes became available. Only last week did we develop penicillin and television and nuclear power, and now if America's new spacecraft succeeds in reaching Venus, we will have literally reached the stars before midnight tonight.

This is a breathtaking pace, and such a pace cannot help but create new ills as it dispels old, new ignorance, new problems, new dangers. Surely the opening vistas of space promise high costs and hardships, as well as high reward.

So it is not surprising that some would have us stay where we are a little longer to rest, to wait. But this city of Houston, this State of Texas, this country of the United States was not built by those who waited and rested and wished to look behind them. This country was conquered by those who moved forward—and so will space.

William Bradford, speaking in 1630 of the founding of the Plymouth Bay Colony, said that all great and honorable actions are accompanied with great difficulties, and both must be enterprised and overcome with answerable courage.

If this capsule history of our progress teaches us anything, it is that man, in his quest for knowledge and progress, is determined and cannot be deterred. The exploration of space will go ahead, whether we join in it or not, and it is one of the great adventures of all time, and no nation which expects to be the leader of other nations can expect to stay behind in this race for space.

Those who came before us made certain that this country rode the first waves of the industrial revolutions, the first waves of modern invention, and the first wave of nuclear power, and this generation does not intend to founder in the backwash of the coming age of space. We mean to be a part of it—we mean to lead it. For the eyes of the world now look into space, to the moon and to the planets beyond, and we have vowed that we shall not see it governed by a hostile flag of conquest, but by a banner of freedom and peace. We have vowed that we shall not see space filled with weapons of mass destruction, but with instruments of knowledge and understanding.

Yet the vows of this Nation can only be fulfilled if we in this Nation are first, and, therefore, we intend to be first. In short, our leadership in science and in industry, our hopes for peace and security, our obligations to ourselves as well as others, all require us to make this effort, to solve these mysteries, to solve them for the good of all men, and to become the world's leading space-faring nation.

We set sail on this new sea because there is new knowledge to be gained, and new rights to be won, and they must be won and used for the progress of all people. For space science, like nuclear science and all technology, has no conscience of its own. Whether it will become a force for good or ill depends on man, and only if the United States occupies a position of preeminence can we help decide whether this new ocean will be a sea of peace or a new terrifying theater of war. I do not say that we should or will go unprotected against the hostile misuse of space any more than we go unprotected against the hostile use of land or sea, but I do say that space can be explored and mastered without feeding the fires of war, without repeating the mistakes that man has made in extending his writ around this globe of ours.

There is no strife, no prejudice, no national conflict in outer space as yet. Its hazards are hostile to us all. Its conquest deserves the best of all mankind, and its opportunity for peaceful cooperation may never come again. But why, some say, the moon? Why choose this as our goal? And they may well ask why climb the highest mountain. Why, 35 years ago, fly the Atlantic? Why does Rice play Texas?

We choose to go to the moon. We choose to go to the moon in this decade and do the other things, not because they are easy, but because they are hard, because that goal will serve to organize and measure the best of our energies and skills, because that challenge is one that we are willing to accept, one we are unwilling to postpone, and one which we intend to win, and the others, too.

It is for these reasons that I regard the decision last year to shift our efforts in space from low to high gear as among the most important decisions that will be made during my incumbency in the Office of the Presidency.

In the last 24 hours we have seen facilities now being created for the greatest and most complex exploration in man's history. We have felt the ground shake and the air shattered by the testing of a Saturn C-1 booster rocket, many times as powerful as the Atlas which launched John Glenn, generating power equivalent to ten thousand automobiles with their accelerators on the floor. We have seen the site where five F-1 rocket engines, each one as powerful as all eight engines of the Saturn combined, will be clustered together to make the advanced Saturn missile, assembled in a new building to be built at Cape Canaveral as tall as a forty-eight-story structure, as wide as a city block, and as long as two lengths of this field.

Within these last 19 months at least 45 satellites have circled the earth. Some 40 of them were "made in the United States of America" and they were far more sophisticated and supplied far more knowledge to the people of the world than those of the Soviet Union.

The Mariner spacecraft now on its way to Venus is the most intricate instrument in the history of space science. The accuracy of that shot is comparable to firing a missile from Cape Canaveral and dropping it in this stadium between the 40-yard lines.

Transit satellites are helping our ships at sea to steer a safer course. Tiros satellites have given us unprecedented warnings of hurricanes and storms, and will do the same for forest fires and icebergs.

We have had our failures, but so have others, even if they do not admit them. And they may be less public.

To be sure, we are behind, and will be behind for some time in manned flight. But we do not intend to stay behind, and in this decade we shall make up and move ahead.

The growth of our science and education will be enriched by new knowledge of our universe and environment, by new techniques of learning and mapping and observation, by new tools and computers for industry, medicine, the home as well as the school. Technical institutions, such as Rice, will reap the harvest of these gains.

And finally, the space effort itself, while still in its infancy, has already created a great number of new companies, and tens of thousands of new jobs. Space and related industries are generating new demands in investment and skilled personnel, and this city and this State, and this region, will share greatly in this growth. What was once the furthest outpost on the old frontier of the West will be the furthest outpost on the new frontier of science and space.

Houston, your City of Houston, with its Manned Spacecraft Center, will become the heart of a large scientific and engineering community. During the next 5 years the National Aeronautics and Space Administration expects to double the number of scientists and engineers in this area, to increase its outlays for salaries and expenses to $60 million a year; to invest some $200 million in plant and laboratory facilities; and to direct or contract for new space efforts over $1 billion from this Center in this City.

To be sure, all this costs us all a good deal of money. This year's space budget is three times what it was in January 1961, and it is greater than the space budget of the previous eight years combined. That budget now stands at $5,400 million a year—a staggering sum, though somewhat less than we pay for cigarettes and cigars every year. Space expenditures will soon rise some more from 40 cents per person per week to more than 50 cents a week for every man, woman, and child in the United States, for we have given this program a high national priority even though I realize that this is in some measure an act of faith and vision, for we do not now know what benefits await us. But if I were to say, my fellow citizens, that we shall send to the moon, 240,000 miles away from the control station in Houston, a giant rocket more than 300 feet tall, the length of this football field, made of new metal alloys, some of which have not yet been invented, capable of standing heat and stresses several times more than have ever been experienced, fitted together with a precision better than the finest watch, carrying all the equipment needed for propulsion, guidance, control, communications, food and survival, on an untried mission, to an unknown celestial body, and then return it safely to earth, reentering the atmosphere at speeds of over twenty five thousand miles per hour, causing heat about half that of the temperature of the sun—almost as hot as it is here today—and do all this, and do it right, and do it first before this decade is out, then we must be bold.

I'm the one who is doing all the work, so we just want you to stay cool for a minute.

However, I think we're going to do it, and I think that we must pay what needs to be paid. I don't think we ought to waste any money, but I think we ought to do the job. And this will be done in the decade of the sixties. It may be done while some of you are still here at school at this college and university. It will be done during the terms of office of some of the people who sit here on this platform. But it will be done. And it will be done before the end of this decade.

I am delighted that this university is playing a part in putting a man on the moon as part of a great national effort of the United States of America.

Many years ago the great British explorer George Mallory, who was to die on Mount Everest, was asked why did he want to climb it. He said, "Because it is there."

Well, space is there, and we're going to climb it, and the moon and the planets are there, and new hopes for knowledge and peace are there. And, therefore, as we set sail we ask God's blessing on the most hazardous and dangerous and greatest adventure on which man has ever embarked.

# John F. Kennedy

## Bracing America for the Cuban Missile Crisis, October 22, 1962

*The cost of freedom is always high,*
*but Americans have always paid it.*
*And one path we shall never choose,*
*and that is the path of surrender or submission.*

White House photograph.

ONE MONTH AFTER JOHN F. KENNEDY pointed the American people to the moon, he appeared on national television to turn their attention to a closer challenge: Cuba.

Most Americans were unaware of the critical dangers they faced in the autumn of 1962. Intelligence photographs had revealed the installation of Soviet missiles in Cuba—capable of devastating attacks against the United States. On October 22, President Kennedy mobilized the American people to face this ominous threat.

Kennedy begins his speech by establishing for the American people the evidence and consequences of Moscow's military buildup in Cuba: "The purpose of these bases can be none other than to provide a nuclear strike capability against the Western Hemisphere." Then he systematically disproves various counterarguments advanced by the Soviets, punctuating each with a terse punctuation that Moscow's explanation "is false."

He unveils a series of initiatives to protect U.S. interests, ranging from a quarantine of military shipments to Cuba to the dramatic promise of retaliation against the Soviet Union.

Finally, Kennedy appeals to the American people to prepare for sacrifice and uncertainty: "My fellow citizens, let no one doubt that this is a difficult and dangerous effort on which we have set out. No one can foresee precisely what course it will take or what costs or casualties will be incurred. Many months of sacrifice and self-discipline lie ahead—months in which both our patience and our will will be tested, months in which many threats and denunciations will keep us aware of our dangers. But the greatest danger of all would be to do nothing."

If there was any doubt in the Kremlin about Kennedy's fortitude that evening, it was dispelled.

---

GOOD EVENING, MY FELLOW CITIZENS:

This Government, as promised, has maintained the closest surveillance of the Soviet military buildup on the island of Cuba. Within the past week, unmistakable evidence has established the fact that a series of offensive missile sites is now in preparation on that imprisoned island. The purpose of these bases can be none other than to provide a nuclear strike capability against the Western Hemisphere.

Upon receiving the first preliminary hard information of this nature last Tuesday morning at 9 AM, I directed that our surveillance be stepped up. And having now confirmed and completed our evaluation of the evidence and our decision on a course of action, this Government feels obliged to report this new crisis to you in fullest detail.

The characteristics of these new missile sites indicate two distinct types of installations. Several of them include medium-range ballistic missiles, capable of carrying a nuclear warhead for a distance of more than 1,000 nautical miles. Each of these missiles, in short, is capable of striking Washington, D.C., the Panama Canal, Cape Canaveral, Mexico City, or any other city in the southeastern part of the United States, in Central America, or in the Caribbean area.

Additional sites not yet completed appear to be designed for intermediate-range ballistic missiles—capable of traveling more than twice as far—and thus capable of striking most of the major cities in the Western Hemisphere, ranging as far north as Hudson Bay, Canada, and as far south as Lima, Peru. In addition, jet bombers, capable of carrying nuclear weapons, are now being uncrated and assembled in Cuba, while the necessary air bases are being prepared.

This urgent transformation of Cuba into an important strategic base—by the presence of these large, long range, and clearly offensive weapons of sudden mass destruction—constitutes an explicit threat to the peace and security of all the Americas, in flagrant and deliberate defiance of the Rio Pact of 1947, the traditions of this Nation and hemisphere, the joint resolution of the 87th Congress, the Charter of the United Nations, and my own public warnings to the Soviets on September 4 and 13. This action also contradicts the repeated assurances of Soviet spokesmen, both publicly and privately delivered, that the arms buildup in Cuba would retain its original defensive character, and that the Soviet Union had no need or desire to station strategic missiles on the territory of any other nation.

The size of this undertaking makes clear that it has been planned for some months. Yet, only last month, after I had made clear the distinction between any introduction of ground-to-ground missiles and the existence of defensive antiaircraft missiles, the Soviet Government publicly stated on September 11 that, and I quote, "the armaments and military equipment sent to Cuba are designed exclusively for defensive purposes," that there is, and I quote the Soviet Government, "there is no need for the Soviet Government to shift its weapons for a retaliatory blow to any other country, for instance Cuba," and that, and I quote their government, "the Soviet Union has so powerful rockets to carry these nuclear warheads that there is no need to search for sites for them beyond the boundaries of the Soviet Union."

That statement was false.

Only last Thursday, as evidence of this rapid offensive buildup was already in my hand, Soviet Foreign Minister Gromyko told me in my office that he was instructed to make it clear once again, as he said his government had already done, that Soviet assistance to Cuba, and I quote, "pursued solely the purpose of contributing to the defense capabilities of Cuba," that, and I quote him, "training by Soviet specialists of Cuban nationals in handling defensive armaments was by no means offensive, and if it were otherwise," Mr. Gromyko went on, "the Soviet Government would never become involved in rendering such assistance."

That statement also was false.

Neither the United States of America nor the world community of nations can tolerate deliberate deception and offensive threats on the part of any nation, large or small. We no longer live in a world where only the actual firing of weapons represents a sufficient challenge to a nation's security to constitute maximum peril. Nuclear weapons are so destructive and ballistic missiles are so swift, that any substantially increased possibility of their use or any sudden change in their deployment may well be regarded as a definite threat to peace.

For many years, both the Soviet Union and the United States, recognizing this fact, have deployed strategic nuclear weapons with great care, never upsetting the precarious status quo which insured that these weapons would not be used in the absence of some vital challenge. Our own strategic missiles have never been transferred to the territory of any other nation under a cloak of secrecy and deception; and our history—unlike that of the Soviets since the end of World War II—demonstrates that we have no desire to dominate or conquer any other nation or impose our system upon its people. Nevertheless, American citizens have become adjusted to living daily on the bull's-eye of Soviet missiles located inside the USSR or in submarines.

In that sense, missiles in Cuba add to an already clear and present danger—although it should be noted the nations of Latin America have never previously been subjected to a potential nuclear threat. But this secret, swift, extraordinary buildup of Communist missiles—in an area well known to have a special and historical relationship to the United States and the nations of the Western Hemisphere, in violation of Soviet assurances, and in defiance of American and hemispheric policy—this sudden, clandestine decision to station strategic weapons for the first time outside of Soviet soil—is a deliberately provocative and unjustified change in the status quo which cannot be accepted by this country, if our courage and our commitments are ever to be trusted again by either friend or foe.

The 1930s taught us a clear lesson: aggressive conduct, if allowed to go unchecked and unchallenged, ultimately leads to war. This nation is opposed to war. We are also true to our word. Our unswerving objective, therefore, must be to prevent the use of these missiles against this or any other country, and to secure their withdrawal or elimination from the Western Hemisphere.

Our policy has been one of patience and restraint, as befits a peaceful and powerful nation which leads a worldwide alliance. We have been determined not to be diverted from our central concerns by mere irritants and fanatics. But now further action is required, and it is under way; and these actions may only be the beginning. We will not prematurely or unnecessarily risk the costs of worldwide nuclear war in which even the fruits of victory would be ashes in our mouth; but neither will we shrink from that risk at any time it must be faced.

Acting, therefore, in the defense of our own security and of the entire Western Hemisphere, and under the authority entrusted to me by the Constitution as endorsed by the resolution of the Congress, I have directed that the following initial steps be taken immediately:

First: To halt this offensive buildup a strict quarantine on all offensive military equipment under shipment to Cuba is being initiated. All ships of any kind bound for Cuba from whatever nation or port will, if found to contain cargoes of offensive weapons, be turned back. This quarantine will be extended, if needed, to other types of cargo and carriers. We are not at this time, however, denying the necessities of life as the Soviets attempted to do in their Berlin blockade of 1948.

Second: I have directed the continued and increased close surveillance of Cuba and its military buildup. The foreign ministers of the OAS, in their communiqué of October 6, rejected secrecy on such matters in this hemisphere. Should these offensive military preparations continue, thus increasing the threat to the hemisphere, further action will be justified. I have directed the Armed Forces to prepare for any eventualities; and I trust that in the interest of both the Cuban people and the Soviet technicians at the sites, the hazards to all concerned of continuing this threat will be recognized.

Third: It shall be the policy of this Nation to regard any nuclear missile launched from Cuba against any nation in the Western Hemisphere as an attack by the Soviet Union on the United States, requiring a full retaliatory response upon the Soviet Union.

Fourth: As a necessary military precaution, I have reinforced our base at Guantanamo, evacuated today the dependents of our personnel there, and ordered additional military units to be on a standby alert basis.

Fifth: We are calling tonight for an immediate meeting of the Organ of Consultation under the Organization of American States, to consider this threat to hemispheric security and to invoke articles 6 and 8 of the Rio Treaty in support of all necessary action. The United Nations Charter allows for regional security arrangements—and the nations of this hemisphere decided long ago against the military presence of outside powers. Our other allies around the world have also been alerted.

Sixth: Under the Charter of the United Nations, we are asking tonight that an emergency meeting of the Security Council be convoked without delay to take action against this latest Soviet threat to world peace. Our resolution will call for the prompt dismantling and withdrawal of all offensive weapons in Cuba, under the supervision of UN observers, before the quarantine can be lifted.

Seventh and finally: I call upon Chairman Khrushchev to halt and eliminate this clandestine, reckless, and provocative threat to world peace and to stable relations between our two nations. I call upon him further to abandon this course of world domination, and to join in an historic effort to end the perilous arms race and to transform the history of man. He has an opportunity now to move the world back from the abyss of destruction by returning to his government's own words that it had no need to station missiles outside its own territory, and withdrawing these weapons from Cuba by refraining from any action which will widen or deepen the present crisis, and then by participating in a search for peaceful and permanent solutions.

This Nation is prepared to present its case against the Soviet threat to peace, and our own proposals for a peaceful world, at any time and in any forum—in the OAS, in the United Nations, or in any other meeting that could be useful—without limiting our freedom of action. We have in the past made strenuous efforts to limit the spread of nuclear weapons. We have proposed the elimination of all arms and military bases in a fair and effective disarmament treaty. We are prepared to discuss new proposals for the removal of tensions on both sides, including the possibilities of a genuinely independent Cuba, free to determine its own destiny. We have no wish to war with the Soviet Union—for we are a peaceful people who desire to live in peace with all other peoples.

But it is difficult to settle or even discuss these problems in an atmosphere of intimidation. That is why this latest Soviet threat—or any other threat which is made either independently or in response to our actions this week—must and will be met with determination. Any hostile move anywhere in the world against the safety and freedom of peoples to whom we are committed, including in particular the brave people of West Berlin, will be met by whatever action is needed.

Finally, I want to say a few words to the captive people of Cuba, to whom this speech is being directly carried by special radio facilities. I speak to you as a friend, as one who knows of your deep attachment to your fatherland, as one who shares your aspirations for liberty and justice for all. And I have watched and the American people have watched with deep sorrow how your nationalist revolution was betrayed—and how your fatherland fell under foreign domination. Now your leaders are no longer Cuban leaders inspired by Cuban ideals. They are puppets and agents of an international conspiracy which has turned Cuba against your friends and neighbors in the Americas, and turned it into the first Latin American country to become a target for nuclear war—the first Latin American country to have these weapons on its soil.

These new weapons are not in your interest. They contribute nothing to your peace and well-being. They can only undermine it. But this country has no wish to cause you to suffer or to impose any system upon you. We know that your lives and land are being used as pawns by those who deny your freedom. Many times in the past, the Cuban people have risen to throw out tyrants who destroyed their liberty. And I have no doubt that most Cubans today look forward to the time when they will be truly free—free from foreign domination, free to choose their own leaders, free to select their own system, free to own their own land, free to speak and write and worship without fear or degradation. And then shall Cuba be welcomed back to the society of free nations and to the associations of this hemisphere.

My fellow citizens, let no one doubt that this is a difficult and dangerous effort on which we have set out. No one can foresee precisely what course it will take or what costs or casualties will be incurred. Many months of sacrifice and self-discipline lie ahead—months in which both our patience and our will will be tested, months in which many threats and denunciations will keep us aware of our dangers. But the greatest danger of all would be to do nothing.

The path we have chosen for the present is full of hazards, as all paths are; but it is the one most consistent with our character and courage as a nation and our commitments around the world. The cost of freedom is always high, but Americans have always paid it. And one path we shall never choose, and that is the path of surrender or submission.

Our goal is not the victory of might, but the vindication of right; not peace at the expense of freedom, but both peace and freedom, here in this hemisphere, and, we hope, around the world. God willing, that goal will be achieved.

# John F. Kennedy

## Ich Bin ein Berliner, June 26, 1963

*Freedom has many difficulties and democracy is not perfect.*
*But we have never had to put a wall up to keep our people in—*
*to prevent them from leaving us.*

Photograph taken 1961.

I N MANY RESPECTS, the moral front of the Cold War was the wall that divided Berlin. There, five months before he would lose his life, John F. Kennedy articulated for the world why the battle was worth fighting.

A million people gathered to hear Kennedy's speech. In a stirring cadence, he described the stark differences between East and West: "There are many people in the world who really don't understand, or say they don't, what is the great issue between the free world and the Communist world. Let them come to Berlin. There are some who say that communism is the wave of the future. Let them come to Berlin. And there are some who say, in Europe and elsewhere, we can work with the Communists. Let them come to Berlin. And there are even a few who say that it is true that communism is an evil system, but it permits us to make economic progress. Lass' sic nach Berlin Kommen. Let them come to Berlin. Freedom has many difficulties and democracy is not perfect. But we have never had to put a wall up to keep our people in—to prevent them from leaving us."

---

I AM PROUD to come to this city as the guest of your distinguished mayor, who has symbolized throughout the world the fighting spirit of West Berlin. And I am proud to visit the Federal Republic with your distinguished chancellor who for so many years has committed Germany to democracy and freedom and progress, and to come here in the company of my fellow American, General Clay, who has been in this city during its great moments of crisis and will come again if ever needed.

Two thousand years ago, the proudest boast was "Civis Romanus sum." Today, in the world of freedom, the proudest boast is "Ich bin ein Berliner."

There are many people in the world who really don't understand, or say they don't, what is the great issue between the free world and the Communist world. Let them come to Berlin. There are some who say that communism is the wave of the future. Let them come to Berlin. And there are some who say, in Europe and elsewhere, we can work with the Communists. Let them come to Berlin. And there are even a few who say that it is true that communism is an evil system, but it permits us to make economic progress. Lass' sic nach Berlin Kommen. Let them come to Berlin.

Freedom has many difficulties and democracy is not perfect. But we have never had to put a wall up to keep our people in—to prevent them from leaving us. I want to say on behalf of my countrymen who live many miles away on the other side of the Atlantic, who are far distant from you, that they take the greatest pride, that they have been able to share with you, even from a distance, the story of the last 18 years. I know of no town, no city, that has been besieged for 18 years that still lives with the vitality and the force, and the hope, and the determination of the city of West Berlin. While the wall is the most obvious and vivid demonstration of the failures of the Communist system—for all the world to see—we take no satisfaction in it; for it is, as your Mayor has said, an offense not only against history but an offense against humanity, separating families, dividing husbands and wives and brothers and sisters, and dividing a people who wish to be joined together.

What is true of this city is true of Germany—real, lasting peace in Europe can never be assured as long as one German out of four is denied the elementary right of free men, and that is to make a free choice. In 18 years of peace and good faith, this generation of Germans has earned the right to be free, including the right to unite their families and their nation in lasting peace, with good will to all people. You live in a defended island of freedom, but your life is part of the main. So let me ask you, as I close, to lift your eyes beyond the dangers of today, to the hopes of tomorrow, beyond the freedom merely of this city of Berlin, or your country of Germany, to the advance of freedom everywhere, beyond the wall to the day of peace with justice, beyond yourselves and ourselves to all mankind.

Freedom is indivisible, and when one man is enslaved, all are not free. When all are free, then we look forward to that day when this city will be joined as one and this country and this great continent of Europe in a peaceful and hopeful globe. When that day finally comes, as it will, the people of West Berlin can take sober satisfaction in the fact that they were in the front lines for almost two decades.

All free men, wherever they may live, are citizens of Berlin, and therefore, as a free man, I take pride in the words "Ich bin ein Berliner."

# Richard Nixon

## ASKING FOR PATIENCE ON VIETNAM,
## NOVEMBER 3, 1969

*So tonight, to you, the great silent majority of my fellow Americans,
I ask for your support. I pledged in my campaign for the Presidency to end the war
in a way that we could win the peace. I have initiated a plan of action
which will enable me to keep that pledge. The more support I can have
from the American people, the sooner that pledge can be redeemed.
For the more divided we are at home, the less likely the enemy
is to negotiate at Paris.*

Official White House portrait.

**M**UCH OF MY TIME IN CONGRESS has been spent addressing issues of war and peace in Iraq. Although initial support for the war was high, it steadily eroded in the face of critical questions about the rationale for the invasion and the mounting casualties and chaotic conditions after Saddam Hussein was toppled. As public criticism increased, I heard President George W. Bush appeal for patience in quiet White House meetings, in large public rallies, and in speeches directly to the American people.

The debate has often touched on whether the situation in Iraq parallels our experience in Vietnam. Future historians will likely debate the analogies between Iraq and Vietnam. What is clear, however, is that President Richard Nixon and President Bush confronted similar public anxieties as both wars dragged on. Indeed, this speech by President Nixon addresses many of the concerns that would arise thirty-five years later.

Near his conclusion, Nixon engages in a shrewd and skillful technique designed to bolster support from those who may be turning skeptical about the war but are troubled by the images of protests on America's streets, referring to them as "the great silent majority of my fellow Americans."

Personal and historic views about Vietnam will be debated for many years. I believe, however, that this speech effectively secured much-needed support for Richard Nixon's wartime policies at a critical moment. It would not be until March 1973—four and a half years after the speech—that the last U.S. combat soldiers would leave Vietnam.

---

GOOD EVENING, MY FELLOW AMERICANS:

Tonight I want to talk to you on a subject of deep concern to all Americans and to many people in all parts of the world—the war in Vietnam.

I believe that one of the reasons for the deep division about Vietnam is that many Americans have lost confidence in what their Government has told them about our policy. The American people cannot and should not be asked to support a policy which involves the overriding issues of war and peace unless they know the truth about that policy.

Tonight, therefore, I would like to answer some of the questions that I know are on the minds of many of you listening to me.

How and why did America get involved in Vietnam in the first place?

How has this administration changed the policy of the previous administration?

What has really happened in the negotiations in Paris and on the battle-front in Vietnam?

What choices do we have if we are to end the war?

What are the prospects for peace?

Now let me begin by describing the situation I found when I was inaugurated on January 20.

The war had been going on for four years. 31,000 Americans had been killed in action.

The training program for the South Vietnamese was behind schedule. 540,000 Americans were in Vietnam with no plans to reduce the number.

No progress had been made at the negotiations in Paris and the United States had not put forth a comprehensive peace proposal.

The war was causing deep division at home and criticism from many of our friends, as well as our enemies, abroad.

In view of these circumstances, there were some who urged that I end the war at once by ordering the immediate withdrawal of all American forces.

From a political standpoint, this would have been a popular and easy course to follow. After all, we became involved in the war while my predecessor was in office. I could blame the defeat, which would be the result of my action, on him—and come out as the peacemaker. Some put it to me quite bluntly: This was the only way to avoid allowing Johnson's war to become Nixon's war.

But I had a greater obligation than to think only of the years of my Administration, and of the next election. I had to think of the effect of my decision on the next generation, and on the future of peace and freedom in America, and in the world.

Let us all understand that the question before us is not whether some Americans are for peace and some Americans are against peace. The question at issue is not whether Johnson's war becomes Nixon's war.

The great question is: How can we win America's peace?

Well, let us turn now to the fundamental issue: Why and how did the United States become involved in Vietnam in the first place?

Fifteen years ago North Vietnam, with the logistical support of Communist China and the Soviet Union, launched a campaign to impose a Communist government on South Vietnam by instigating and supporting a revolution.

In response to the request of the Government of South Vietnam, President Eisenhower sent economic aid and military equipment to assist the people of South Vietnam in their efforts to prevent a Communist takeover. Seven years ago, President Kennedy sent 16,000 military personnel to Vietnam as combat advisers. Four years ago, President Johnson sent American combat forces to South Vietnam.

Now, many believe that President Johnson's decision to send American combat forces to South Vietnam was wrong. And many others—I among them—have been strongly critical of the way the war has been conducted.

But the question facing us today is: Now that we are in the war, what is the best way to end it?

In January I could only conclude that the precipitate withdrawal of all American forces from Vietnam would be a disaster not only for South Vietnam but for the United States and for the cause of peace.

For the South Vietnamese, our precipitate withdrawal would inevitably allow the Communists to repeat the massacres which followed their takeover in the North 15 years before.

They then murdered more than 50,000 people and hundreds of thousands more died in slave labor camps.

We saw a prelude of what would happen in South Vietnam when the Communists entered the city of Hue last year. During their brief rule there, there was a bloody reign of terror in which 3,000 civilians were clubbed, shot to death, and buried in mass graves.

With the sudden collapse of our support, these atrocities at Hue would become the nightmare of the entire nation and particularly for the million and a half Catholic refugees who fled to South Vietnam when the Communists took over in the North.

For the United States this first defeat in our nation's history would result in a collapse of confidence in American leadership not only in Asia but throughout the world.

Three American Presidents have recognized the great stakes involved in Vietnam and understood what had to be done.

In 1963, President Kennedy, with his characteristic eloquence and clarity said: ". . . We want to see a stable Government there, carrying on the struggle to maintain its national independence.

"We believe strongly in that. We are not going to withdraw from that effort. In my opinion, for us to withdraw from that effort would mean a collapse not only of South Vietnam but Southeast Asia. So we're going to stay there."

President Eisenhower and President Johnson expressed the same conclusion during their terms of office.

For the future of peace, precipitate withdrawal would be a disaster of immense magnitude.

A nation cannot remain great if it betrays its allies and lets down its friends.

Our defeat and humiliation in South Vietnam without question would promote recklessness in the councils of those great powers who have not yet abandoned their goals of world conquest.

This would spark violence wherever our commitments help maintain the peace—in the Middle East, in Berlin, eventually even in the Western Hemisphere.

Ultimately, this would cost more lives. It would not bring peace; it would bring more war.

For these reasons I rejected the recommendation that I should end the war by immediately withdrawing all of our forces. I chose instead to change American policy on both the negotiating front and the battlefront. In order to end the war fought on many fronts, I initiated a pursuit for peace on many fronts.

In a television speech on May 14, in a speech before the United Nations, on a number of other occasions, I set forth our peace proposals in great detail.

We have offered the complete withdrawal of all outside forces within one year.

We have proposed a cease-fire under international supervision.

We have offered free elections under international supervision with the Communists participating in the organization and conduct of the elections as an organized political force. And the Saigon government has pledged to accept the result of the elections.

We have not put forth our proposals on a take-it-or-leave-it basis. We have indicated that we're willing to discuss the proposals that have been put forth by the other side. We have declared that anything is negotiable, except the right of the people of South Vietnam to determine their own future. At the Paris peace conference, Ambassador Lodge has demonstrated our flexibility and good faith in 40 public meetings.

Hanoi has refused even to discuss our proposals. They demand our unconditional acceptance of their terms which are that we withdraw all American forces immediately and unconditionally and that we overthrow the government of South Vietnam as we leave.

We have not limited our peace initiatives to public forums and public statements. I recognized in January that a long and bitter war like this usually cannot be settled in a public forum. That is why in addition to the public statements and negotiations, I have explored every possible private avenue that might lead to a settlement.

Tonight I am taking the unprecedented step of disclosing to you some of our other initiatives for peace—initiatives we undertook privately and secretly because we thought we thereby might open a door which publicly would be closed.

I did not wait for my inauguration to begin my quest for peace.

Soon after my election, through an individual who was directly in contact on a personal basis with the leaders of North Vietnam, I made two private offers for a rapid, comprehensive settlement. Hanoi's replies called in effect for our surrender before negotiations.

Since the Soviet Union furnishes most of the military equipment for North Vietnam, Secretary of State Rogers, my assistant for national security affairs, Dr. Kissinger, Ambassador Lodge and I personally have met on a number of occasions with representatives of the Soviet Government to enlist their assistance in getting meaningful negotiations started. In addition, we have had extended discussions directed toward that same end with representatives of other governments which have diplomatic relations with North Vietnam. None of these initiatives have to date produced results.

In mid-July I became convinced that it was necessary to make a major move to break the deadlock in the Paris talks. I spoke directly in this office, where I'm now sitting, with an individual who had known Ho Chi Minh on a personal basis for twenty-five years. Through him I sent a letter to Ho Chi Minh.

I did this outside of the usual diplomatic channels with the hope that with the necessity of making statements for propaganda removed, there might be constructive progress toward bringing the war to an end.

Let me read from that letter to you now:

Dear Mr. President:

I realize that it is difficult to communicate meaningfully across the gulf of four years of war. But precisely because of this gulf I wanted to take this opportunity to reaffirm in all solemnity my desire to work for a just peace. I deeply believe that the war in Vietnam has gone on too long and delay in bringing it to an end can benefit no one, least of all the people of Vietnam. . . .

The time has come to move forward at the conference table toward an early resolution of this tragic war. You will find us forthcoming and open-minded in a common effort to bring the blessings of peace to the brave people of Vietnam. Let history record that at this critical juncture both sides turned their face toward peace rather than toward conflict and war.

I received Ho Chi Minh's reply on August 30, 3 days before his death. It simply reiterated the public position North Vietnam had taken at Paris and flatly rejected my initiative.

The full text of both letters is being released to the press.

In addition to the public meetings that I have referred to, Ambassador Lodge has met with Vietnam's chief negotiator in Paris in 11 private sessions.

We have taken other significant initiatives which must remain secret to keep open some channels of communications which may still prove to be productive.

But the effect of all the public, private, and secret negotiations which have been undertaken since the bombing halt a year ago, and since this Administration came into office on January 20th, can be summed up in one sentence: No progress whatever has been made except agreement on the shape of the bargaining table.

Well, now, who's at fault? It has become clear that the obstacle in negotiating an end to the war is not the President of the United States. It is not the South Vietnamese Government.

The obstacle is the other side's absolute refusal to show the least willingness to join us in seeking a just peace. And it will not do so while it is convinced that all it has to do is to wait for our next concession, and our next concession after that one, until it gets everything it wants.

There can now be no longer any question that progress in negotiation depends only on Hanoi's deciding to negotiate, to negotiate seriously.

I realize that this report on our efforts on the diplomatic front is discouraging to the American people, but the American people are entitled to know the truth—the bad news as well as the good news—where the lives of our young men are involved.

Now let me turn, however, to a more encouraging report on another front.

At the time we launched our search for peace, I recognized we might not succeed in bringing an end to the war through negotiations. I therefore put into effect another plan to bring peace—a plan which will bring the war to an end regardless of what happens on the negotiating front.

It is in line with the major shift in U.S. foreign policy which I described in my press conference at Guam on July 25. Let me briefly explain what has been described as the Nixon Doctrine—a policy which not only will help end the war in Vietnam but which is an essential element of our program to prevent future Vietnams.

We Americans are a do-it-yourself people—we're an impatient people. Instead of teaching someone else to do a job, we like to do it ourselves. And this trait has been carried over into our foreign policy. In Korea, and again in Vietnam, the United States furnished most of the money, most of the arms, and most of the men to help the people of those countries defend their freedom against Communist aggression.

Before any American troops were committed to Vietnam, a leader of another Asian country expressed this opinion to me when I was traveling in Asia as a private citizen. He said: "When you are trying to assist another nation defend its freedom, U.S. policy should be to help them fight the war, but not to fight the war for them."

Well in accordance with this wise counsel, I laid down in Guam three principles as guidelines for future American policy toward Asia:

First, the United States will keep all of its treaty commitments.

Second, we shall provide a shield if a nuclear power threatens the freedom of a nation allied with us, or of a nation whose survival we consider vital to our security.

Third, in cases involving other types of aggression, we shall furnish military and economic assistance when requested in accordance with our treaty commitments. But we shall look to the nation directly threatened to assume the primary responsibility of providing the manpower for its defense.

After I announced this policy, I found that the leaders of the Philippines, Thailand, Vietnam, South Korea, other nations which might be threatened by Communist aggression, welcomed this new direction in American foreign policy.

The defense of freedom is everybody's business—not just America's business. And it is particularly the responsibility of the people whose freedom is threatened. In the previous Administration, we Americanized the war in Vietnam. In this Administration, we are Vietnamizing the search for peace.

The policy of the previous Administration not only resulted in our assuming the primary responsibility for fighting the war, but even more significant did not adequately stress the goal of strengthening the South Vietnamese so that they could defend themselves when we left.

The Vietnamization plan was launched following Secretary Laird's visit to Vietnam in March. Under the plan, I ordered first a substantial increase in the training and equipment of South Vietnamese forces. In July, on my visit to Vietnam, I changed General Abrams' orders, so that they were consistent with the objectives of our new policies. Under the new orders, the primary mission of our troops is to enable the South Vietnamese forces to assume the full responsibility for the security of South Vietnam. Our air operations have been reduced by over 20 percent.

And now we have begun to see the results of this long-overdue change in American policy in Vietnam.

After five years of Americans going into Vietnam we are finally bringing American men home. By December 15 over 60,000 men will have been withdrawn from South Vietnam, including 20 percent of all of our combat forces.

The South Vietnamese have continued to gain in strength. As a result, they've been able to take over combat responsibilities from our American troops.

Two other significant developments have occurred since this Administration took office.

Enemy infiltration, infiltration which is essential if they are to launch a major attack over the last three months, is less than 20 percent of what it was over the same period last year.

And most important, United States casualties have declined during the last two months to the lowest point in three years.

Let me now turn to our program for the future.

We have adopted a plan which we have worked out in cooperation with the South Vietnamese for the complete withdrawal of all U.S. combat ground forces and their replacement by South Vietnamese forces on an orderly scheduled timetable. This withdrawal will be made from strength and not from weakness. As South Vietnamese forces become stronger, the rate of American withdrawal can become greater.

I have not, and do not, intend to announce the timetable for our program, and there are obvious reasons for this decision which I'm sure you will understand. As I've indicated on several occasions, the rate of withdrawal will depend on developments on three fronts.

One of these is the progress which can be, or might be, made in the Paris talks. An announcement of a fixed timetable for our withdrawal would completely remove any incentive for the enemy to negotiate an agreement. They would simply wait until our forces had withdrawn and then move in.

The other two factors on which we will base our withdrawal decisions are the level of enemy activity and the progress of the training programs of the South Vietnamese forces. And I am glad to be able to report tonight progress on both of these fronts has been greater than we anticipated when we started the program in June for withdrawal. As a result, our timetable for withdrawal is more optimistic now than when we made our first estimates in June. Now this clearly demonstrates why it is not wise to be frozen in on a fixed timetable.

We must retain the flexibility to base each withdrawal decision on the situation as it is at that time, rather than on estimates that are no longer valid. Along with this optimistic estimate, I must in all candor leave one note of caution. If the level of enemy activity significantly increases, we might have to adjust our timetable accordingly.

However, I want the record to be completely clear on one point. At the time of the bombing halt just a year ago there was some confusion as to whether there was an understanding on the part of the enemy that if we stopped the bombing of North Vietnam, they would stop the shelling of cities in South Vietnam. I want to be sure that there is no misunderstanding on the part of the enemy with regard to our withdrawal program.

We have noted the reduced level of infiltration, the reduction of our casualties and are basing our withdrawal decisions partially on those factors.

If the level of infiltration or our casualties increase while we are trying to scale down the fighting, it will be the result of a conscious decision by the enemy.

Hanoi could make no greater mistake than to assume that an increase in violence will be to its advantage. If I conclude that increased enemy action jeopardizes our remaining forces in Vietnam, I shall not hesitate to take strong and effective measures to deal with that situation.

This is not a threat. This is a statement of policy which as Commander in Chief of our Armed Forces, I am making and meeting my responsibility for the protection of American fighting men wherever they may be.

My fellow Americans, I am sure you can recognize from what I have said that we really only have two choices open to us if we want to end this war.

I can order an immediate precipitate withdrawal of all Americans from Vietnam without regard to the effects of that action.

Or we can persist in our search for a just peace through a negotiated settlement, if possible, or through continued implementation of our plan for Vietnamization, if necessary—a plan in which we will withdraw all of our forces from Vietnam on a schedule in accordance with our program as the South Vietnamese become strong enough to defend their own freedom.

I have chosen this second course.

It is not the easy way.

It is the right way.

It is a plan which will end the war and serve the cause of peace—not just in Vietnam but in the Pacific and in the world.

In speaking of the consequences of a precipitous withdrawal, I mentioned that our allies would lose confidence in America.

Far more dangerous, we would lose confidence in ourselves. Oh, the immediate reaction would be a sense of relief that our men were coming home. But as we saw the consequences of what we had done, inevitable remorse and divisive recrimination would scar our spirit as a people.

We have faced other crises in our history and we have become stronger by rejecting the easy way out and taking the right way in meeting our challenges. Our greatness as a nation has been our capacity to do what has to be done when we knew our course was right.

I recognize that some of my fellow citizens disagree with the plan for peace I have chosen. Honest and patriotic Americans have reached different conclusions as to how peace should be achieved.

In San Francisco a few weeks ago, I saw demonstrators carrying signs reading, "Lose in Vietnam, bring the boys home."

Well, one of the strengths of our free society is that any American has a right to reach that conclusion and to advocate that point of view. But as President of the United States, I would be untrue to my oath of office if I allowed the policy of this nation to be dictated by the minority who hold that point of view and who try to impose it on the nation by mounting demonstrations in the street.

For almost two hundred years, the policy of this nation has been made under our Constitution by those leaders in the Congress and the White House elected by all the people. If a vocal minority, however fervent its cause, prevails over reason and the will of the majority, this nation has no future as a free society.

And now, I would like to address a word, if I may, to the young people of this Nation who are particularly concerned, and I understand why they are concerned, about this war.

I respect your idealism.

I share your concern for peace.

I want peace as much as you do.

There are powerful personal reasons I want to end this war. This week I will have to sign 83 letters to mothers, fathers, wives, and loved ones of men who have given their lives for America in Vietnam. It's very little satisfaction to me that this is only one-third as many letters as I signed the first week in office. There is nothing I want more than to see the day come when I do not have to write any of those letters.

I want to end the war to save the lives of those brave young men in Vietnam.

But I want to end it in a way which will increase the chance that their younger brothers and their sons will not have to fight in some future Vietnam some place in the world.

And I want to end the war for another reason. I want to end it so that the energy and dedication of you, our young people, now too often directed into bitter hatred against those responsible for the war, can be turned to the great challenges of peace, a better life for all Americans, a better life for all people on this earth.

I have chosen a plan for peace. I believe it will succeed.

If it does not succeed, what the critics say now won't matter. Or if it does succeed, what the critics say now won't matter. If it does not succeed, anything I say then won't matter.

I know it may not be fashionable to speak of patriotism or national destiny these days, but I feel it is appropriate to do so on this occasion.

Two hundred years ago this nation was weak and poor. But even then, America was the hope of millions in the world. Today we have become the strongest and richest nation in the world, and the wheel of destiny has turned so that any hope the world has for the survival of peace and freedom will be determined by whether the American people have the moral stamina and the courage to meet the challenge of free world leadership.

Let historians not record that, when America was the most powerful nation in the world, we passed on the other side of the road and allowed the last hopes for peace and freedom of millions of people to be suffocated by the forces of totalitarianism.

And so tonight—to you, the great silent majority of my fellow Americans, I ask for your support.

I pledged in my campaign for the Presidency to end the war in a way that we could win the peace. I have initiated a plan of action which will enable me to keep that pledge.

The more support I can have from the American people, the sooner that pledge can be redeemed, for the more divided we are at home, the less likely the enemy is to negotiate at Paris.

Let us be united for peace. Let us also be united against defeat. Because let us understand: North Vietnam cannot defeat or humiliate the United States. Only Americans can do that.

Fifty years ago, in this room, and at this very desk, President Woodrow Wilson spoke words which caught the imagination of a war-weary world. He said: "This is the war to end wars." His dream for peace after World War I was shattered on the hard reality of great power politics. And Woodrow Wilson died a broken man.

Tonight, I do not tell you that the war in Vietnam is the war to end wars, but I do say this: I have initiated a plan which will end this war in a way that will bring us closer to that great goal to which—to which Woodrow Wilson and every American President in our history has been dedicated—the goal of a just and lasting peace.

As President I hold the responsibility for choosing the best path for that goal and then leading the nation along it.

I pledge to you tonight that I shall meet this responsibility with all of the strength and wisdom I can command, in accordance with your hopes, mindful of your concerns, sustained by your prayers.

# Nelson Mandela

## UNITE! MOBILIZE! FIGHT ON!
## JUNE 10, 1980

*We face an enemy that is deep rooted;*
*an enemy entrenched and determined not to yield.*
*Our march to freedom is long and difficult.*
*But both within and beyond our borders*
*the prospects of victory grow bright.*

Photograph from 1993.

JUNE **1976 WAS A CRITICAL MOMENT** in the battle against apartheid. The South African police had just demonstrated their overwhelming power—and their willingness to use it—when they unleashed dogs, tear gas, and munitions against an unarmed group of students protesting in Soweto. This might have been enough to deflate and defeat the antiapartheid movement. But Nelson Mandela used it to ignite continued opposition. This message was smuggled from his prison cell and officially published in June 1980. It fortified those who battled apartheid against crushing force.

Mandela's leadership would bear extraordinary fruit. By 1991 apartheid would be abolished. He was released from prison on February 11, 1990, and became the first black president of the state, serving from 1994 to 1999.

---

### RACISTS RULE BY THE GUN!

The gun has played an important part in our history. The resistance of the black man to white colonial intrusion was crushed by the gun. Our struggle to liberate ourselves from white domination is held in check by force of arms. From conquest to the present the story is the same. Successive white regimes have repeatedly massacred unarmed defenseless blacks. And wherever and whenever they have pulled out their guns the ferocity of their fire has been trained on the African people.

Apartheid is the embodiment of the racialism, repression and inhumanity of all previous white supremacist regimes. To see the real face of apartheid we must look beneath the veil of constitutional formulas, deceptive phrases and playing with words.

The rattle of gunfire and the rumbling of Hippo armored vehicles since June 1976 have once again torn aside that veil. Spread across the face of our country, in black townships, the racist army and police have been pouring a hail of bullets killing and maiming hundreds of black men, women and children. The toll of the dead and injured already surpasses that of all past massacres carried out by this regime.

Apartheid is the rule of the gun and the hangman. The Hippo, the FN rifle and the gallows are its true symbols. These remain the easiest resort, the ever ready solution of the race-mad rulers of South Africa.

## VAGUE PROMISES, GREATER REPRESSION

IN THE MIDST OF THE PRESENT CRISIS, while our people count the dead and nurse the injured, they ask themselves: what lies ahead?

From our rulers we can expect nothing. They are the ones who give orders to the soldier crouching over his rifle: theirs is the spirit that moves the finger that caresses the trigger.

Vague promises, tinkerings with the machinery of apartheid, constitution juggling, massive arrests and detentions side by side with renewed overtures aimed at weakening and forestalling the unity of us blacks and dividing the forces of change—these are the fixed paths along which they will move. For they are neither capable nor willing to heed the verdict of the masses of our people.

## THE VERDICT OF JUNE 16!

THAT VERDICT IS LOUD AND CLEAR: apartheid has failed. Our people remain unequivocal in its rejection. The young and the old, parent and child, all reject it. At the forefront of this 1976/77 wave of unrest were our students and youth. They come from the universities, high schools and even primary schools. They are a generation whose whole education has been under the diabolical design of the racists to poison the minds and brainwash our children into docile subjects of apartheid rule. But after more than twenty years of Bantu Education the circle is closed and nothing demonstrates the utter bankruptcy of apartheid as the revolt of our youth.

The evils, the cruelty and the inhumanity of apartheid have been there from its inception. And all blacks—Africans, Coloureds and Indians—have opposed it all along the line. What is now unmistakable, what the current wave of unrest has sharply highlighted, is this: that despite all the window-dressing and smooth talk, apartheid has become intolerable.

This awareness reaches over and beyond the particulars of our enslavement. The measure of this truth is the recognition by our people that under apartheid our lives, individually and collectively, count for nothing.

# UNITE!

WE FACE AN ENEMY that is deep rooted; an enemy entrenched and determined not to yield. Our march to freedom is long and difficult. But both within and beyond our borders the prospects of victory grow bright.

The first condition for victory is black unity. Every effort to divide the blacks, to woo and pit one black group against another, must be vigorously repulsed. Our people—African, Coloured, Indian and democratic whites—must be united into a single massive and solid wall of resistance, of united mass action.

Our struggle is growing sharper. This is not the time for the luxury of division and disunity. At all levels and in every walk of life we must close ranks. Within the ranks of the people differences must be submerged to the achievement of a single goal—the complete overthrow of apartheid and racist domination.

# VICTORY IS CERTAIN!

THE REVULSION OF THE WORLD against apartheid is growing and the frontiers of white supremacy are shrinking. Mozambique and Angola are free and the war of liberation gathers force in Namibia and Zimbabwe. The soil of our country is destined to be the scene of the fiercest fight and the sharpest battles to rid our continent of the last vestiges of white minority rule.

The world is on our side. The OAU, the UN and the anti-apartheid movement continue to put pressure on the racist rulers of our country. Every effort to isolate South Africa adds strength to our struggle.

At all levels of our struggle, within and outside the country, much has been achieved and much remains to be done. But victory is certain!

# WE SALUTE ALL OF YOU!

WE WHO ARE CONFINED within the grey walls of the Pretoria regime's prisons reach out to our people. With you we count those who have perished by means of the gun and the hangman's rope. We salute all of you—the living, the injured and the dead. For you have dared to rise up against the tyrant's might.

Even as we bow at their graves we remember this: the dead live on as martyrs in our hearts and minds, a reproach to our disunity and the host of shortcomings that accompany divisions among the oppressed, a spur to our efforts to close ranks, and a reminder that the freedom of our people is yet to be won.

We face the future with confidence. For the guns that serve apartheid cannot render it unconquerable. Those who live by the gun shall perish by the gun.

## UNITE! MOBLISE! FIGHT ON!

Between the anvil of united mass action and the hammer of the armed struggle we shall crush apartheid and white minority racist rule.

# Ronald Reagan

## TEAR DOWN THIS WALL!
## JUNE 12, 1987

*Come here to this gate!*
*Mr. Gorbachev, open this gate!*
*Mr. Gorbachev, tear down this wall!*

Official White House portrait, 1985.

**M**OST OF THE SPEECHES IN THIS BOOK were delivered for "domestic consumption"—to mobilize a population to resist and defeat external threat. This speech by President Ronald Reagan was directly aimed at a different audience: the leaders of the Soviet Union and the oppressed populations across Eastern Europe who struggled for freedom.

Twenty-four years after President John F. Kennedy delivered his famous "Ich bin ein Berliner" speech to the people of West Berlin, President Ronald Reagan visited the divided city.

For the audience of the oppressed, Reagan offers a vivid contrast: "In the 1950's, Khrushchev predicted: 'We will bury you.' But in the West today, we see a free world that has achieved a level of prosperity and well-being unprecedented in all human history. In the Communist world, we see failure, technological backwardness, declining standards of health, even want of the most basic kind—too little food. Even today, the Soviet Union still cannot feed itself. After these four decades, then, there stands before the entire world one great and inescapable conclusion: Freedom leads to prosperity. Freedom replaces the ancient hatreds among the nations with comity and peace. Freedom is the victor."

In the most famous passage from the speech, Reagan acknowledges the emergence of democratic reforms in the Soviet Union, but demands more: "There is one sign the Soviets can make that would be unmistakable, that would advance dramatically the cause of freedom and peace. General Secretary Gorbachev, if you seek peace, if you seek prosperity for the Soviet Union and Eastern Europe, if you seek liberalization: Come here to this gate! Mr. Gorbachev, open this gate! Mr. Gorbachev, tear down this wall!"

Two and a half years later, on November 9, 1989, men and women took sledgehammers to the Berlin Wall—on both sides. Communism came to a crushing defeat; and the forty-year Cold War came to an end.

———•◦•———

**T**HANK YOU VERY MUCH. Chancellor Kohl, Governing Mayor Diepgen, ladies and gentlemen: Twenty-four years ago, President John F. Kennedy visited Berlin, speaking to the people of this city and the world at the city hall. Well, since then two other presidents have come, each in his turn, to Berlin. And today I, myself, make my second visit to your city.

We come to Berlin, we American Presidents, because it's our duty to speak, in this place, of freedom. But I must confess, we're drawn here by other things as well: by the feeling of history in this city, more than five hundred years older than our own nation; by the beauty of the Grunewald and the Tiergarten; most of all, by your courage and determination. Perhaps the composer Paul Lincke understood something about American Presidents. You see, like so many Presidents before me, I come here today because wherever I go, whatever I do: "Ich hab noch einen koffer in Berlin" [I still have a suitcase in Berlin].

Our gathering today is being broadcast throughout Western Europe and North America. I understand that it is being seen and heard as well in the East. To those listening throughout Eastern Europe, I extend my warmest greetings and the good will of the American people. To those listening in East Berlin, a special word: Although I cannot be with you, I address my remarks to you just as surely as to those standing here before me. For I join you, as I join your fellow countrymen in the West, in this firm, this unalterable belief: Es gibt nur ein Berlin. [There is only one Berlin.]

Behind me stands a wall that encircles the free sectors of this city, part of a vast system of barriers that divides the entire continent of Europe. From the Baltic, south, those barriers cut across Germany in a gash of barbed wire, concrete, dog runs, and guard towers. Farther south, there may be no visible, no obvious wall. But there remain armed guards and checkpoints all the same—still a restriction on the right to travel, still an instrument to impose upon ordinary men and women the will of a totalitarian state. Yet it is here in Berlin where the wall emerges most clearly; here, cutting across your city, where the news photo and the television screen have imprinted this brutal division of a continent upon the mind of the world. Standing before the Brandenburg Gate, every man is a German, separated from his fellow men. Every man is a Berliner, forced to look upon a scar.

President von Weizsacker has said: "The German question is open as long as the Brandenburg Gate is closed." Today I say: As long as this gate is closed, as long as this scar of a wall is permitted to stand, it is not the German question alone that remains open, but the question of freedom for all mankind. Yet I do not come here to lament. For I find in Berlin a message of hope, even in the shadow of this wall, a message of triumph.

In this season of spring in 1945, the people of Berlin emerged from their air-raid shelters to find devastation. Thousands of miles away, the people of the United States reached out to help. And in 1947 Secretary of State—as you've been told—George Marshall announced the creation of what would become known as the Marshall plan. Speaking precisely forty years ago this month, he said: "Our policy is directed not against any country or doctrine, but against hunger, poverty, desperation, and chaos."

In the Reichstag a few moments ago, I saw a display commemorating this fortieth anniversary of the Marshall plan. I was struck by the sign on a burnt-out, gutted structure that was being rebuilt. I understand that Berliners of my own generation can remember seeing signs like it dotted throughout the

Western sectors of the city. The sign read simply: "The Marshall plan is help-ing here to strengthen the free world." A strong, free world in the West, that dream became real. Japan rose from ruin to become an economic giant. Italy, France, Belgium—virtually every nation in Western Europe saw political and economic rebirth; the European Community was founded.

In West Germany and here in Berlin, there took place an economic miracle, the Wirtschaftswunder. Adenauer, Erhard, Reuter, and other leaders under-stood the practical importance of liberty—that just as truth can flourish only when the journalist is given freedom of speech, so prosperity can come about only when the farmer and businessman enjoy economic freedom. The Ger-man leaders reduced tariffs, expanded free trade, lowered taxes. From 1950 to 1960 alone, the standard of living in West Germany and Berlin doubled.

Where four decades ago there was rubble, today in West Berlin there is the greatest industrial output of any city in Germany—busy office blocks, fine homes and apartments, proud avenues, and the spreading lawns of parkland. Where a city's culture seemed to have been destroyed, today there are two great universities, orchestras and an opera, countless theaters, and museums. Where there was want, today there's abundance—food, clothing, automo-biles—the wonderful goods of the Ku'damm. From devastation, from utter ruin, you Berliners have, in freedom, rebuilt a city that once again ranks as one of the greatest on Earth. The Soviets may have had other plans. But, my friends, there were a few things the Soviets didn't count on Berliner herz, Berliner humor, ja, und Berliner schnauze. [Berliner heart, Berliner humor, yes, and a Berliner nose.]

In the 1950s, Khrushchev predicted: "We will bury you." But in the West today, we see a free world that has achieved a level of prosperity and well-being unprecedented in all human history. In the Communist world, we see failure, technological backwardness, declining standards of health, even want of the most basic kind—too little food. Even today, the Soviet Union still can-not feed itself. After these four decades, then, there stands before the entire world one great and inescapable conclusion: Freedom leads to prosperity. Freedom replaces the ancient hatreds among the nations with comity and peace. Freedom is the victor.

And now the Soviets themselves may, in a limited way, be coming to under-stand the importance of freedom. We hear much from Moscow about a new policy of reform and openness. Some political prisoners have been released. Certain foreign news broadcasts are no longer being jammed. Some eco-nomic enterprises have been permitted to operate with greater freedom from state control. Are these the beginnings of profound changes in the Soviet state? Or are they token gestures, intended to raise false hopes in the West, or to strengthen the Soviet system without changing it? We welcome change and openness; for we believe that freedom and security go together, that the advance of human liberty can only strengthen the cause of world peace.

There is one sign the Soviets can make that would be unmistakable, that would advance dramatically the cause of freedom and peace. General Secretary Gorbachev, if you seek peace, if you seek prosperity for the Soviet Union and Eastern Europe, if you seek liberalization: Come here to this gate! Mr. Gorbachev, open this gate! Mr. Gorbachev, tear down this wall!

I understand the fear of war and the pain of division that afflict this continent—and I pledge to you my country's efforts to help overcome these burdens. To be sure, we in the West must resist Soviet expansion. So we must maintain defenses of unassailable strength. Yet we seek peace; so we must strive to reduce arms on both sides. Beginning ten years ago, the Soviets challenged the Western alliance with a grave new threat, hundreds of new and more deadly SS-20 nuclear missiles, capable of—striking every capital in Europe. The Western alliance responded by committing itself to a counter-deployment unless the Soviets agreed to negotiate a better solution; namely, the elimination of such weapons on both sides. For many months, the Soviets refused to bargain in earnestness. As the alliance, in turn, prepared to go forward with its counterdeployment, there were difficult days—days of protests like those during my 1982 visit to this city—and the Soviets later walked away from the table.

But through it all, the alliance held firm. And I invite those who protested then—I invite those who protest today—to mark this fact: Because we remained strong, the Soviets came back to the table. And because we remained strong, today we have within reach the possibility, not merely of limiting the growth of arms, but of eliminating, for the first time, an entire class of nuclear weapons from the face of the Earth. As I speak, NATO ministers are meeting in Iceland to review the progress of our proposals for eliminating these weapons. At the talks in Geneva, we have also proposed deep cuts in strategic offensive weapons. And the Western allies have likewise made far-reaching proposals to reduce the danger of conventional war and to place a total ban on chemical weapons.

While we pursue these arms reductions, I pledge to you that we will maintain the capacity to deter Soviet aggression at any level at which it might occur. And in cooperation with many of our allies, the United States is pursuing the Strategic Defense Initiative research to base deterrence not on the threat of offensive retaliation, but on defenses that truly defend; on systems, in short, that will not target populations, but shield them. By these means we seek to increase the safety of Europe and all the world. But we must remember a crucial fact: East and West do not mistrust each other because we are armed; we are armed because we mistrust each other. And our differences are not about weapons but about liberty. When President Kennedy spoke at the City Hall those twenty-four years ago, freedom was encircled, Berlin was under siege. And today, despite all the pressures upon this city, Berlin stands secure in its liberty. And freedom itself is transforming the globe.

In the Philippines, in South and Central America, democracy has been given a rebirth. Throughout the Pacific, free markets are working miracle after miracle of economic growth. In the industrialized nations, a technological revolution is taking place—a revolution marked by rapid, dramatic advances in computers and telecommunications.

In Europe, only one nation and those it controls refuse to join the community of freedom. Yet in this age of redoubled economic growth, of information and innovation, the Soviet Union faces a choice: It must make fundamental changes, or it will become obsolete. Today thus represents a moment of hope. We in the West stand ready to cooperate with the East to promote true openness, to break down barriers that separate people, to create a safer, freer world.

And surely there is no better place than Berlin, the meeting place of East and West, to make a start. Free people of Berlin: Today, as in the past, the United States stands for the strict observance and full implementation of all parts of the Four Power Agreement of 1971. Let us use this occasion, the seven hundred and fiftieth anniversary of this city, to usher in a new era, to seek a still fuller, richer life for the Berlin of the future. Together, let us maintain and develop the ties between the Federal Republic and the Western sectors of Berlin, which is permitted by the 1971 agreement.

And I invite Mr. Gorbachev: Let us work to bring the Eastern and Western parts of the city closer together, so that all the inhabitants of all Berlin can enjoy the benefits that come with life in one of the great cities of the world. To open Berlin still further to all Europe, East and West, let us expand the vital air access to this city, finding ways of making commercial air service to Berlin more convenient, more comfortable, and more economical. We look to the day when West Berlin can become one of the chief aviation hubs in all central Europe.

With our French and British partners, the United States is prepared to help bring international meetings to Berlin. It would be only fitting for Berlin to serve as the site of United Nations meetings, or world conferences on human rights and arms control or other issues that call for international cooperation. There is no better way to establish hope for the future than to enlighten young minds, and we would be honored to sponsor summer youth exchanges, cultural events, and other programs for young Berliners from the East. Our French and British friends, I'm certain, will do the same. And it's my hope that an authority can be found in East Berlin to sponsor visits from young people of the Western sectors.

One final proposal, one close to my heart: Sport represents a source of enjoyment and ennoblement, and you many have noted that the Republic of Korea—South Korea—has offered to permit certain events of the 1988 Olympics to take place in the North. International sports competitions of all kinds could take place in both parts of this city. And what better way to demonstrate to the world the openness of this city than to offer in some future year to hold the Olympic games here in Berlin, East and West?

In these four decades, as I have said, you Berliners have built a great city. You've done so in spite of threats—the Soviet attempts to impose the East-mark, the blockade. Today the city thrives in spite of the challenges implicit in the very presence of this wall. What keeps you here? Certainly there's a great deal to be said for your fortitude, for your defiant courage. But I believe there's something deeper, something that involves Berlin's whole look and feel and way of life—not mere sentiment. No one could live long in Berlin without being completely disabused of illusions. Something instead, that has seen the difficulties of life in Berlin but chose to accept them, that continues to build this good and proud city in contrast to a surrounding totalitarian presence that refuses to release human energies or aspirations. Something that speaks with a powerful voice of affirmation, that says yes to this city, yes to the future, yes to freedom. In a word, I would submit that what keeps you in Berlin is love—love both profound and abiding.

Perhaps this gets to the root of the matter, to the most fundamental distinction of all between East and West. The totalitarian world produces backwardness because it does such violence to the spirit, thwarting the human impulse to create, to enjoy, to worship. The totalitarian world finds even symbols of love and of worship an affront. Years ago, before the East Germans began rebuilding their churches, they erected a secular structure: the television tower at Alexander Platz. Virtually ever since, the authorities have been working to correct what they view as the tower's one major flaw, treating the glass sphere at the top with paints and chemicals of every kind. Yet even today when the Sun strikes that sphere—that sphere that towers over all Berlin—the light makes the sign of the cross. There in Berlin, like the city itself, symbols of love, symbols of worship, cannot be suppressed.

As I looked out a moment ago from the Reichstag, that embodiment of German unity, I noticed words crudely spray-painted upon the wall, perhaps by a young Berliner, "This wall will fall. Beliefs become reality." Yes, across Europe, this wall will fall. For it cannot withstand faith; it cannot withstand truth. The wall cannot withstand freedom.

And I would like, before I close, to say one word. I have read, and I have been questioned since I've been here about certain demonstrations against my coming. And I would like to say just one thing, and to those who demonstrate so. I wonder if they have ever asked themselves that if they should have the kind of government they apparently seek, no one would ever be able to do what they're doing again.

PART 5

# 9/11 AND BEYOND

*I can hear you. I can hear you.*
*The rest of the world hears you.*
*And the people who knocked these buildings down*
*will hear all of us soon.*

—GEORGE W. BUSH, 2001

# George W. Bush

## RALLYING AMERICA AFTER 9/11,
## SEPTEMBER 20, 2001

*And tonight a few miles from the damaged Pentagon,*
*I have a message for our military: Be ready.*
*I have called the armed forces to alert, and there is a reason.*
*The hour is coming when America will act,*
*and you will make us proud.*

Official White House portrait, 2003.

NINE DAYS AFTER THE SEPTEMBER 11TH ATTACKS, I stood on the floor of the House of Representatives as the president entered the chamber and made his way down the center aisle to thunderous applause. That night, the aisle did not separate Democrats and Republicans. Although I had—and continue to have—significant differences with the president's policies, all disagreements dissipated in the face of the barbaric attacks on our country.

As I watched the president approach the rostrum, I took note of a great historic irony: President George W. Bush would address the Congress from the same place that Franklin Delano Roosevelt summoned America after the attacks on Pearl Harbor.

Like Roosevelt, President Bush faced multiple challenges: to inspire confidence after the trauma of the attacks only nine days before; to describe for the American people what the future held; to define our individual and collective roles in responding to the attacks.

"How will we fight and win this war?" The president asked, echoing a question that dominated kitchen tables and television news shows and congressional meetings. "We will direct every resource at our command—every means of diplomacy, every tool of intelligence, every instrument of law enforcement, every financial influence and every necessary weapon of war—to the destruction and to the defeat of the global terror network."

Perhaps one of the most dramatic moments in the speech came when the president held before the entire Congress a small police shield that glittered in the lights. "And I will carry this. It is the police shield of a man named George Howard, who died at the World Trade Center trying to save others. It was given to me by his mom, Arlene, as a proud memorial to her son. It is my reminder of lives that ended and a task that does not end."

The task does not end.

Although President Bush's speech concludes this volume, it will not be the last speech that motivates men and women forward even when times are perilous and the hours grim. However, the words here echo—and preview—similar pronouncements in the face of challenge.

Washington addressing his troops and preventing an insurrection against our new government; Lincoln mobilizing a nation to defeat slavery and then imploring the same nation to demonstrate both charity and justice; Franklin D. Roosevelt calling every American to serve and sacrifice in the battle against Nazism and Fascism; John Kennedy challenging us to conquer the seemingly unconquerable distance of space.

President Bush's words that night summoned America to equal tasks. Sadly, the unity of purpose the president achieved that evening would, before long, dissipate. Many had the sense that the words themselves were not supported by the other indispensable tools of victory: shared sacrifice, patient planning, focused military priorities, adequate funding of our troops and our veterans, diplomacy that is both muscular and smart. Despite those criticisms (which I find entirely valid), the speech itself was a beacon to a nation gripped with trauma, a nation seeking a sense of direction toward a peaceful, stable, decent world for their children.

A nation that faced challenge was inspired that evening to meet the challenge, as it has in its past, as it will in its future.

---

MR. SPEAKER, MR. PRESIDENT PRO TEMPORE, MEMBERS OF CONGRESS, AND FELLOW AMERICANS:

In the normal course of events, presidents come to this chamber to report on the state of the Union. Tonight, no such report is needed. It has already been delivered by the American people.

We have seen it in the courage of passengers who rushed terrorists to save others on the ground. Passengers like an exceptional man named Todd Beamer. And would you please help me welcome his wife Lisa Beamer here tonight?

We have seen the state of our Union in the endurance of rescuers working past exhaustion. We've seen the unfurling of flags, the lighting of candles, the giving of blood, the saying of prayers in English, Hebrew and Arabic. We have seen the decency of a loving and giving people who have made the grief of strangers their own.

My fellow citizens, for the last nine days, the entire world has seen for itself the state of union, and it is strong.

Tonight, we are a country awakened to danger and called to defend freedom. Our grief has turned to anger and anger to resolution. Whether we bring our enemies to justice or bring justice to our enemies, justice will be done.

I thank the Congress for its leadership at such an important time. All of America was touched on the evening of the tragedy to see Republicans and Democrats joined together on the steps of this Capitol singing "God Bless America." And you did more than sing. You acted, by delivering forty billion dollars to rebuild our communities and meet the needs of our military. Speaker Hastert, Minority Leader Gephardt, Majority Leader Daschle and Senator Lott, I thank you for your friendship, for your leadership and for your service to our country.

And on behalf of the American people, I thank the world for its outpouring of support. America will never forget the sounds of our national anthem playing at Buckingham Palace, on the streets of Paris and at Berlin's Brandenburg Gate. We will not forget South Korean children gathering to pray outside our embassy in Seoul, or the prayers of sympathy offered at a mosque in Cairo. We will not forget moments of silence and days of mourning in Australia and Africa and Latin America. Nor will we forget the citizens of eighty other nations who died with our own. Dozens of Pakistanis, more than one hundred and thirty Israelis, more than two hundred and fifty citizens of India, men and women from El Salvador, Iran, Mexico and Japan, and hundreds of British citizens.

America has no truer friend than Great Britain. Once again, we are joined together in a great cause. I'm so honored the British prime minister has crossed an ocean to show his unity with America. Thank you for coming, friend.

On September the 11th, enemies of freedom committed an act of war against our country. Americans have known wars, but for the past one hundred and thirty-six years they have been wars on foreign soil, except for one Sunday in 1941. Americans have known the casualties of war, but not at the center of a great city on a peaceful morning. Americans have known surprise attacks, but never before on thousands of civilians. All of this was brought upon us in a single day, and night fell on a different world, a world where freedom itself is under attack.

Americans have many questions tonight. Americans are asking, "Who attacked our country?"

The evidence we have gathered all points to a collection of loosely affiliated terrorist organizations known as al-Qaida. They are some of the murderers indicted for bombing American embassies in Tanzania and Kenya and responsible for bombing the USS *Cole*. Al-Qaida is to terror what the Mafia is to crime. But its goal is not making money. Its goal is remaking the world and imposing its radical beliefs on people everywhere.

The terrorists practice a fringe form of Islamic extremism that has been rejected by Muslim scholars and the vast majority of Muslim clerics; a fringe movement that perverts the peaceful teachings of Islam. The terrorists' directive commands them to kill Christians and Jews, to kill all Americans and make no distinctions among military and civilians, including women and children. This group and its leader, a person named Osama bin Laden, are linked to many other organizations in different countries, including the Egyptian Islamic Jihad, the Islamic Movement of Uzbekistan.

There are thousands of these terrorists in more than sixty countries. They are recruited from their own nations and neighborhoods and brought to camps in places like Afghanistan, where they are trained in the tactics of terror. They are sent back to their homes or sent to hide in countries around the world to plot evil and destruction.

The leadership of al-Qaida has great influence in Afghanistan and supports the Taliban regime in controlling most of that country. In Afghanistan we see al-Qaida's vision for the world. Afghanistan's people have been brutal-ized, many are starving and many have fled. Women are not allowed to attend school. You can be jailed for owning a television. Religion can be practiced only as their leaders dictate. A man can be jailed in Afghanistan if his beard is not long enough.

The United States respects the people of Afghanistan—after all, we are currently its largest source of humanitarian aid—but we condemn the Taliban regime. It is not only repressing its own people, it is threatening people every-where by sponsoring and sheltering and supplying terrorists.

By aiding and abetting murder, the Taliban regime is committing murder. And tonight the United States of America makes the following demands on the Taliban.

Deliver to United States authorities all of the leaders of al-Qaida who hide in your land.

Release all foreign nationals, including American citizens you have unjustly imprisoned. Protect foreign journalists, diplomats and aid workers in your country. Close immediately and permanently every terrorist training camp in Afghanistan. And hand over every terrorist and every person and their sup-port structure to appropriate authorities.

Give the United States full access to terrorist training camps, so we can make sure they are no longer operating.

These demands are not open to negotiation or discussion. The Taliban must act and act immediately. They will hand over the terrorists, or they will share in their fate.

I also want to speak tonight directly to Muslims throughout the world. We respect your faith. It's practiced freely by many millions of Americans and by millions more in countries that America counts as friends. Its teach-ings are good and peaceful, and those who commit evil in the name of Allah blaspheme the name of Allah.

The terrorists are traitors to their own faith, trying, in effect, to hijack Islam itself. The enemy of America is not our many Muslim friends. It is not our many Arab friends. Our enemy is a radical network of terrorists and every government that supports them.

Our war on terror begins with al-Qaida, but it does not end there. It will not end until every terrorist group of global reach has been found, stopped and defeated.

Americans are asking, "Why do they hate us?"

They hate what they see right here in this chamber: a democratically elected government. Their leaders are self-appointed. They hate our freedoms: our freedom of religion, our freedom of speech, our freedom to vote and assemble and disagree with each other. They want to overthrow existing governments in many Muslim countries such as Egypt, Saudi Arabia and Jordan. They want to drive Israel out of the Middle East. They want to drive Christians and Jews out of vast regions of Asia and Africa. These terrorists kill not merely to end lives, but to disrupt and end a way of life. With every atrocity, they hope that America grows fearful, retreating from the world and forsaking our friends. They stand against us because we stand in their way.

We're not deceived by their pretenses to piety. We have seen their kind before. They're the heirs of all the murderous ideologies of the twentieth century. By sacrificing human life to serve their radical visions, by abandoning every value except the will to power, they follow in the path of fascism, Nazism and totalitarianism. And they will follow that path all the way to where it ends in history's unmarked grave of discarded lies.

Americans are asking, "How will we fight and win this war?" We will direct every resource at our command—every means of diplomacy, every tool of intelligence, every instrument of law enforcement, every financial influence and every necessary weapon of war—to the destruction and to the defeat of the global terror network.

Now this war will not be like the war against Iraq a decade ago, with a decisive liberation of territory and a swift conclusion. It will not look like the air war above Kosovo two years ago, where no ground troops were used and not a single American was lost in combat.

Our response involves far more than instant retaliation and isolated strikes. Americans should not expect one battle, but a lengthy campaign unlike any other we have ever seen. It may include dramatic strikes visible on TV and covert operations secret even in success. We will starve terrorists of funding, turn them one against another, drive them from place to place until there is no refuge or no rest. And we will pursue nations that provide aid or safe haven to terrorism. Every nation in every region now has a decision to make: Either you are with us, or you are with the terrorists.

From this day forward, any nation that continues to harbor or support terrorism will be regarded by the United States as a hostile regime. Our nation has been put on notice, we're not immune from attack. We will take defensive measures against terrorism to protect Americans.

Today, dozens of federal departments and agencies, as well as state and local governments, have responsibilities affecting homeland security. These efforts must be coordinated at the highest level. So tonight, I announce the creation of a Cabinet-level position reporting directly to me, the Office of Homeland Security. And tonight, I also announce a distinguished American to lead this effort, to strengthen American security: a military veteran, an effective governor, a true patriot, a trusted friend, Pennsylvania's Tom Ridge. He will lead, oversee and coordinate a comprehensive national strategy to safeguard our country against terrorism and respond to any attacks that may come.

These measures are essential. The only way to defeat terrorism as a threat to our way of life is to stop it, eliminate it and destroy it where it grows.

Many will be involved in this effort, from FBI agents, to intelligence operatives, to the reservists we have called to active duty. All deserve our thanks, and all have our prayers.

And tonight a few miles from the damaged Pentagon, I have a message for our military: Be ready. I have called the armed forces to alert, and there is a reason. The hour is coming when America will act, and you will make us proud.

This is not, however, just America's fight. And what is at stake is not just America's freedom. This is the world's fight. This is civilization's fight. This is the fight of all who believe in progress and pluralism, tolerance and freedom.

We ask every nation to join us. We will ask and we will need the help of police forces, intelligence services and banking systems around the world. The United States is grateful that many nations and many international organizations have already responded with sympathy and with support—nations from Latin America, to Asia, to Africa, to Europe, to the Islamic world.

Perhaps the NATO charter reflects best the attitude of the world: An attack on one is an attack on all. The civilized world is rallying to America's side. They understand that if this terror goes unpunished, their own cities, their own citizens may be next. Terror unanswered cannot only bring down buildings, it can threaten the stability of legitimate governments.

And you know what? We're not going to allow it.

Americans are asking, What is expected of us?

I ask you to live your lives and hug your children. I know many citizens have fears tonight, and I ask you to be calm and resolute, even in the face of a continuing threat. I ask you to uphold the values of America and remember why so many have come here. We're in a fight for our principles, and our first responsibility is to live by them. No one should be singled out for unfair treatment or unkind words because of their ethnic background or religious faith.

I ask you to continue to support the victims of this tragedy with your contributions. Those who want to give can go to a central source of information, libertyunites.org, to find the names of groups providing direct help in New York, Pennsylvania and Virginia.

The thousands of FBI agents who are now at work in this investigation may need your cooperation, and I ask you to give it. I ask for your patience with the delays and inconveniences that may accompany tighter security and for your patience in what will be a long struggle.

I ask your continued participation and confidence in the American economy. Terrorists attacked a symbol of American prosperity; they did not touch its source. America is successful because of the hard work and creativity and enterprise of our people. These were the true strengths of our economy before September 11, and they are our strengths today.

And finally, please continue praying for the victims of terror and their families, for those in uniform and for our great country. Prayer has comforted us in sorrow and will help strengthen us for the journey ahead.

Tonight I thank my fellow Americans for what you have already done and for what you will do.

And ladies and gentlemen of the Congress, I thank you, their representatives, for what you have already done and for what we will do together.

Tonight we face new and sudden national challenges.

We will come together to improve air safety, to dramatically expand the number of air marshals on domestic flights and take new measures to prevent hijacking. We will come together to promote stability and keep our airlines flying with direct assistance during this emergency. We will come together to give law enforcement the additional tools it needs to track down terror here at home. We will come together to strengthen our intelligence capabilities to know the plans of terrorists before they act and to find them before they strike. We will come together to take active steps that strengthen America's economy and put our people back to work.

Tonight, we welcome two leaders who embody the extraordinary spirit of all New Yorkers, Governor George Pataki and Mayor Rudolf Giuliani. As a symbol of America's resolve, my administration will work with Congress and these two leaders to show the world that we will rebuild New York City.

After all that has just passed, all the lives taken and all the possibilities and hopes that died with them, it is natural to wonder if America's future is one of fear.

Some speak of an age of terror. I know there are struggles ahead and dangers to face. But this country will define our times, not be defined by them. As long as the United States of America is determined and strong, this will not be an age of terror. This will be an age of liberty here and across the world.

Great harm has been done to us. We have suffered great loss. And in our grief and anger, we have found our mission and our moment. Freedom and fear are at war. The advance of human freedom, the great achievement of our time and the great hope of every time, now depends on us.

Our nation, this generation, will lift the dark threat of violence from our people and our future. We will rally the world to this cause by our efforts, by our courage. We will not tire, we will not falter, and we will not fail.

It is my hope that in the months and years ahead life will return almost to normal. We'll go back to our lives and routines, and that is good. Even grief recedes with time and grace.

But our resolve must not pass. Each of us will remember what happened that day and to whom it happened. We will remember the moment the news came, where we were and what we were doing.

Some will remember an image of a fire or story or rescue. Some will carry memories of a face and a voice gone forever.

And I will carry this. It is the police shield of a man named George Howard, who died at the World Trade Center trying to save others. It was given to me by his mom, Arlene, as a proud memorial to her son. It is my reminder of lives that ended and a task that does not end.

I will not forget the wound to our country and those who inflicted it. I will not yield, I will not rest, I will not relent in waging this struggle for freedom and security for the American people.

The course of this conflict is not known, yet its outcome is certain. Freedom and fear, justice and cruelty, have always been at war, and we know that God is not neutral between them.

Fellow citizens, we'll meet violence with patient justice, assured of the rightness of our cause and confident of the victories to come. In all that lies before us, may God grant us wisdom, and may he watch over the United States of America.

# NOTES ON SOURCES

The speech texts in this volume are provided from the following sources:

All Napoléon Bonaparte speeches were taken from Tarbell, Ida. *Napoléon's Addresses*. Boston: Joseph Knight, 1896.

The following speeches are reproduced with permission of Curtis Brown Ltd., London, on behalf of the Estate of Winston Churchill; copyright Winston S. Churchill: "Winston Churchill: Victory at All Costs," "Winston Churchill: We Shall Never Surrender," "Winston Churchill: We Can Take It Again," "Winston Churchill: On Refusing to 'Give In.'"

The following speeches were taken from Safire, William. *Lend Me Your Ears*. New York: W. W. Norton and Company, 1997: "Queen Elizabeth I: Supporting Her Troops against the Spanish Armada," "Harold Ickes: Imploring Americans to Fight," "General Sir Bernard Montgomery: No Retreat," "General George Patton: Exhorting the Third Army," "Empress Theodora: Fight, Not Flight," "George Washington: Calming His Rebellious Troops."

The following speeches were taken from taken from www.jfklibrary.org, accessed February 9, 2007: "John F. Kennedy: Challenging America to Reach the Moon," "John F. Kennedy: Bracing America for the Cuban Missile Crisis," "John F. Kennedy: Ich Bin ein Berliner."

The following speeches were taken from www.presidency.ucsb.edu, accessed February 9, 2006: "John F. Kennedy: What You Can Do for Your Country," "Woodrow Wilson: To the U.S. Naval Academy."

The following speeches are from Thucydides. Translation by Rex Warner. *History of the Pelopennesian War*. New York: Penguin Books. 1954: "Pericles:

Reply to Sparta," "Pericles: At the Funeral of Fallen Soldiers," "Pericles: Lifting the Morale of Athens."

The following speeches were taken from www.fdrlibrary.marist.edu, accessed February 23, 2007: "Franklin D. Roosevelt: 9/11 Address," "Franklin D. Roosevelt: On Preparing America for War."

The following speeches were taken from Copeland, Lewis, Lawrence W. Lamm, and Stephen J. McKenna. *The World's Great Speeches*. New York: Dover Publications, Inc., 1999: "St. Bernard: On the Second Crusade," "Catiline: To His Troops," "Georges Clemenceau: Defend to the Death," "Marshal Ferdinand Foch: Tribute to Napoléon," "Frederick the Great: Before Invading Silesia," "Frederick the Great: Before the Battle of Leuthen," "Giuseppe Garibaldi: Farewell Address: Fight On!" "John Hancock: On the Boston Massacre," "Hannibal: To His Soldiers," "Patrick Henry: Liberty or Death," "Isocrates: On Resisting Persia," "Abraham Lincoln: Second Inaugural Address," "Vyacheslav Molotov: Responding to Germany's Invasion," "Josef Stalin: Defend Every Inch," "Henry Stimson: Asking for Sacrifice."

"Menachem Begin: Preparing Israel for an Arab Attack," was provided by the Menachem Begin Heritage Foundation.

"George W. Bush: Rallying American after 9/11," was taken from *The Congressional Record*. Washington, D.C. September 21, 2001.

"Frederick Douglass: Men of Color, To Arms" was taken from www.teaching americanhistory.org, accessed February 20, 2007.

"General Dwight D. Eisenhower: Ordering the Normandy Invasion," was taken from www.eisenhower.archives.gov, accessed February 25, 2007.

"Abraham Lincoln: Gettysburg Address," was taken from www.loc.gov, accessed February 20, 2007.

"Abraham Lincoln: To the 166th Ohio Regiment," was taken from www.repeatafterus.com, accessed February 20, 2007.

"General Douglas MacArthur: Duty, Honor, Country," was taken from www. west-point.org, accessed February 23, 2006.

"Nelson Mandela: Unite! Moblize! Fight On!" was provided by the Nelson Mandela Foundation.

"Moses: Instructing His People to March without Him," reprinted from Judaica Press, Book of Deuteronomy (www.judaicapress.com).

"Richard Nixon: Asking for Patience on Vietnam," was taken from nixon foundation.org, accessed February 25, 2007.

"Ronald Ronald: Tear Down This Wall!" was taken from www.reagan.utexas. edu, accessed February 25, 2007.

"Franklin D. Roosevelt: Declaring War on Japan," was taken from www. remember.gov, accessed February 24, 2007. Web site by the White House Commission on Remembrance.

"William Shakespeare: 'Battle of Agincourt,'" from *Henry V*, was taken from www.shakespeare-literature.com, accessed February 18, 2007.

"Josef Stalin: Demanding Courage," was taken from mishalov.com/Stalin_ 28July42, accessed February 25, 2007.

"Harry S. Truman: Calling America to the Cold War," was taken from www. trumanlibrary.org, accessed February 25, 2007.

"Woodrow Wilson: War Message to Congress," was taken from woodrow wilson.org, accessed February 20, 2007.

"Eleazar ben Yair: Death, Not Slavery," was taken from Israel, Steve, and Seth Forman. *Great Jewish Speeches throughout History.* New Jersey: Jason Aronson, 1994.

# ILLUSTRATION CREDITS

Moses: Instructing His People to March without Him (circa 1260 BCE), p. 3. *Moses Smashing the Tables of the Law*, by Rembrandt (1601–1669). The Yorck Project, *10.000 Meisterwerke der Malerei* (DVD-ROM, 2002). (Wikimedia Commons, http://commons.wikimedia.org/wiki/Image:Rembrandt_Harmensz._van_Rijn_079.jpg)

Pericles: Reply to Sparta (432 BCE), p. 8. Marble bust of Pericles wearing Corinthian helmet, artist unknown. Located at Museo Chiaramonti, Vatican City, section I, #14. (Marie-Lan Nguyen / WikimediaCommons, http://commons.wikimedia.org/wiki/Image:Bust_Pericles_Chiaramonti.jpg)

Pericles: At the Funeral of Fallen Soldiers (431 BCE), p. 14. Marble bust of Pericles, copy of Ktesilas. Located at Museo Pio-Clementino, Vatican City, Muses Hall. (Marie-Lan Nguyen / Wikimedia Commons, http://commons.wikimedia.org/wiki/Image:Pericles_PioClementino_Inv269_n2.jpg)

Pericles: Lifting the Morale of Athens (430 BCE), p. 21. Bust of Pericles, Roman copy of Greek work. Located at Altes Museum, Berlin. (Gunnar Bach Pedersen / Wikimedia Commons, http://commons.wikimedia.org/wiki/Image:Perikles_altes_Museum.jpg)

Isocrates: On Resisting Persia (380 BCE), p. 26. Engraving by an unnamed artist (1778) from a marble bust at Rome. (Mary Evans Picture Library)

Hannibal: To His Soldiers (218 BCE), p. 33. Portrait bust of Hannibal. Located at the Museo Archeologico Nazionale, Naples, Italy. (Alinari / Art Resources, NY)

Catiline: To His Troops (62 BCE), p. 37. *Cicero Denounces Catiline*, by Cesare Maccari (1840–1919). (Wikimedia Commons, http://commons.wiki media.org/wiki/Image:Maccari-Cicero.jpg)

Eleazar ben Yair: Death, Not Slavery (May 73), p. 40. Aerial view of the ruins of the Masada in the Judean Desert, Israel. (Ester Inbar / Wikimedia Com mons, http://commons.wikimedia.org/wiki/Image:Masada01_ST_04.jpg)

Empress Theodora: Fight, Not Flight (January 18, 532), p. 46. Byzantine mosaic depicting Empress Theodora flanked by a chaplain and court lady. Located at the Basilica of San Vitale, Ravenna, Italy. (Wikimedia Commons, http://commons.wikimedia.org/wiki/Image:Empress_Theodora.jpg)

St. Bernard: On the Second Crusade (1146), p. 48. (From *A Short History of Monks and Monasteries*, by Alfred Wesley Wishart, 1865–1933; http://www.gutenberg.net/etext/13206)

William Shakespeare: "Battle of Agincourt" (1599), p. 51. Portrait of William Shakespeare, 1623. Located at the British Museum in London. (Erich Lessing / Art Resource, NY)

Queen Elizabeth I: Supporting Her Troops against the Spanish Armada (July 1588), p. 54. Coronation portrait of Elizabeth I, ca. 1558, artist unknown. Located at the National Portrait Gallery, London. (Edward Buehler, http://www.tudor-portraits.com)

Frederick the Great: Before Invading Silesia (December 11, 1740), p. 57. Frederick the Great of Prussia. (Library of Congress, LC-USZ62-28680)

Frederick the Great: Before the Battle of Leuthen (December 3, 1757), p. 59. Frederick the Great. (Utopia Portrait Gallery, University of Texas, Austin)

John Hancock: On the Boston Massacre (March 5, 1774), p. 65. *Jean Hancock, President au Congres des XIII Provinces Unies d'Amerique, né à Boston*. (Publisher: Thomas Hart, London, ca. 1776; copy of an English print by C. Corbutt. http://www.donaldheald.com/search/dtail_01.php?booknr=3935133&ordernr=3737 and http://commons.wikimedia.org/wiki/Image:John_Hancock_c_1776.jpg)

Patrick Henry: Liberty or Death (March 23, 1775), p. 70. Painting by George Bagby Matthews (1857–1943). Located in the U.S. Senate. (U.S. Senate, http://www.senate.gov/artandhistory/art/artifact/Painting_31_00011.htm)

George Washington: Calming His Rebellious Troops (March 15, 1783), p. 74. The Lansdowne Portrait. Located in the National Portrait Gallery, Smithsonian Institution. (Wikimedia Commons, http://commons.wiki media.org/wiki/Image:Washington_%283%29.jpg)

Napoléon Bonaparte: Speeches of 1796–1815, p. 78. *Napoleon in His Study*, by Jacques-Louis David (1748–1825). (Wikimedia Commons, http://com mons.wikimedia.org/wiki/Image:Napoleon_Bonaparte.jpg)

Giuseppe Garibaldi: Farewell Address: Fight On! (September 1860), p. 91. (from *Portrait Gallery of Eminent Men and Women in Europe and America*, by Evert A. Duyckinick. Utopia Portrait Gallery, University of Texas, Austin)

Frederick Douglass: Men of Color, To Arms! (March 21, 1863), p. 94. Photograph taken ca. 1879. (National Archives, FILE #: 200-FL-22)

Abraham Lincoln: Gettysburg Address (November 19, 1863), p. 98. Photograph taken November 8, 1863. (Library of Congress, LC-USZ62-13016)

Abraham Lincoln: To the 166th Ohio Regiment (August 22, 1864), p. 101. Photograph taken February 9, 1864. (Library of Congress, LC-USP6-2415-A)

Abraham Lincoln: Second Inaugural Address (March 4, 1865), p. 103. Herline & Hensel lithograph, ca 1860–70. (Library of Congress, LC-DIG-pga-03364)

Woodrow Wilson: To the U.S. Naval Academy (June 5, 1914), p. 109. (Library of Congress, LC-USZC2-6247)

Woodrow Wilson: War Message to Congress (April 2, 1917), p. 114. President Woodrow Wilson addressing Congress, 1917. (Library of Congress, LC-USZ62-113662)

Georges Clemenceau: Defend to the Death (June 4, 1918), p. 123. Photograph by Gaspar-Félix Tournachon (1820–1910). (Wikimedia Commons, http://commons.wikimedia.org/wiki/Image:Georges_Clemenceau_Nadar.jpg

Marshal Ferdinand Foch: Tribute to Napoléon (May 5, 1921), p. 128. Photograph ca. 1918–20, by Emilie Cambier. Issued in the book by Rene Weiss, *La Ville de Paris et les Fêtes de la Victoire, 13–14 juillet 1919*, Paris, Imprimerie Nationale, 1920. (Réunion des Musées Nationaux / Art Resource, NY)

Winston Churchill: Victory at All Costs (May 13, 1940), p. 131. Photograph taken 1940. (Library of Congress, LC-USZ62-64419)

Winston Churchill: We Shall Never Surrender (June 4, 1940), p. 134. Photograph taken ca. 1942. (Library of Congress, LC-USW33-019093-C)

Henry Stimson: Asking for Sacrifice (May 6, 1941), p. 142. Photograph taken August 8, 1929. (Library of Congress, LC-USZ62-54011)

Harold Ickes: Imploring Americans to Fight (May 18, 1941), p. 146. Harold Ickes as he leaves the White House, 1938. (Library of Congress, LC-USZ62-106292)

Vyacheslav Molotov: Responding to Germany's Invasion (June 22, 1941), p. 152. Photograph taken ca. 1955. (Library of Congress, LC-USZ62-101609)

Josef Stalin: Defend Every Inch (July 3, 1941), p. 156. Soviet propaganda photo. (Wikimedia Commons, http://commons.wikimedia.org/wiki/Image: Stalin1.jpg)

Winston Churchill: We Can Take It Again (July 14, 1941), p. 163. Churchill at a conference in Quebec. (Franklin D. Roosevelt Presidential Library)

Franklin D. Roosevelt: 9/11 Address (September 11, 1941), p. 166. Photograph taken December 27, 1933. (Library of Congress, LC-USZ62-117121)

Winston Churchill: On Refusing to "Give In" (October 29, 1941), p. 175. Churchill arrives for the start of the Potsdam Conference. (U.S. Army Signal Corps, Harry S. Truman Library)

Franklin D. Roosevelt: Declaring War on Japan (December 8, 1941), p. 178. President Roosevelt signing the declaration of war against Japan, 1941. (National Archives, 79-AR-82)

Franklin D. Roosevelt: On Preparing America for War (December 9, 1941), p. 181. President Roosevelt at Arlington National Cemetery. (Franklin D. Roosevelt Presidential Library)

Josef Stalin: Demanding Courage (July 28, 1942), p. 190. Secretary-general of the Communist Party of Soviet Russia, ca. 1942. (Library of Congress, LC-USW33- 019081-C)

General Sir Bernard Montgomery: No Retreat (August 13, 1942), p. 195. Photograph taken ca. 1942. (U.S. Department of Defense photo)

General George Patton: Exhorting the Third Army (Spring 1944), p. 199. Patton as lieutenant general, March 30, 1943. (Library of Congress, LC-USZ62-25122)

General Dwight D. Eisenhower: Ordering the Normandy Invasion (June 6, 1944), p. 204. Photograph taken November 19, 1947. (U.S. Naval Institute Photo Archive)

Harry S. Truman: Calling America to the Cold War (March 12, 1947), p. 209. Photograph taken November 1945. (U.S. Naval Institute Photo Archive)

Menachem Begin: Preparing Israel for an Arab Attack (May 14, 1948), p. 213. Photograph from 1978. (© The Nobel Foundation)

John F. Kennedy: What You Can Do for Your Country (January 20, 1961), p. 219. Photograph by Fabian Bachrach, 1961. (U.S. Naval Institute Photo Archive)

General Douglas MacArthur: Duty, Honor, Country (May 12, 1962), p. 224. General MacArthur surveying the beachhead on Leyte Island, 1944. (U.S. Naval Institute Photo Archive)

John F. Kennedy: Challenging America to Reach the Moon (September 12, 1962), p. 230. President Kennedy in the Oval Office, 1963. Photograph by Cecil Stoughton, White House. (John F. Kennedy Presidential Library and Museum, Boston)

John F. Kennedy: Bracing America for the Cuban Missile Crisis (October 22, 1962), p. 237. White House photograph. (John F. Kennedy Presidential Library and Museum, Boston)

John F. Kennedy: Ich Bin ein Berliner (June 26, 1963), p. 244. Photograph taken 1961. (Library of Congress, LC-USZ62-117124)

Richard Nixon: Asking for Patience on Vietnam (November 3, 1969), p. 247. Official White House Portrait. (Library of Congress, LC-USZ62-13037 DLC)

Nelson Mandela: Unite! Mobilize! Fight On! (June 10, 1980), p. 259. Photograph from 1993. (© The Nobel Foundation)

Ronald Reagan: Tear Down This Wall! (June 12, 1987), p. 264. Official White House portrait. (Ronald Reagan Presidential Library)

George W. Bush: Rallying America after 9/11 (September 20, 2001), p. 275. Official White House portrait. (U.S. Department of Defense photo / Eric Draper)

# INDEX

# ABOUT THE AUTHOR

Steve Israel has been a Member of the U.S. Congress since 2001, representing New York's 2nd congressional delegation on Long Island. Formerly a member of the House Armed Services Committee, Representative Israel is considered a leading voice in Congress on military and energy security issues. He currently sits on the House Appropriations Committee.

Israel has led efforts in Congress to promote professional military education and use the lessons of military history to guide today's warriors and policymakers on issues of strategy, doctrine, and tactics. He founded the Congressional Battlefield Preservation Caucus and has lectured at the U.S. Military Academy at West Point, the National Defense University, and elsewhere. He appears frequently on CNN, Fox News, and MSNBC.

Israel drafted the Next Generation Energy Security Initiative—a comprehensive plan to reduce our oil dependence based on the historic tools used to win the Space Race and Cold War.

He founded the House Democratic Study Group on National Security and the bipartisan House Defense Energy Working Group. He also organized and chairs the House Center Aisle Caucus—a group of Democrats and Republicans committed to finding consensus on national challenges. As Israel has said: "Democrats and Republicans may disagree on 70 percent of issues. But that gives us an obligation to focus on passing the 30 percent we do agree on, which would make America 100 percent better off."

The congressman lives on Long Island with his wife, a family court judge. He has two daughters.